Other Books by HENRY STEELE COMMAGER

THE AMERICAN MIND
THE BLUE AND THE GRAY
CRUSADERS FOR FREEDOM
DOCUMENTS OF AMERICAN HISTORY
THE ERA OF REFORM, 1830–1860
THE FIRST BOOK OF AMERICAN HISTORY
FREEDOM, LOYALTY, DISSENT
THE GROWTH OF THE AMERICAN REPUBLIC
2 vols. (with Samuel Eliot Morison)
THE HERITAGE OF AMERICA
(with Allan Nevins)
MAJORITY RULE AND MINORITY RIGHTS
THE NEW AMERICAN NATION
50 vols. (editor, with Richard B. Morris)
PROLOGUE TO THE SIXTIES
THEODORE PARKER: YANKEE CRUSADER
A SHORT HISTORY OF THE UNITED STATES
(with Allan Nevins)
THE SPIRIT OF SEVENTY-SIX
(editor, with Richard B. Morris)
FREEDOM AND ORDER
LIVING IDEAS IN AMERICA *(editor)*
THE NATURE AND STUDY OF HISTORY
LESTER WARD AND THE WELFARE STATE

The Search for a Usable Past

THE SEARCH FOR
A USABLE PAST

and *Other Essays*
in Historiography

by Henry Steele Commager

NEW YORK : Alfred · A · Knopf

1967

Library of Congress Catalog Card Number:
67–11142

THIS IS A BORZOI BOOK
PUBLISHED BY ALFRED A. KNOPF. INC.

Manufactured in the United States of America

PUBLISHED MAY 22, 1967
SECOND PRINTING, OCTOBER 1967

TO
JACQUES BARZUN

WHO ILLUSTRATES
THE MAXIM
OF
JUSTICE HOLMES:

LIFE IS PAINTING A PICTURE,
NOT DOING A SUM

CONTENTS

viii   *Contents*

INTRODUCTION

I DO NOT suppose that these essays represent or shadow forth anything so pretentious as a philosophy of history, and indeed I trust that they do not, for I have long subscribed to George Macaulay Trevelyan's sagacious dictum that philosophy is not something you take to the study of history, but something which, if you are lucky, you carry away from that study. I do think these miscellaneous papers represent fairly enough interests and points of view which have persisted through a good many years. Those interests—in the history and practice of reform, the interpretation of the law, the Enlightenment in the Old World and the New—are expressions of a larger concern with nationalism and national character. The study of nationalism has flourished mightily in recent years—and no wonder, with some sixty new nations clamoring for explanation and attention—but the study of national character has encountered skepticism and scorn and, in some quarters, the concept itself has been repudiated. But banished from the front door of orthodox history, it has been re-admitted by the back door of the behavioral sciences, and cultural anthropologists now permit us to speak, without apology, of national habits and traits. There are, as we know, many ways of approaching the study of national character, from the full-dress study of Literature and Law to the somewhat disheveled consideration of courting habits and prestige ratings; interestingly enough Tocqueville, who is a very touchstone of respectability, anticipated most of these. Who can doubt that one of the most interesting and rewarding is the examination of how a people first reconstructs (or imagines) and then interprets its past, and the way in which it uses that past? It is fair to say that American scholarship has so far largely neglected this approach to the history of national character. We have, by now, a substantial library on American historiography, but only rarely and, as it were, parenthetically, do our scholars relate the writing of history to the philosophy, popular or academic, about the nature and uses of history. The explanation of this situation is probably to be found in a kind of historical paradox: that while the past itself has been almost wholly an Old World possession and preoccupation, Americans have resolutely studied themselves as if they were an isolated chapter in history and exempt from the processes of history.

For half a century after 1893 the shadow of Frederick Jackson Turner lay athwart the writing of American history. It was not merely that he so successfully imposed the frontier thesis on historical studies; more important, he encouraged, unconsciously no doubt, the habit of thinking of the American experience as unique, and the readiness to be content with the study of that experience or with the study of other nations only as their history illuminated the American. In his presidential address to the American Historical Association in 1946 Professor Carlton Hayes protested vigorously against this parochialism inherent in the Turner thesis and prevalent in the study of American history, but only slowly and reluctantly did Americans turn from preoccupation with their own experience to an earlier tradition of comparative history —the tradition of great romantics like Prescott, Motley, Parkman, and Henry Adams. Of the three major developments in historiography in the past quarter-century, two —the quantitative broadening of the scope of historical studies to embrace non-Western societies, and the qualitative deepening of these studies through the exploitation of the materials and techniques of the behavioral sciences— have encouraged American historians to break away from their traditional parochialism. The third, however—what Herbert Butterfield has happily called "technical history" —may encourage parochialism anew, not by virtue of any inherent principle, but because it requires an intense cultivation of minutiae, which are almost inevitably of only local and passing interest, and leaves little time for those larger studies of historical philosophy and comparative culture so essential to an understanding of the uses to which a people puts its various pasts.

Already there is a perceptible change. The concept of historiography has broadened greatly—the much-abused Vernon Parrington deserves some credit here—and it has deepened as well. What is more, it attracts increasingly those scholars whose primary and pervasive interest is in the history of ideas. We do not as yet have anything quite comparable to Meinecke's *Die Entstehung des Historismus,* or Ernst Cassirer's *The Philosophy of the Enlightenment,* or Paul Hazard's study of the *Crisis of the European Conscience,* or Werner Jaeger's *Paideia,* but such affluent scholars as S. E. Morison and Perry Miller, Howard Mumford Jones and Stow Persons, Richard Hofstadter and Peter Gay show us what can be done with historiography when it is used imaginatively to illuminate the thought of the past and when it is wed to mythology and religion, art and literature. I should be happy if some of these

essays might serve to stimulate interest in that history of
American historical thought which is as yet unwritten.

   Some of the essays printed here appeared first in historical journals, some were written as introductions to
books, and a few emerged first as addresses to scholarly
audiences. I have not tried to bring any of these up to
date nor, except for the occasional elimination of rhetoric
and jargon, have I imposed any literary revision upon
them.

Henry Steele Commager

Amherst, December 31, 1966

The Search for a Usable Past

THE SEARCH FOR
A USABLE PAST

THE UNITED STATES was the first of the "new" nations. As the American colonies were the first to rebel against a European mother country, so the American states were the first to create—we can use Lincoln's term, to bring forth—a new nation. Modern nationalism was inaugurated by the American, not the French, Revolution. But the new United States faced problems unknown to the new nations of nineteenth-century Europe—and twentieth. For in the Old World the nation came before the state; in America the state came before the nation. In the Old World, nations grew out of well-prepared soil, built upon a foundation of history and traditions; in America the foundations were still to be laid, the seeds still to be planted, the traditions still to be formed.

The problem which confronted the new United States then was radically different from that which confronted, let us say, Belgium, Italy, Greece, or Germany in the nineteenth century, or Norway, Finland, Iceland, and Israel in the twentieth. These "new" states were already

SOURCE: *American Heritage*, XVI : 2 (February 1965). Copyright © 1965 by Henry Steele Commager.

amply equipped with history, tradition, and memory—as well as with most of the other essential ingredients of nationalism except political independence. Of them it can be said that the nation was a product of history. But with the United States, history was rather a creation of the nation, and it is suggestive that in the New World the self-made nation was as familiar as the self-made man.

It is unnecessary to emphasize anything as familiar as the importance of history, tradition, and memory to successful nationalism. On this matter statesmen, historians, and philosophers of nationalism are all agreed. It was the very core of Edmund Burke's philosophy: the nation—society itself—is a partnership of past, present, and future; we (the English) "derive all we possess as an inheritance from our forefathers." It is indeed not merely the course of history but of nature itself. Thus Friedrich von Schlegel, trying to quicken a sense of nationalism in the Germans, urged that "nothing is so important as that the Germans . . . return to the course of their own language and poetry, and liberate from the old documents of their ancestral past that power of old, that noble spirit which . . . is sleeping in them." And Mazzini, in his struggle for the unification of Italy, was ever conscious that "the most important inspiration for nationalism is the awareness of past glories and past sufferings."

So, too, with the philosophers of nationalism, and the historians as well. Listen to Ernest Renan. In that famous lecture "What Is a Nation?" he emphasized "the common memories, sacrifices, glories, afflictions, and regrets," and submitted that the worthiest of all cults was "the cult of ancestors." So, too, with the hard-headed John Stuart Mill, across the Channel: "The strongest cause [for the feeling of nationality] is identity of political antecedents, the possession of a national history, and consequent community of recollections, collective pride and humiliation, pleasure and regret." The moderns all agree on this—Europeans and Americans alike.

But if an historical past and an historical memory are indeed essential ingredients for a viable nationalism, what was the new United States to do in 1776, or in 1789, or for that matter at almost any time before the Civil War? How does a country without a past of her own acquire one, or how does she provide a substitute for it? Where could such a nation find the stuff for patriotism, for sentiment, for pride, for memory, for collective character? It was a question that came up very early, for Americans have always been somewhat uncomfortable about their lack of history and of antiquity, somewhat embarrassed about being historical *nouveaux riches*.

It was Henry James who put the question in most memorable form. I refer to that famous passage about the historical and intellectual environment in which the young Nathaniel Hawthorne found himself in 1840. It takes a great deal of history to make a little literature, said James, and how could Hawthorne make literature with a history so meager and so thin: "No state, in the European sense of the word, and indeed barely a specific national name. No sovereign, no court, no personal loyalty, no aristocracy, no church, no clergy, no army, no diplomatic service, no country gentlemen, no palaces, no castles, nor manors, nor old country houses, nor parsonages, nor thatched cottages, nor ivied ruins; no cathedrals, nor abbeys, nor little Norman churches; no great Universities, nor public schools, no Oxford nor Eton nor Harrow; no literature, no novels, no museums, no pictures, no political society, no sporting class—no Epsom nor Ascot!"

There is almost too much here; the indictment, as James himself remarked, is a lurid one, and he noted, too, with some satisfaction, that Hawthorne had not been wholly frustrated by the thinness of his materials—for a good deal remained; that was, said James wryly, our secret, our private joke. It is suggestive that James's famous outburst was inspired by Hawthorne himself; he had, so he wrote, delighted in a place which had "no shadow, no antiquity, no mystery, no picturesque and gloomy wrong, nor anything but a commonplace prosperity, in broad and simple daylight, as is happily the case with my dear native land." It is worth dwelling on this for a moment, for this is from the author of *The Scarlet Letter*, and of *The House of Seven Gables*, and of a score of stories which did precisely dwell on shadows, antiquities, gloomy wrongs—witchcraft, for example. If a Hawthorne, who all his life felt it necessary to immerse himself in New England antiquities and inherited wrongs, could yet contrast his own dear native land with the Old World in these terms, think how unshadowed were the lives of most Americans—or how empty, if you want to adopt the James point of view.

A host of Americans had anticipated all this, but with different emphasis. Thus the poet Philip Freneau, introducing the Abbé Robin's *New Travels in America:* "They who would saunter over half the Globe to copy the inscription on an antique column, to measure the altitude of a pyramid, or describe the ornaments on the Grand Seigneur's State Turban, will scarcely find anything in American Travels to gratify their taste. The works of art are there comparatively trivial and inconsiderable, the splendor of pageantry rather obscure, and consequently few or none but the admirers of simple Nature can either travel with pleasure themselves or read the travels of others with satisfaction, through this country." And half a century later James Fenimore Cooper, caught in that dilemma of New World innocence and Old World corruption so pervasive in the first century of our history, admitted that in America "there are no annals for the histo-

rian, no follies beyond the most vulgar and commonplace for the satirist; no manners for the dramatist; no
obscure fictions for the writer of romance; no gross and
hardy offenses against decorum for the moralist; nor any
of the rich artificial auxiliaries of poetry."

But if there were "no annals for the historian," and if a
historical past was necessary to successful nation-making,
what were Americans to do? Americans had, in fact,
several courses open to them, and with characteristic
self-confidence, took them all.

Over a century before the Revolution it had been observed of the Virginians that they had no need of ancestors, for they themselves were ancestors. The variations
of this theme were infinite, but the theme itself was
simple and familiar: that Americans had no need of a
past because they were so sure of a future. Goethe had
congratulated them on their good fortune in a famous
but almost untranslatable poem, *Amerika, du hast es
besser*: "no ruined castles, no venerable stones, no useless memories, no vain feuds [he said]. . . . may a kind
providence preserve you from tales of knights and robber
barons and ghosts."

Americans took up the refrain with enthusiasm. The
romantic artist Thomas Cole observed that though American scenery was "destitute of the vestiges of antiquity" it
had other features that were reassuring, for "American
associations are not so much with the past as of the
present and the future, and in looking over the unculti-
vated scene, the mind may travel far into futurity."

This theme runs like a red thread through early American literature and oratory, and finally connects itself tri-
umphantly with Manifest Destiny. It began, appropriately enough, with Crèvecoeur: "I am sure I cannot be
called a partial American when I say that the spectacle
afforded by these pleasing scenes must be more enter-
taining and more philosophical than that which arises

from beholding the musty ruins of Rome. Here everything would inspire the reflecting traveller with the most
philanthropic ideas; his imagination, instead of submit-
ting to the painful and useless retrospect of revolutions,
desolations, and plagues, would, on the contrary, wisely
spring forward to the anticipated fields of future cultivation and improvement, to the future extent of those
generations which are to replenish and embellish this
boundless continent." Washington Irving's friend and
collaborator, James Paulding, entertained the same sentiment: "It is for the other nations to boast of what they
have been, and, like garrulous age, muse over the history
of their youthful exploits that only renders decrepitude
more conspicuous. Ours is the more animating sentiment
of hope, looking forward with prophetic eye."

Best of all is Cooper's John Cadwallader in *Notions of
the Americans,* rebuking his travelling companion, the
bachelor Count, for his unmanly longing for antiquity:
"You complain of the absence of association to give its
secret, and perhaps greatest charm which such a sight is
capable of inspiring. You complain unjustly. The moral
feeling with which a man of sentiment and knowledge
looks upon the plains of your [Eastern] Hemisphere is
connected with his recollections; here it should be min-
gled with his hopes. The same effort of the mind is as
equal to the one as to the other."

The habit of looking forward instead of back blended
readily enough with Manifest Destiny. Thus John Louis
O'Sullivan, who all but invented Manifest Destiny, cheerfully dismissed the past in favor of the future: "We have
no interest in scenes of antiquity, only as lessons of
avoidance of nearly all their examples. The expansive
future is our arena. We are entering on its untrodden
space with the truth of God in our minds, beneficent
objects in our hearts, and with a clear conscience unsul-
lied by the past. We are the nation of human progress,

and who will, what can, set limits on our onward march? . . . the far-reaching, the boundless future will be the era of American greatness. . . ."

There was nothing surprising in Emerson's conclusion that America had no past. "All," he said, "has an outward and prospective look." For transcendentalism—the first genuine expression of the American temperament in philosophy, or New England's at least—was impatient with origins, put its confidence in inspiration, looked upon each day as a new epoch and each man as an Adam. It is difficult to exaggerate the impatience of the transcendentalists with the past. It was not so much that they were opposed to it as that they found it irrelevant. And note that New England's major historians—Bancroft, Prescott, Ticknor, Motley, and Parkman—were all outside the mainstream of transcendentalism.

This was all very well, this confidence in the future. But it was, after all, pretty thin fare for nationalism to feed on at a time when other self-conscious nations were rejoicing in an ancient and romantic past. To be sure, the past became ancient and the future became present more rapidly in America than anywhere else: thus Thomas Jefferson could write from Paris in 1787 that much was to be said for keeping the "good, old, venerable, fabrick" of the six-year-old Articles of Confederation. And thus, too, John Randolph, in the Virginia ratifying convention, could "take farewell of the Confederation, with reverential respect, as an old benefactor."

Happily, there was a second formula to which Americans had recourse, and one no less convenient than the first: that America had, in fact, the most impressive of all pasts; *all* Europe was the American past. After all, we speak the tongue that Shakespeare spake—and for good measure, the tongues of Luther and Racine and Dante and Cervantes as well. Just because they had crossed the Atlantic Ocean, Americans had not forfeited or repudiated their heritage. Americans enjoyed, in fact, the richest and most varied of all heritages. Other benighted peoples had only their past—the Danes a Danish, the Germans a German—but Americans had them all. Were we not in very truth a teeming nation of nations? Edward Everett asserted this as early as 1820: "We suppose that in proportion to our population Lord Byron and Walter Scott are more read in America than in England, nor do we see why we are not entitled to our full share of all that credit which does not rest . . . in the person of the author. . . ." Whitman made this the burden of "Thou Mother With Thy Equal Brood":

Sail, sail thy best, ship of Democracy,
Of value is thy freight, 'tis not the Present only,
The Past is also stored in thee,
Thou holdest not the venture of thyself alone, not of the
     Western Continent alone,
Earth's résumé entire floats on thy keel O ship, is steadied
     by thy spars, . . .
Steer then with good strong hand, and wary eye O helms-
     man, thou carriest great companions,
Venerable priestly Asia sails this day with thee,
And royal feudal Europe sails with thee.

All very well, but a risky business, this assimilation of the Old World past. For could the Old World be trusted? Could the past be trusted? We come here to one of the major themes of American intellectual history, and one of the most troublesome of all the problems in the creation of a usable past.

The theme of New World innocence and Old World corruption emerged early, and persisted all through the nineteenth century: it is a constant of American literature as of American politics, and if it no longer haunts our literature, it still bedevils our politics and diplomacy.

How deeply they were shocked, these innocent Americans, by the goings on in Europe! Benjamin Franklin, after a long residence in England, could deprecate the notion of a reconciliation between the Americans and the mother country on moral grounds: "I have not heard what Objections were made to the Plan in the Congress, nor would I make more than this one, that, when I consider the extreme Corruption prevalent among all Orders of Men in this old rotten State, and the glorious publick Virtue so predominant in our rising Country, I cannot but apprehend more Mischief than Benefit from a closer Union." Dr. Benjamin Rush, who had studied in Edinburgh and in London, never ceased to preach the danger of contamination from abroad. With Jefferson—surely the most cosmopolitan American of his generation—New World innocence and Old World corruption was almost an *idée fixe*. How illuminating, that famous letter to John Banister about the education of his son. "Why send an American youth to Europe for education? . . . Let us view the disadvantages. . . . To enumerate them all, would require a volume. I will select a few. If he goes to England, he learns drinking, horse racing, and boxing. These are the peculiarities of English education. The following circumstances are common to education in that, and the other countries of Europe. He acquires a fondness for European luxury and dissipation, and a contempt for the simplicity of his own country; he is fascinated with the privileges of the European aristocrats and sees, with abhorrence, the lovely equality which the poor enjoy with the rich, in his own country; he contracts a partiality for aristocracy or monarchy; he forms foreign friendships which will never be useful to him . . . he is led, by the strongest of all the human passions, into a spirit for female intrigue, destructive of his own and others' happiness, or a passion for whores, destructive of his health, and, in both cases, learns to consider fidelity

to the marriage bed as an ungentlemanly practice. . . .
It appears to me, then, that an American coming to Europe for education, loses in his knowledge, in his morals, in his health, in his habits, and in his happiness. . . ."

The theme, and the arguments, persisted. Hezekiah Niles wrote on the eve of the War of 1812 that "the War, dreadful as it is, will not be without its benefits in . . . separating us from the *strumpet governments of Europe.*" It is the most persistent theme in American literature from Crèvecœur to Tocqueville, from Hawthorne's *Marble Faun* to James' *Daisy Miller* and *Portrait of a Lady,* from *Innocents Abroad* to *The Sun Also Rises.* Something of its complexity and difficulty can be seen in the position of the expatriate. Here Americans long maintained a double standard; it was taken for granted not only that European immigrants to the United States give up their nationality and identify themselves with their adopted country, but that they do so exuberantly. But for Americans to give up their nationality and identify themselves with a foreign country was another matter altogether.

Needless to say, there are philosophical and psychological implications here which we ignore at our peril. For this concept of New World innocence and Old World corruption encouraged that sense of being a people apart which nature herself had already sufficiently dramatized. How characteristic that Jefferson should have combined nature and morality in his first inaugural: "Kindly separated by nature from one quarter of the globe; too high-minded to endure the degradations of the others. . . ." To this day Americans are inclined to think that they are somehow outside the stream of history, somehow exempt from its burden.

But quite aside from the theme of Old World corruption, the availability of the European past was not a simple matter of chronological assimilation or absorption. It was available, to be sure, but only on limited terms. It was there more for purposes of contrast than for enrichment; it pointed the moral of American superiority, and adorned the tale of American escape from contamination. It was there, too, as a museum, a curio shop, and a moral playground. But for practical purposes it contributed little to the juices of American Life.

Americans had a third choice: They could use what they had. "We have not, like England and France, centuries of achievements and calamities to look back on," wrote the indefatigable diarist George Templeton Strong, "but being without the eras that belong to older nationalities—Anglo-Saxon, Carolingian, Hohenstaufen, Ghibelline, and so forth—we dwell on the details of our little all of historic life and venerate every trivial fact about our first settlers and colonial governors and revolutionary heroes." Not all Americans struck so modest a pose. All their past lacked, after all, was antiquity, and antiquity was relative; in any event, this meant that the American past was better authenticated than the European.

Nothing in the history of American nationalism is more impressive than the speed and the lavishness with which Americans provided themselves with a usable past: history, legends, symbols, paintings, sculpture, monuments, shrines, holy days, ballads, patriotic songs, heroes, and—with some difficulty—villains. Henry James speaks somewhere of his old friend Emerson dwelling for fifty years "within the undecorated walls of his youth." To Emerson they did not seem undecorated, for he embellished them with a rich profusion of historical association and out of memory: the author of "Concord Hymn" was not unaware of the past.

Not every American, to be sure, was as deeply rooted as Emerson, but even to newcomers America soon ceased to be undecorated. Uncle Sam was quite as good as John Bull, and certainly more democratic. The bald eagle

(Franklin sensibly preferred the turkey, but was over-
ruled) did not compare badly with the British lion and
was at least somewhat more at home in America than the
lion in Britain. The Stars and Stripes, if it did not fall
straight out of heaven like Denmark's *Dannebrog,* soon
had its own mythology, and it had, besides, one inesti-
mable advantage over all other flags, in that it provided
an adjustable key to geography and a visible evidence of
growth. Soon it provided the stuff for one of the greatest
of all national songs—the tune difficult but the sentiments elevated—and one becoming to a free people. The
Declaration of Independence was easier to understand
than Magna Carta, and parts of it could be memorized
and recited—as Magna Carta could not. In addition it
had a Liberty Bell to toll its fame, which was something
the British never thought of. There were no less than two
national mottoes—*E pluribus unum,* selected, so appropriately, by Franklin, Jefferson, and John Adams, and
Novus ordo seclorum, with their classical origins. There
were no antiquities, but there were shrines: Plymouth
Rock, of course, and Independence Hall and Bunker Hill
and Mount Vernon and Monticello; eventually there was
to be the Log Cabin in which Lincoln was born, as inde-
structible as the hull of the *Mayflower.*

These were some of the insignia, as it were, the insistent manifestations of the possession of an historical
past. The stuff of that past was crowded and rich; it is
still astonishing that Americans managed to fill their
historical canvas so elaborately in so short a time. The
colonial era provided a remote past: Pocahontas saving
John Smith; the Pilgrims landing on the sandy coast of
Plymouth, and celebrating the first Thanksgiving; Roger
Williams fleeing through the wintry storms to Narragan-
sett Bay; William Penn treating with the Indians; Deer-
field going up in flames, its captives trekking through the
snow to distant Canada; Franklin walking the streets of

Philadelphia, munching those "three great puffy rolls" that came to be permanent props.

The Revolution proved a veritable cornucopia of heroic episodes and memories: Washington crossing the Delaware; Washington kneeling at Valley Forge; the signing of the Declaration; Captain Parker at Lexington Common: "If they mean to have a war, let it begin here!"; Prescott at Bunker Hill: "Don't fire until you see the whites of their eyes!"; John Paul Jones closing with the *Serapis:* "I have not yet begun to fight!"; Nathan Hale on the gallows: "I only regret that I have but one life to lose for my country"; Tom Paine writing the first *Crisis* on the flat of a drum, by the flickering light of campfires; George Rogers Clark wading through the flooded Wabash bottom lands to capture Vincennes; Washington at Yorktown: "The World Turned Upside Down"; Washington, again, fumbling for his glasses at Newburgh: "I have grown gray in your service, and now find myself growing blind"; Washington even in Heaven, not a pagan Valhalla but a Christian Heaven, doubly authenticated by a parson and a historian—one person to be sure—the incomparable Parson Weems.

The War of 1812, for all its humiliations, made its own contributions to national pride. Americans conveniently forgot the humiliations and recalled the glories: Captain Lawrence off Boston Harbor: "Don't give up the ship"; the *Constitution* riddling the *Guerrière;* Francis Scott Key peering through the night and the smoke to see if the flag was still there; Perry at Put-in-Bay: "We have met the enemy and they are ours"; the hunters of Kentucky repulsing Pakenham—

> *There stood John Bull in Martial pomp*
> *But here was old Kentucky.*

No wonder Old Hickory went straight to the White House.

The West, too—not one West but many—provided a continuous flow of memories and experiences and came to be, especially for immigrants, a great common denominator. There was the West of the Indian; of Washington at Fort Necessity; John Finley and Daniel Boone; of Lewis and Clark; of the Santa Fe Trail and the Oregon Trail and the California Gold Rush; the West of the miner and the cowboy; the West of the Union Pacific and the other transcontinentals. "If it be romance, if it be contrast, if it be heroism that we require," asked Robert Louis Stevenson, "what was Troytown to this?" What indeed?

Richest of all in its contribution to the storehouse of American memory was the Civil War, with its hero, Lincoln: it produced the best literature and the best songs of any modern war; it was packed with drama and with heroism. To one part of America it gave the common bond of defeat and tragedy, but a defeat that fed sentiment so powerful that it was metamorphosed into victory. It gave to the whole of America a dramatic sense of unity; to Negroes it associated national unity with freedom; and to all it gave the most appealing of national heroes, probably the only modern hero to rank with Alfred and Barbarossa and Joan of Arc. Certainly, of all modern heroes it is Lincoln who lends himself most readily to mythology; his birth humble and even mysterious; his youth gentle and simple; his speech pithy and wise; his wit homely and earthy; his counsels benign. He emerged briefly to save his nation and free the slaves, and died tragically as the lilacs bloomed; no wonder the poets and the myth-makers have exhausted themselves on this theme.

No less remarkable was the speed and comprehensiveness with which the new nation provided itself with an artistic record. From the beginning, to be sure, Americans had been fortunate in this realm; no other nation, it is safe to say, has had its entire history so abundantly recorded as the American, from the first contributions by Le Moyne and De Bry and John White to the realism of the Ash Can school of the early twentieth century. Never before in recorded history had anything excited the imagination like the discovery of the New World—O brave new world, O strange new world; new world that was Utopia and Paradise. Everything about it excited the explorers and conquerors: the Patagonian giants and the Amazons of Brazil and the pygmies of the Far North; the mountains that soared fifty miles into the clouds and the lakes as vast as continents and the caves of solid gold; the natives who were descended from the Tartars or the Jews or the Norwegians or the Welsh; the flora and fauna so strange they all but defied description. How make clear the wonder and the terror of it all?

All the explorers were historians, to be sure; almost all of them were artists as well, and soon all Europe could share the wonder of those who had seen what men had never seen before. It was as if cartographers had given us maps of the voyages of the Phoenicians or of the Vikings; it was as if artists had pictured Hector and Agamemnon before the walls of Troy or Romulus founding the city that would bear his name, or Hengist and Horsa on the shores of Ebbsfleet!

Political independence brought with it artistic freedom, and an ardent preoccupation with the birth of the nation created the stirring political drama; the scenes of battle, lurid and triumphant; the Founding Fathers, grave, as became men occupying a sure place in history. In a generation when Franklin doubted the possibility and John Adams the propriety of art, a host of artists emerged, as if in defiance of counsels too sober; if they were not Rembrandts or Turners, they were better than anyone had any right to expect. It is not, however, their artistic merits that interest us, but their historical function. John Singleton Copley gave us a rich and crowded portrait gallery of colonial society in the process of becoming American—the merchants, the statesmen, the captains, and their ladies as well. John Trumbull regarded himself as the official painter of the Revolution and covered that chapter of history systematically though not comprehensively. Scarcely less impressive was the contribution of the versatile Charles Willson Peale, who left us a whole gallery of Founding Fathers as well as an academy of artistic sons, while the achievement of Gilbert Stuart in impressing on future generations his image of the Father of His Country is almost without parallel in the history of art. This school of artistic historians came to an end when its work was done, when it had provided posterity with artistic archives and monuments of its birth and its youth. Then the new nation, secure in the possession of an artistic record, could afford to indulge the romanticism of an Allston or a Cole, of the Hudson River school, or of genre painters like the puckish John Quidor—worthy companion to Washington Irving—or William Sidney Mount.

The celebration of independence and the founding of the republic was but one chapter in the history of the creation of an artistic image of the American past. Another school seized, almost instinctively, on the inexhaustible theme of the Indian and the winning of the West. Thus, while scores of American artists sailed for the Italian Arcadia, others, untrained, or trained in the irrelevant school of Düsseldorf, moved quite as confidently across the Alleghenies and on to the prairies and the plains and the mountains of the West. What a romantic group they were: the Swiss Carl Bodmer, who went with Prince Maximilian of Wied up the Missouri River in the early 1830's, and who gave us a crowded gallery of Sioux, Crees, Assiniboins, and Mandans; the indefatigable George Catlin with his hundreds of Indian portraits—surely the fullest artistic re-creation of the

West before photography; Alfred Jacob Miller, who was the artist for Captain Stewart's explorations in the Far West and who sketched not only Indians but the landscape—Chimney Rock and Independence Rock and the Tetons and the Wind River Mountains; the luckless John Mix Stanley, who was ubiquitous, from the lead mines of Galena to the Cherokee country, with Kearny on the Santa Fe Trail, one thousand miles by canoe up the Columbia, even to distant Hawaii—the work of a lifetime lost in the great Smithsonian fire of 1865.

Not all of these artists of the early West re-created the past for their own generation. Miller, for example, was not really known in his own day, nor was Stanley. Far more important in the creation of the popular image of America were two artist-ornithologists, Alexander Wilson and John James Audubon, who captured for all time the flora and fauna of America in its pastoral age. Wilson's nine-volume *American Ornithology* was perhaps the most ambitious work of science in the early republic. Soon came Audubon's *Birds of America,* less scientific than Wilson's *Ornithology* but more splendid, "the most magnificent monument" said Cuvier, "which art has ever raised to ornithology." And Audubon, of course, contributed more: his own extraordinary life and legend.

The sumptuous paintings of Wilson and Audubon reached the public only gradually, and in cheap reproductions. More effective was the impact of the almost forgotten school of panoramists. The hapless John Vanderlyn, who had dared display his nude *Ariadne* to an outraged public, introduced the panorama, in a specially built rotunda in New York's City Hall Park. But it was Versailles and Athens and Mexico which he chose to display; perhaps that is why he failed. His successors preferred to reveal America, and particularly the Father of Waters, which had the advantage of being almost the only object of nature longer than their paintings. One John Rowson

Smith did a panorama of the Mississippi as early as 1844;
when he displayed it at Saratoga Springs, New York, he
took in twenty thousand dollars in six weeks. Soon there
were a dozen rivals in the field: John Banvard, for example, who claimed that his Mississippi panorama was
three miles long (actually it was only a quarter of a mile
—a bad calculation, that). Poor John Stanley, who had
so little luck with his Indian paintings, scored a tremendous success with a panorama of the *Western Wilds,*
forty-two episodes, no less, requiring a minimum of two
hours to view! Greatest of all the panoramists was Henry
Lewis, who managed to cover almost three-quarters of a
mile of canvas with his paintings; his earnings from his
great panorama enabled him to settle in Düsseldorf and
learn to paint. Whatever their artistic merits, or demerits,
the panoramas helped give a whole generation of Americans some feeling for the spaciousness and the beauty of
the early West.

   Writing in 1841, Emerson had lamented that "banks
and tariffs, the newspaper and caucus, Methodism and
Unitarianism, are flat and dull to dull people but rest on
the same foundations of wonder as the town of Troy and
the temple of Delphi. . . . Our logrolling, our stumps
and their politics, our fisheries, our Negroes and Indians,
our boasts and our repudiations . . . the northern trade,
the southern planting, the western clearing, Oregon and
Texas, are yet unsung. Yet America is a poem in our eyes;
its ample geography dazzles the imagination." Poets and
artists had responded, but none had quite encompassed
American nature. Even Whitman and Winslow Homer
could not quite do that. For nature played a special role in
American history and in the process of creating a sense
of history and a national consciousness. Since the seventeenth century, Europeans have not had to concern them-

selves energetically with the conquest of nature, for nature, like history, was given. For Americans, on the other
hand, the relationship to nature was more personal, and
more complex. They had an empty continent to settle and
successive frontiers to conquer, and for them nature had
always played a twofold role: her ruggedness was a challenge, and her richness a manifestation of divine favor.
How suggestive it is that for over two hundred years
Europeans could not make up their minds whether the
New World was Paradise or an accursed place, whether
its natives were Noble Savages or degenerate men without souls. But however nature was to be interpreted—and
by the nineteenth century the paradisiacal interpretation
had triumphed—it was, in a peculiar way, the great common denominator and the great common experience. Virginians, Pilgrims, and Quakers alike could rejoice in the
abundance of nature, and generations of pioneers, even
those who were not *Mayflower* descendants or FFV's,
could cherish the common memory of hardship endured
and overcome.

Because they had conquered nature, Americans came
in time to think that they had created it and to display
toward it a proprietary interest. The stupendous flow of
Niagara, the luxuriance of the Bluegrass, the power and
majesty of the Father of Waters, the limitless expanse of
prairie and plain, the glory of the Rockies—all of these
came to be regarded as national attributes, and failure to
appreciate them, like failure to appreciate political attributes, an affront. How interesting that from "Swanee
River" to "Ol' Man River" songs celebrating nature have
usurped the place of formal patriotic music—"Dixie," for
example, or "My Old Kentucky Home," or "On the Banks
of the Wabash," or "Home on the Range," or best of all,
"America, the Beautiful."

And how interesting, too, that where in other countries
topography is local, in America it is national. In the Old

World, plains, valleys, and mountains belong to the people who happen to inhabit them, but in America the whole country, "from sea to shining sea," belongs to the whole people. The Italians and Germans traditionally celebrate their own cities, their particular churches or bridges; the English write two-volume works on Fly-casting in the Dart, or Cricket in Lower Slaughter, but until recently there has been little of this local possessiveness about Americans. "We have so much country that we have no country at all," Hawthorne lamented back in 1837, but Hawthorne was far from typical, and newcomers who could find little satisfaction in the slums of New York or the coal mines of Pennsylvania or the steel mills of Gary might yet rejoice in the Great Lakes and Yosemite. Movement, especially westward movement, is an essential ingredient in the American memory; when, in 1960, John F. Kennedy hit on the slogan, "Get America moving," he touched a responsive chord.

The task of providing themselves with a historical past was peculiarly difficult for Americans because it was not something that could be taken for granted, as with most peoples, or arranged once and for all. It was something that had to be done over and over again, for each new wave of newcomers, and that had to be kept up to date, as it were, continually reinvigorated and modernized. Above all, it had to be a past which contained an ample supply of easily grasped common denominators for a heterogeneous people, English and German, Irish and Norse, white and black, gentile and Jew, Protestant, Mormon, and Catholic, old stock and newcomer. Almost inevitably the common denominators tended to be pictorial and symbolic: the Pilgrims and Valley Forge, Washington and Lincoln, cowboy and Indian, and along with them ideas and institutions like Democracy, Liberty, Equality, the American Dream, and the American Way of Life.

One consequence of this emphasis on the simple, the

symbolic, and the ideological is that American patriotism tended to be more artificial, labored, and ostentatious than that of most Old World peoples. It was almost inevitably calculated and artificial: after all, the process of drawing the juices of tradition for a German boy newly arrived in America was very different from that for a French or an English lad at home, where everything could be taken for granted, or left to nature. Tradition in America had to be labored, for it was not born into the young; it did not fill the horizon, as the glory of Joan of Arc or the fame of Nelson filled the horizons of French and English boys and girls. The American past could not be absorbed from childhood on in the art and architecture of every town and village, in song and story and nursery rhyme, in novel and history, in the names of streets and squares and towns. Growing up in Pittsburgh or Chicago was a very different experience, historically, from growing up in London or Edinburgh, Paris or Rome. And patriotism probably had to be ostentatious; in any event, it is. Ostentation characterizes new wealth, and new loyalties as well. This is doubtless one reason there is so much emphasis on the overt observance of patriotism in America. Americans dedicate a large number of days to ceremonial patriotism: the Fourth of July, Memorial Day, Confederate Memorial Day, Veterans Day, Washington's Birthday, Lincoln's Birthday, Columbus Day, Loyalty Day, and many others, and for good measure many states have their own special holidays—Patriots' Day in Massachusetts or Texas Independence Day. Americans require children to "pledge allegiance to the flag," impose loyalty oaths for every conceivable occasion, and march in "I Am an American Day" parades, and there is no W. S. Gilbert to satirize what so many take with passionate seriousness. Perhaps nowhere else in the Western world is loyalty such a touchstone as in the United States, perhaps nowhere else are there so many organizations dedicated to fostering patriotism: the Daughters of the American Revolution, the Sons of the American Revolution, the Colonial Dames, the United Daughters of the Confederacy, the Americanism committees of the great veterans' organizations, and, more recently but no less ardently, the Minute Women.

The process of acquiring a usable past was immensely facilitated by two extraordinary circumstances. The first was the eagerness of almost all newcomers from every part of the globe to slough off their pasts and take on an American habit, an eagerness so avid and so pervasive that it made nonsense of the compunctions and fears of native Americans from Fisher Ames to Thomas Bailey Aldrich a century later. Perhaps no other society in the process of transforming itself into a nation had more co-operative material to work with. The American new-comer, as he told us over and over again, was under both moral and practical compulsions to achieve acceptance for himself and for his children by becoming completely American as rapidly and as thoroughly as possible. Crève-coeur, who saw so much, saw this, and so too the magisterial Tocqueville, but it is a lesson that has had to be relearned in every generation.

That it was possible for newcomers to become American overnight was the second circumstance. The explanation here lies in large part in the high degree of literacy that obtained in America, even in the eighteenth century, and the tradition of literacy and of education that flourished in that and the next century. Schools proved, in the long run, the most effective agencies for the creation and the transmission of an American memory. If they did not deliberately inculcate Americanism, that was because they did not need to: Noah Webster's Spellers, McGuffey's many Readers, Jedidiah Morse's Geographies and Peter Parley's Histories—these and scores of books like them conjured up an American past and provided, for generations of children, the common denominators, the stories and songs and poems, the memories and symbols. And it was the children, in turn, who educated the parents, for America is the only country where, as a matter of course, it is assumed that each new generation is wiser and more sophisticated than the old, and where parents adopt the standards of their children rather than children adopting those of their parents. For newcomers too old for school, and too inflexible to learn from their children, the work of providing an American past was carried on by those many voluntary organizations which have always performed the most miscellaneous of social tasks: churches, political parties, labor unions, lyceums, fraternal and filiopietistic organizations, and so forth.

What this meant was that the sentiment of American nationalism was, to an extraordinary degree, a literary creation, and that the national memory was a literary and, in a sense, a contrived memory. The contrast here with the Old World is sharp. There the image of the past was conjured up and sustained by a thousand testimonials: folklore and folk song, the vernacular and the patois, church music and architecture, monuments, paintings and murals, the pageantry of the court and of popular feasts and holidays. To be sure, literature—poetry and drama and formal histories—came to play a role, but only when it was quarried from cultural foundations that went deep. In America the image of the past was largely the creation of the poets and the storytellers, and chiefly of the New England-New York group who flourished between the War of 1812 and the War for the Union, that group familiar to an earlier generation through the amiable game of Authors: Irving, Cooper, and Bryant; Longfellow, Hawthorne, and Whittier; Emerson, Lowell, and Holmes. These were the Founding

Fathers of American literary nationalism, and their
achievement was scarcely less remarkable than that of
the Founding Fathers of political nationalism.

In a single generation these men of letters gave Americans the dramas, the characters, the settings, which were
to instruct and delight succeeding generations: Uncas
and Deerslayer and Long Tom Coffin; Rip Van Winkle
and the Headless Horseman; Miles Standish, Paul Revere, Evangeline, and Hiawatha; Goodman Brown, the
Gray Champion, and Hester Prynne, as well as the Salem
Customs House, the House of Seven Gables, the Old
Manse, and the Great Stone Face; Skipper Ireson and
Concord Bridge and Old Ironsides and the One-Hoss Shay
and Hosea Biglow with all his Yankee company.

This richly embroidered image of the past which the
literary Founding Fathers created and imposed upon
Americans was very largely a New England image, and
much that was most distinctive about American nationalism was to be conditioned by this circumstance. It meant
that Americans on Iowa prairies or the plains of Texas
would sing *"I love thy rocks and rills, thy woods and.
templed hills"* with no sense of incongruity; that Plymouth
would supplant Jamestown as the birthplace of America;
that Thanksgiving would be everywhere a New England
holiday; that Paul Revere would be the winged horseman
of American history and Concord Bridge the American
equivalent of the Rubicon; that Boston's Statehouse would
vindicate its claim—or Holmes's—to be the "hub of the
solar system." If all this was hard on the South, southerners had only themselves to blame for their indifference to
their own men of letters. The most familiar of southern
symbols came from the North: Harriet Beecher Stowe of
New England gave us Uncle Tom and Little Eva and
Topsy and Eliza, and it was Stephen Foster of Pittsburgh
who sentimentalized the Old South, while even "Dixie"
had northern origins.

The literary task of creating a usable past was largely performed by 1865; after that date perhaps only Mark Twain, Bret Harte, and Louisa May Alcott added anything substantial to the treasure house of historical memories. This was, in perspective, the most significant achievement of American literature and one almost without parallel in the literature of any other country in a comparable period; perhaps Norway provides the closest parallel. How interesting that a people supposed to be indifferent to literature—supposed by some to have no literature—should depend so largely upon literature for the nourishment of its historical self-consciousness. Certainly the speed and effectiveness with which Americans rallied their resources to supply themselves with an historical past cannot but excite astonishment. And what a past it was—splendid, varied, romantic, and all but blameless, in which there were heroes but no villains, victories but no defeats—a past that was all prologue to the Rising Glory of America.

CONSTITUTIONAL HISTORY
AND THE
HIGHER LAW

"SHOULD an act of parliament be against any of His natural laws, which are immutably true, their declaration would be contrary to eternal truth, equity and justice, and consequently void." [1]

"There are eternal principles of justice which no government has a right to disregard. . . . Some acts, although not expressly forbidden, may be against the plain and obvious dictates of reason." [2]

"It is conceded . . . that there are certain limitations upon this power, not prescribed in express terms by any constitutional provision, but inherent in the subject itself, which attend its exercise under all circumstances and which are as inflexible and absolute in their restraints as if directly imposed in the most positive of words." [3]

SOURCE: *The Constitution Reconsidered,* ed. Conyers Read. Copyright 1938 Columbia University Press, New York. Reprinted by permission.

[1] James Otis: *Rights of the British Colonies Asserted and Proved,* p. 70.
[2] Bank of State v. Cooper, 2 Yerg. (Tenn.) 599.
[3] People v. Salem, 20 Mich. 452.

"It is true that no one has a vested right in any particular rule of common law, but it is also true that the legislative power of a state can only be exerted in subordination to the fundamental principles of right and justice which the guaranty of due process in the Fourteenth Amendment is intended to preserve." [4]

Here are four *obiter dicta*. The first is from James Otis's famous argument against parliamentary tyranny in 1764, the second from Justice Green's opinion in the Tennessee bank case of 1831, the third from the great Cooley's ruling on the nature of a public purpose in 1870, the fourth from Chief Justice Taft's defense of the use of the injunction in labor disputes in 1921. Approximately half a century separates each of these four dicta; the philosophy, even the language, is the same. Nor would it be difficult to discover similar expressions of juristic philosophy for every decade of our history; [5] such an exercise

[4] Truax v. Corrigan, 257 U.S. 312.

[5] Writing in 1894, Judge Dillon pointed out that "rules regulating civil conduct may . . . be imported by the tribunals, when necessary for the purposes of actual decisions of causes, from the field of morality. Such rules, however, become invested with the quality of law only when and to the extent that the judges authenticate or adopt, or set upon them the *imprimatur* of the State,— that is, recognize and enforce them by their judgments. . . . It is a mistake to suppose that this process has ceased. In consequence of modern inventions, aggregations of capital, and changed social conditions, I am inclined to think that at no previous periods has this method of legal growth and change been in more constant and active operation than at the present time." John F. Dillon: *The Laws and Jurisprudence of England and America* (Boston, 1894), p. 5. For examples and discussion of higher law pronouncements from state and federal bench, see C. G. Haines: *Revival of Natural Law Concepts* (Cambridge, 1930) and *The American Doctrine of Judicial Review* (New York, 1914); Benjamin F. Wright: *American Interpretations of Natural Law* (Cambridge, 1931); J. R. Commons: *Legal Foundations of Capitalism* (New York, 1924); John Dickinson: *Administrative Justice and the Supremacy of the Law in the United States* (Cambridge, 1927); Edouard Lambert: *Le Gouvernement des juges et la lutte contre la législation sociale aux États-Unis* (Paris, 1921); Louis Boudin: *Government by Judiciary*, 2 vols. (New York, 1932); E. S. Corwin: "A Basic Doctrine of American Constitutional Law,"

is, however, scarcely necessary to emphasize what these brief excerpts illustrate—the persistence of the doctrine of the higher law, a persistence all the more remarkable in that the philosophy which justifies it has been repudiated now for three quarters of a century.[6]

It is as dangerous, perhaps, and as gratuitous, for the historian to suggest a definition of the higher law as for the courts to attempt a definition of due process or the police power, and we would have irreproachable precedent for evading the task. Yet we may submit a characterization. We suggest that higher law is that body of law which is grounded in the nature of man and finds its inspiration and derives its authority from *a priori* or intuitive rather than experimental facts. Such a law was natural, perhaps inevitable, in the eighteenth century. It fitted a universe ruled, it might be supposed, by reason, and susceptible to understanding. It was the logical expression of the philosophy of the Englightenment, and served well as the constitution for the heavenly city of the eighteenth-century philosophers.[7] It is superfluous here to observe, what has been observed so often and so learnedly, that it served, too, the purpose of Americans in their struggle with the mother country and in their effort to construct a political system grounded on reason [8]—su-

Michigan Law Review, XII, 247, and "The Doctrine of Due Process of Law before the Civil War," *Harvard Law Review*, XXIV, 366, 460; John Dickinson: "The Law behind the Law," *Columbia Law Review*, XXIX, 113; C. G. Haines: "Implied Limitations on Legislatures," *Texas Law Review*, II, 269, and "Law of Nature in State and Federal Decisions," *Yale Law Journal*, XXV, 617; and Louis Boudin: "Anarchic Element in the Notion of a Higher Law," *New York University Law Quarterly*, VIII, 1.

[6] "To defend a doctrine of natural rights today requires either insensibility to the world's progress or else considerable courage in the face of it"—Morris Cohen: "Jus Naturale Redivivum," *Philosophical Review*, XXV, 761.

[7] See Carl Becker's masterly *Heavenly City of the Eighteenth Century Philosophers* (New Haven, 1932).

[8] See especially C. F. Mullett: *Fundamental Law and the American Revolution* (New York, 1933); B. F. Wright: op. cit.; R. G.

perfluous to recall Jefferson's appeal in the Declaration to self-evident truths and to the laws of Nature and Nature's God, or John Adams's faith in rights "rooted in the constitution of the intellectual and moral world," or the youthful Hamilton's joyous assurance that "the sacred rights of mankind are . . . written as with a sunbeam in the whole volume of human nature, by the hand of Divinity itself, and can never be erased or obscured by mortal power." [9]

This concept of law, which was to Americans the common sense of the matter, implied that law was a science, followed a fixed and regular course, and was the same yesterday, today, and forever. The principles of law were like the Axioms of Euclid, nor did they appeal with any less compelling force to the understanding of right-minded men. This attitude toward law, like the concept of higher law itself, was a tenacious one. It persisted well into the thirties in what Dean Pound called mechanical jurisprudence,[1] Professor Cohen the phonographic theory of the law; [2] and in the decisions of the courts and the lucubrations of the bar,[3] and few things are more suggestive than

---

Adams: *Political Ideas of the American Revolution* (Durham, 1912); A. C. McLaughlin: *Courts, Constitutions and Parties,* Ch. i (Chicago, 1912).

[9] Quoted in C. E. Merriam: *American Political Theories,* p. 48.

[1] Pound: "Mechanical Jurisprudence," *Columbia Law Review,* VIII, 605. The great John Austin referred to "the childish fiction employed by our judges that judiciary or common law is not made by them, but is a miraculous something made by nobody, existing, I suppose, from eternity and merely declared from time to time by the judges." *Lectures on Jurisprudence,* 4th cdn., p. 655.

[2] Morris R. Cohen: "Legal Theories and Social Science," New York State Bar Association *Proceedings,* XXXVIII, 177.

[3] "The judges make no laws, they establish no policy, they never enter into the domain of public action. They do not govern." Justice Brewer, in *The Movement of Coercion* (1893), quoted in Dickinson: "Law behind the Law," *Columbia Law Review,* XXIX, 113, 115; and in South Carolina v. U.S., 199 U.S. 437 at 448. Justice Brewer said, "The Constitution is a written instrument. As such its meaning does not alter. That which it meant when adopted it means now." "Any intimation that the Constitution is

the cavalier and even contemptuous manner in which
Professor Cohens's masterly analysis of this phonographic
theory was dismissed by members of the Bar Association
of New York.[4] We have here to recognize what Justice
Holmes called the illusion of certainty,[5] and that it is an
essential part of the concept of natural law.

Americans, having discovered the usefulness of natural law, elaborated it, and having justified its application
by success, protected that success by transforming natural into constitutional law: the state and federal constitutions. And in so far as natural law had found refuge in

flexible, even in response to the police power, is unsound. . . .
That a state may not impair the obligations of a contract or that a
person can not be deprived of his property without due process of
law, are principles fundamental, and if the Legislature, in response to public clamor for an experimental social reform, may
break down these constitutional guaranties . . . all guaranties of
the Constitution . . . may be exchanged, modified, or totally
eliminated." Judge Van Orsdel, in Adkins v. Children's Hospital,
quoted in Boudin: *Government by Judiciary,* II, 551. "The provisions of the Constitution seem so direct and definite as to need no
reinforcing words and to leave no other inquiry than, Does the
statute under review come within their prohibition? . . . By the
Fifth Amendment no person can be deprived of property without
due process of law. The prohibitions need no strengthening comment. They are as absolute as axioms." Dissenting opinion of
Justice McKenna, in Block v. Hirsh, 256 U.S. 135. And as recently
as 1937, we may read, "It is urged that the question involved
should now receive fresh consideration . . . because of the 'economic conditions which have supervened,' but the meaning of the
Constitution does not change with the ebb and flow of economic
events." Justice Sutherland, in West Coast Hotel Co. v. Parrish,
75th Cong. 1st Sess. Sen. Doc. No. 46, p. 10.

[4] See discussion of Professor Cohen's address, in New York
State Bar Association *Proceedings,* XXXVIII, 177.

[5] "Perhaps one of the reasons why judges do not like to discuss
questions of policy, or to put decisions in terms upon their views
as lawmakers, is that the moment you leave the path of merely
logical deduction you lose the illusion of certainty which makes
legal reasoning seem like mathematics. But the certainty is only
an illusion nevertheless." *Collected Legal Papers,* p. 126. See also
"The Path of the Law," ibid., p. 167; and W. N. Hohfeld: "Fundamental Legal Conceptions as Applied to Judicial Reasoning," *Yale
Law Journal,* XXVI, 711.

written law, there was little reason to invoke it; it was automatically invoked whenever the constitution was invoked, and this was the logic of Marshall in the Marbury case.[6] There were, to be sure, occasions when judges of state and federal courts found it desirable to suggest natural law limitations distinct from and superior to even written constitutions,[7] but the impressive thing is the paucity of such occasions in the first half century of our history.[8]

Not until the rise of transcendentalism in the 1840s did the doctrine of the higher law become again significant, and then it was applied more realistically, more radically, and more honestly, than at any other time in our history.[9] Judges such as Marshall, Chase, Story, or Kent, and their successors, were always under compulsion to circumscribe their interpretation of the higher law by written constitutions, precedents, and juridical philosophy; this left some room for intuition, but only in limited fields. Emerson, Channing, Parker, Sumner, Phillips, and Garrison were embarrassed by no such considerations. They recognized readily enough that the higher law was intuitive, recognized it even where they made concessions to the skepticism of men by substantiating facts of intuition with facts of experimental observation. And they applied the higher law not only to the institution of slavery—the most familiar application—but to all hu-

[6] 1 Cranch 137.

[7] See, for example, the early case of Calder v. Bull, 3 Dallas 386 and the much later case of Wynehamer v. The People, 13 N.Y. 378, and other cases discussed in E. S. Corwin: "Doctrine of Due Process before the Civil War," *Harvard Law Review*, XXIV, 366, and "Extension of Judicial Review in New York State, 1783–1905," *Michigan Law Review*, XV, 281; and Rosenthal: "Massachusetts Acts and Resolves Declared Unconstitutional by the Supreme Court of Massachusetts," *Massachusetts Law Quarterly*, I, 301.

[8] Corwin, Haines, and Wright are all agreed on this point.

[9] H. S. Commager: *Theodore Parker* (Boston, 1936), *passim*.

man institutions: church, state, the family, property; and
not the least of these was property.[1] They challenged
society to show, before the bar of reason, its title to the
accepted order of things.[2]

It was not difficult for philosophers to do this, only
courageous, for consistency demanded the philosophical
conclusion but did not require its practical application.
Men breathed still the intellectual atmosphere of the Enlightenment, lived in a universe guided by reason and
guarded by a beneficent providence, cherished faith in
virtue and in the ultimate authority of justice and morality. The appeal to the higher law was valid; it was inevitable. And it was made on behalf of human rights rather
than of property rights.

It was, to be sure, a matter of emphasis. The Revolutionary Fathers had invoked the higher law on behalf of
life and liberty as well as of property, but did not assume
or even suspect the existence of any conflict; the transcendentalists discovered a basic conflict between liberty
and property, and invoked the higher law on behalf of the
former.[3] Justice Shaw had already defined the police
power,[4] but the possibilities of the police power for the

[1] See, for example, Parker's sermons on "The Mercantile
Classes," "The Perishing Classes," "The Dangerous Classes," and
"The Moral Dangers Incident to Prosperity," in *Works*, Centenary
edn., Vol. X.

[2] Emerson's "New England Reformers" is still the best account
of this.

[3] See, for example, Parker's sermon on "The Function of Conscience in Relation to the Laws of Men," *Works*, Vol. XI: "The
law of God has eminent domain everywhere, over the private
passions of Oliver and Charles, the special interests of Carthage
and Rome, over all official business, all precedents, all human
statutes, over all the conventional affairs of one man or of mankind. My own conscience is to declare that law to me, yours to
you, and is before all private passions or public interests, the
decision of majorities and a world full of precedents." For a fuller
discussion, see Commager, op. cit., Ch. x, "Slavery and the Higher
Law."

[4] Commonwealth v. Alger, 7 Cushing 53 (Massachusetts Reports).

regulation or even destruction of property devoted to anti-social or immoral uses was not apprehended. So transcendentalism, instead of formulating a socio-legal philosophy which would have permitted the state, in the exercise of its police power, to strike down slavery, intemperance, immorality, and the inequitable accumulation of wealth, encouraged instead a highly individualistic and personal repudiation of evil. It was a natural attitude, for transcendentalism is necessarily individualistic, but the failure of the transcendental reformers to socialize their conscience or to develop a legal instrument with which to implement their higher law concepts was significant. Had they been able to formulate a rationale for the identification of the individual conscience with the social conscience, had they been able, in short, to socialize the higher law, it is probable that much of the later conflict between due process and police power would have been avoided. It is probable, indeed, that the courts might have been forced to recognize the consonance of higher law and police power instead of arraying the two in opposition.

The world of reason, the universe of law, was shattered by the doctrine of evolution; the kingdom of law gave way to the principalities of laws, the law of nature to the laws of men. Transcendentalism was abandoned for experimentalism, idealism for pragmatism. Science, theology, politics, education, economics even, all accommodated themselves to the new philosophy, all recognized the evolutionary and pragmatic character of their data. Yet the doctrine of natural law, repudiated in all the sciences and in most of the social sciences, found refuge in jurisprudence, or, at least, in the courts. It found not only refuge here, it found implementation.

This, the third chapter in the history of the higher law in America, begins properly with the due process clause of the Fourteenth Amendment. That clause was not a

new one in our Constitution, but it was new as a limitation upon states, and the meaning which was read into it
was new. That property rights constituted one of the
sacred trinity of natural rights was not a discovery of
either Justice Field or Justice Brewer; the fact had been
observed by the Fathers and adumbrated by the courts on
numerous occasions. But in the half-century after Reconstruction the courts managed to broaden immensely
the concept of property, to read property into the concept
of liberty, and to apply extra-constitutional guarantees to
both by interpreting due process as an implied limitation
upon legislative action.[5]

This is a thrice-told tale. What must be emphasized is
that the court, in interpreting due process, police power,
property, liberty, reasonable, fair return, public interest,
public purpose, and so forth, has been engaged not only
in legislation but in superlegislation.[6] The function of the
courts, in importing higher law doctrine into the Constitution, has been constitutional rather than legislative
merely, and it may be said that since the 1880s the
Supreme Court has sat as a continuous constitutional
convention. For the laws which the Court has formulated

[5] Haines: *Revival of Natural Law Concepts.* See also Ray
Brown: "Due Process, Police Power, and the Supreme Court,"
Harvard Law Review, XL, 943.
[6] "The chief law-makers in our country may be, and often are,
the judges, because they are the final seat of authority. Every time
they interpret contract, property, vested rights, due process, liberty, they necessarily enact into law parts of a system of social
philosophy; and since such interpretation is fundamental, they
give direction to all law-making." Theodore Roosevelt, Message to
Congress, Dec. 8, 1908. "The Court in addition to the proper use
of its judicial function has improperly set itself up as a third
House of the Congress—a superlegislature, as one of the Justices
has called it. . . ." F. D. Roosevelt, Address on Reorganization of
the Federal Judiciary, March 9, 1937. "Denying that they are
applying anything but the express terms of written constitutions
the justices of higher courts in the United States have in effect
created a superconstitution, a superior law which in certain respects is regarded as unchangeable by the people themselves."
Haines: *Revival of Natural Law Concepts,* p. 227.

are in very fact higher laws. They have not only legislative but constitutional validity. They are not subject to repeal by ordinary political action, but only by the most laborious and uncertain processes.[7]

What we have to consider, then, is a body of legislation and of constitutional provisions formulated by the courts with the particular purpose of protecting property against legislative restrictions or exactions. It would be superfluous to recall particular examples of such higher law legislation; it may be suggested that wherever the due process clause has been given substantive rather than merely procedural significance, and wherever police power has been challenged to show its credentials, such judicial legislation has occurred.[8] It may be suggested more specifically that every attempt by the judiciary to discover what property is clothed with a public interest,[9] what action constitutes a public purpose,[1] what occupations or

[7] The failure of President Roosevelt's effort to reform the federal judiciary in 1937 is evidence enough on this point.

[8] Note Judge Story's reference to the due process clause of the Fifth Amendment: "This clause in effect affirms the right of trial according to the process and proceedings of the common law." *Commentaries on the Constitution*, sec. 1789. The literature on this subject is immense. See especially R. L. Mott: *Due Process of Law: an Historical and Analytical Treatise* (Indianapolis, 1926); L. P. McGehee: *Due Process of Law under the Federal Constitution* (Northport, Long Island, 1906); E. Freund: *The Police Power, Public Policy, and Constitutional Rights* (Chicago, 1904); C. E. Hughes: *The Supreme Court of the United States* (New York, 1928); H. E. Willis: "Due Process of Law under the U.S. Constitution," *University of Pennsylvania Law Review*, LXX, 331; C. M. Hough: "Due Process of Law—Today," *Harvard Law Review*, XXXII, 218.

[9] Munn v. Illinois, 94 U.S. 113. But see Taft's opinion in Wolff Packing Co. v. Kansas Court of Industrial Relations, 262 U.S. 522, Holmes's dissent in Tyson v. Banton, 273 U.S. 418, Brandeis's dissent in New State Ice Company v. Liebmann, 285 U.S. 262, and the admirable discussion in W. Hamilton: "Affectation with a Public Interest," *Yale Law Journal*, XXXIX, 1104.

[1] By 1880 the courts had arrived at the position, announced by Judge Cooley in his *Constitutional Limitations*, that it is for the courts to determine what is a public purpose. The leading case is Loan Association v. Topeka, 20 Wallace 655. But note Judge

what conditions are of a nature to justify state regulation,[2] what constitutes liberty in the economic order,[3] and
what may be a reasonable and what a confiscatory return
on investment,[4] is higher law legislation.

And this judicial higher law, like all higher law, is
intuitive and transcendental; Dean Pound characterized
it more bluntly as "purely personal and arbitrary." [5] For,
as Professor Corwin has observed, "in relation to constitutional law . . . the constitutional document has become

---

Clifford's dissent, and the modification of the doctrine in Green v.
Frazier, 253 U.S. 233. "A careful reading of the numerous cases
in which this doctrine has been announced impels the conclusion
that none of them progressed very far in the direction of finding
constitutional basis for the doctrine either in express provisions or
reasonable implication." McBain: "Taxation for a Private Purpose," *Political Science Quarterly*, XXIX, 185. See also illuminating study of the subject in F. Goodnow: *Social Reform and the
Constitution*, Ch. 7.

[2] The cases are too numerous to list, but see *in re* Jacobs, 98
New York 98; Holden v. Hardy, 169 U.S. 366; Lochner v. New
York, 198 U.S. 45; Adkins v. Children's Hospital, 261 U.S. 525;
and any wage or hour or factory law cases.

[3] See Pound: "Liberty of Contract," *Yale Law Journal*, XXIII,
472. Most important labor cases involve a consideration of the
nature and meaning of "liberty" in the Fourteenth Amendment.
H. R. Seager: "Attitude of American Courts toward Restrictive
Labor Legislation," *Political Science Quarterly*, XIX, 589; T. R.
Powell: "The Judiciality of Minimum Wage Legislation," *Harvard
Law Review*, XXXIX, 545.

[4] In Munn v. Illinois this question was resigned to the legislative branch, but by the end of the following decade the Court had
beat a retreat from this dangerous position, and the requirement
of judicial review, e.g., judicial determination, was clear by 1889.
Chicago, Milwaukee and St. Paul R. R. Co., v. Minnesota, 134 U.S.
418. See H. Hull: "Reasonable Rates," *Michigan Law Review*, XV,
478; R. Brown: "Due Process of Law, Police Power and the Supreme Court," *Harvard Law Review*, XL, 943; and D. Richberg:
"Value—by Judicial Fiat," *Harvard Law Review*, XL, 567.

[5] "Common Law and Legislation," *Harvard Law Review*, XXI,
383, at 393. John Dickinson has put it well: "The body of considerations which chance to operate on a judge or court at the
moment of bringing a new rule of law into existence may properly
be regarded as the determining factor in the creation of law. The
theory of the 'higher law' . . . is nothing but a persistent assumption that these considerations must themselves take the form of,
or at least be conceived as constituting, jural law." "The Law
behind the Law," *Columbia Law Review*, XXIX, 307.

hardly more than a formal point of reference. For most of the Court's excursions in the constitutional sphere the constitutional document is little more than a taking-off ground; the journey out and back occurs in a far different medium of selected precedents, speculative views regarding the nature of the Constitution and the purposes designed to be served by it, and unstated judicial preferences." [6]

These views and preferences are conditioned by precedents, but the choice of precedents is almost limitless,[7] and a long record of decisions and dissents have revealed that judges rarely find themselves embarrassed by the absence of precedents that appear controlling on either side of an issue.[8] The question is not one of precedents, but of the choice of precedents, and what conditions this choice is what Mr. Holmes has called the "inarticulate major premise." [9] Whenever the court is called upon to determine whether mining is a hazardous occupation,[1] whether labor in a bakeshop is fatiguing,[2] whether ware-

[6] "Standpoint in Constitutional Law," *Boston University Law Review*, XVII, 513.

[7] There is an illuminating discussion of this in E. C. Corwin: *Twilight of the Supreme Court* (New Haven, 1934), Ch. 3.

[8] Many of the New Deal decisions have taken the form of elaborate debates between liberal and conservative members of the court. Note Justice Harlan's frank statement in Monongahela Bridge Co. v. U.S., 216 U.S. 177, at 195: "The courts have rarely, if ever, felt themselves so restrained by technical rules that they could not find some remedy consistent with the law, for acts . . . that violated natural justice or were hostile to the fundamental principles devised for the protection of the essential rights of property."

[9] Lochner v. New York, 198 U.S. 45, at 74. See also "The Path of the Law," *Collected Legal Papers*, p. 167. "I think that the judges themselves have failed adequately to recognize their duty of weighing considerations of social advantage. The duty is inevitable, and the result of the often proclaimed judicial aversion to deal with such considerations is simply to leave the very ground and foundation of judgments inarticulate, and often unconscious."

[1] Holden v. Hardy, 106 U.S. 366.

[2] Lochner v. New York, 198 U.S. 45.

houses,[3] slaughterhouses,[4] insurance,[5] banks,[6] ice plants,[7] employment agencies,[8] theaters,[9] are businesses clothed with a public interest, whether women are physiologically different from men,[1] whether the decision of a commission conforms to due process,[2] whether a minimum wage [3] or a limitation upon hours [4] or a prohibition of a yellow-dog contract [5] constitutes deprivation of property without due process, whether education,[6] or the distribution of seed,[7] or the amelioration of the lot of the blind [8] are public purposes—whenever the Court is called upon

[3] Munn v. Illinois, 94 U.S. 113.
[4] Slaughter House Cases, 16 Wallace 36.
[5] German Alliance Insurance Co. v. Lewis, 233 U.S. 389.
[6] Noble State Bank v. Haskell, 219 U.S. 110.
[7] New State Ice Co. v. Liebmann, 285 U.S. 262.
[8] Adams v. Tanner, 244 U.S. 590 and Ribnik v. McBride, 277 U.S. 350.
[9] Tyson v. Banton, 273 U.S. 418.
[1] Muller v. Oregon, 208 U.S. 412 and Adkins v. Children's Hospital, 261 U.S. 525.
[2] C. M. and St. P.R.R. Co. v. Minn., 134 U.S. 418, and Smyth v. Ames, 169 U.S. 466.
[3] Adkins v. Children's Hospital, 261 U.S. 525; Morehead v. N.Y. ex. rel. Tipaldo, 298 U.S. 587; West Coast Hotel Co. v. Parrish (March 29, 1937), U.S. 75th Cong. 1 Sess. Sen. Doc. No. 46.
[4] Bunting v. Oregon, 243 U.S. 426, and *supra*, note 37, 38.
[5] Hitchman Coal and Coke Co. v. Mitchell, 245 U.S. 229.
[6] The Supreme Court of Missouri invalidated a law providing for progressive inheritance tax for purposes of scholarships at the State University. "Paternalism," said the Court, "is an assumption by the government of a quasi-fatherly relation to the citizen and his family, involving excessive governmental regulation of the private affairs and business methods and interests of the people . . . and is pernicious in its tendencies. . . . Paternalism is a plant which should receive no nourishment upon the soil of Missouri." State v. Switzler, 143 Missouri 287.
[7] State v. Osawkee Township, 14 Kansas 418, invalidating a state law providing for the free distribution of seed to farmers.
[8] Lucas Co. v. State, 75 Ohio 114, invalidating a county ordinance providing for allowances to indigent blind. "If the power of the legislature to confer an annuity upon any class of needy citizens is admitted upon the ground that its tendency will be to prevent them from becoming a public charge," said the court, "innumerable cases may clamor for similar bounties, . . . and it is doubted that any line could be drawn short of an equal distribution of property."

to decide any of these questions, it makes a choice of precedents and invokes the higher law to invalidate the choice.

The character of that choice becomes more apparent if we note some of the alternatives among which the Court has chosen. Why, for example, has the Court permitted a liberal interpretation of due process where state control over personal rights was at stake, but insisted upon a narrow and traditional interpretation where regulation of property was involved? [9] Why has the Court chosen to read a broad interpretation into the word property, but a narrow interpretation into the phrase property clothed with a public interest? [1] Why has it seen fit to sustain uniformity of railroad rates in intrastate as well as interstate commerce as a proper instrument for regulation,[2] but rejected protection of the right of railway labor to

[9] See for example Spies v. Illinois, 123 U.S. 131, Brooks v. Missouri, 124 U.S. 394, and, above all, Hurtado v. Calif., 110 U.S. 516. In his dissent in Maxwell v. Dow, Justice Harlan said, "If due process of law, required by the Fourteenth Amendment, does not allow a state to take private property without just compensation, but does allow the life and liberty of the citizen to be taken in a mode that is repugnant to the settled usages and modes of proceeding authorized at the time the constitution was adopted . . . it would seem that the protection of private property is of more consequence than the protection of the life and liberty of the citizen." 176 U.S. 581, at 614. And Holmes, in his dissent in the Frank case, expressed the same idea even more bluntly: "We see no reason for a less liberal rule in a matter of life and death." Frank v. Magnum, 237 U.S. 309. See also J. R. Commons: *Legal Foundations of Capitalism*, pp. 341 ff.

[1] The best analysis of the relation of the judiciary to the protection of property is to be found in R. Ely's masterly *Property and Contract in Their Relation to the Distribution of Wealth*, 2 vols. (New York, 1914). Commons: *Legal Foundations of Capitalism*, and Goodnow: *Social Reform and the Constitution*, are scarcely less valuable. See also A. T. Hadley: "The Constitutional Position of Property in America," *The Independent*, April 18, 1908; J. Orton: "Confusion of Property with Privilege," *The Independent*, Aug. 19 and Aug. 26, 1909; and Kales: "Due Process, the Inarticulate Major Premise, and the Adamson Act," *Yale Law Journal*, XXVI, 519.

[2] R.R. Commission of Wisconsin v. C.B. & Q. R.R. Co., 257 U.S. 563.

organize as an improper extension of the commerce power? [3] Why has it recognized the concept of public purpose and public interest with reference to the advantageous exploitation of natural resources,[4] but not with respect to the advantageous conservation of human resources? [5] Why has it imported the rule of reason into the Sherman Act with respect to industry [6] but ignored it with reference to labor? [7] The questions could be multiplied almost indefinitely, but these will suffice for illustration. In no instance was the answer inescapably determined by the words of the Constitution and by precedents. In every instance the answer was given on the basis of considerations of higher law imported into the Constitution by the judges themselves.

We come here, at long last, to the business of the constitutional historian. In so far as our constitutional history, especially since the Fourteenth Amendment, is judicial legislation inspired by higher law, his business is to trace that legislation and analyze that law. The historian cannot be content with recording the conclusions of the Court, as if they were self-explanatory. Conclusions may be sufficient for the professional lawyer and are—if we may trust the casebooks—sufficient for constitutional law, but the historian can no more read constitutional history through decisions than he can read political history through statutes. He is required to discover the philo-

[3] Adair v. U.S., 208 U.S. 161.

[4] See the thoughtful remarks in Goodnow: *Social Reform and the Constitution,* pp. 325 ff., and citations.

[5] It is unnecessary here to recapitulate the long history of judicial review of wage and hour, tenement house and factory inspection and compensation legislation. Ives v. South Buffalo, 201 N.Y. 271 and Adkins v. Children's Hospital, 261 U.S. 525, are typical.

[6] Standard Oil Co. of N.J. v. U.S., 221 U.S. 1.

[7] I imply that a "rule of reason" for labor would have resulted in a different decision in Duplex Printing Press Co. v. Deering, 254 U.S. 443, and in Bedford Cut Stone Co. v. Journeymen Stonecutters, 274 U.S. 37, both involving some phase of the secondary boycott.

sophical and temperamental bases of judicial legislation, required, particularly, to discover the nature of the higher-law concepts which control so many of the more important decisions.

We live under governments whose limits are set by courts,[8] and with reference to intuitive ideas that find expression in the slippery phrases of due process, police power, liberty, public purpose, and so forth. Nor are these limits negative merely; the application of limitations is a positive act. Yet we lack appreciation of the nature of these intuitive concepts, and we lack a codification of legislation inspired by them. We confess that the judiciary is a constitutional convention, but we have not inquired into its membership, credentials, purposes, or achievements; we confess that it is a legislative chamber, but we do not know what laws it has made. We have not even analyzed the psychology of popular acquiescence in the higher law, though it constitutes obviously a basic paradox in our political system. How does it happen that democracy not only tolerates but encourages the application by courts of higher law restrictions upon itself? Hamilton, who approved of judicial review, pointed out that abuse of this power, if it ever occurred, would be speedily rebuked by impeachment;[9] how does it happen

[8] "We are governed by our judges and not by our legislatures. . . . It is our judges who formulate our public policies and our basic laws." Bruce: *The American Judge* (New York, 1924), pp. 6, 8. On judicial government see also Brooks Adams: *The Theory of Social Revolutions* (New York, 1914); Cardozo: *Nature of the Judicial Process* (New Haven, 1921); Holmes: *The Common Law*, pp. 34 ff.

[9] *The Federalist*, No. 81. "It may in the last place be observed that the supposed danger of judiciary encroachments on the legislative authority . . . is in reality a phantom. Particular misconstructions and contraventions of the will of the legislature may now and then happen; but they can never be so extensive as to amount to an inconvenience, or in any sensible degree to affect the order of the political system. . . . And the inference is greatly fortified by the consideration of the important constitutional check which the power of instituting impeachments in one

that the sanction of impeachment, as a weapon of democracy, has never been effectively invoked to restrain judicial abuse of power? An elective rather than an appointive judiciary held promise of articulating the courts to democracy; can it be shown that elective judges have been less eager to apply higher law limitations upon democratic processes than have appointive judges? [1]

The fact is that a certain divinity has hedged the Court and its cabalistic oracles, until it has come to seem almost blasphemous for historians to suggest that the Court is a political institution or that jurisprudence is sociological, though deans of law schools may, apparently, make these observations with impunity.[2] The historian has no hesitation in investigating the mechanism of the legislative or executive departments or the history of tariff or land or banking legislation, but he has avoided a realistic consideration of the mechanism of the judiciary or the history of judicial legislation. He abandons Plutarch and embraces Boswell or even Strachey as a model for political biography, but he has scarcely attempted to write biographies of judges, and when he does he dons his most somber robes.[3] He assumes cheerfully

---

part of the legislative body and of determining them in another, would give to that body upon the members of the judicial department. This is alone a complete security. . . ."

[1] Dean Frank Sommer of the New York University School of Law has investigated this subject and concludes that elective judges are, on the whole, no more responsive to democratic opinion than are appointive judges.

[2] Pound, "Scope and Purpose of Sociological Jurisprudence," *Harvard Law Review*, XXIV, 591; XXV, 140, 489. See also his *Law and Morals* (Chapel Hill, 1926) and *Interpretations of Legal History* (New York, 1923).

[3] See, for example, the reverent approach of Beveridge in his biography of *Marshall* or of Trimble in his recent *Waite*. Silas Bent, *Justice Oliver Wendell Holmes* (New York, 1932) and Mason, *Brandeis and the Modern State* (Princeton, 1933) escape the taint. Happily this situation is now (1966) completely changed. Mark D. Howe: *Justice Oliver Wendell Holmes*, 2 vols. (Cambridge, Mass.; 1957, 1963); Henry Pringle: *Life and Times of William Howard Taft*, 2 vols. (New York and Toronto, 1939);

enough the rôle of social or economic or intellectual historian where the executive or legislative departments are concerned, but does not willingly confess the same technique applicable to the study of courts.

Yet the character of the modern higher law, subjective as it is, is no more elusive than the character of Jeffersonian democracy or Manifest Destiny or other concepts which the historian has managed to pin down and survey. Certainly it is subject to investigation and susceptible to interpretation. We cannot discover with finality just how and why the Court imported into the Constitution higherlaw doctrines of *laissez-faire* capitalism, any more than we can discover with finality just how American business embraced Spencerian philosophy. But we can achieve an awareness of the fact and we can perhaps illuminate the process.

"The very considerations which judges so rarely mention," said Justice Holmes, in his memorable study of the common law, "and always with an apology, are the secret roots from which the law draws all the juices of life. I mean, of course, considerations of what is expedient to the community concerned. Every important principle which is developed by litigation is in fact and at bottom the result of more or less definitely understood views of public policy; most generally, to be sure, under our practice and traditions, the unconscious result of instinctive preferences and inarticulate convictions, but none the less traceable to views of public policy in the last analysis." [4] What Judge Holmes had in mind was in part, and

Alpheus T. Mason: *Harlan Fiske Stone: Pillar of the Law* (New York, 1956); Charles Fairman: *Mr. Justice Miller and the Supreme Court, 1862–1890* (Cambridge, Mass., 1939); Donald G. Morgan: *Justice William Johnson: The First Dissenter* (Columbia, S.C., 1954); Fowler v. Harper: *Justice Rutledge and the Bright Constellation* (Indianapolis, 1965), and many others abandon the filiopietistic attitude for realism.

[4] *The Common Law*, pp. 35–6. See also dissenting opinion in Vegelahn v. Guntner, 167 Mass. 92: "The true grounds of deci-

only in part, the intellectual climate in which judges lived and wrote. Thus it is easy to discover the judicial reaction to the philosophy of laissez faire, easy to remark, as Holmes himself remarked in the most hackneyed of his asides, that judges wrote into the Constitution Herbert Spencer's *Social Statics*.[5] We need not subscribe to Mr. Dooley's conclusion that the Supreme Court follows the election returns in order to appreciate the fact that courts cannot be insensitive to public opinion or fail to reflect it; [6] a comparison of the New York [7] and the Washington minimum-wage decisions,[8] the Schechter [9] and the Jones and Laughlin [1] cases, illuminates this generalization. Nor is it an original observation that judicial opinions are often political as well as constitutional. We know that *Marbury* v. *Madison* was concerned with something more than the right of Marbury to his job,[2] that *Cohens* v. *Virginia* squinted toward state rights,[3] that *Scott* v. *Sand-*

---

sions are considerations of policy and of social advantage, and it is vain to suppose that solutions can be attained merely by logic and the general propositions of law which nobody disputes," and perspicacious observations in "The Path of the Law," *Collected Legal Papers:* "I think that the judges themselves have failed to recognize their duty of weighing considerations of social advantage. . . . I cannot but believe that if the training of lawyers led them habitually to consider more definitely and explicitly the social advantage on which the rule they lay down must be justified, they sometimes would hesitate where now they are confident, and see that really they were taking sides upon debatable and often burning questions" (p. 184).

[5] Lochner v. N.Y., 198 U.S. 45.

[6] See, for comparison, A. V. Dicey: *Lectures on the Relation between Law and Public Opinion in England during the Nineteenth Century* (New York, 1905), esp. pp. 361 ff.

[7] Morehead v. N.Y. ex. rel. Tipaldo, 298 U.S. 587.

[8] West Coast Hotel Co. v. Parrish (March 29, 1937), U.S. 75th Cong. 1st Sess. Sen. Doc. No. 46.

[9] Schechter Poultry Corp. v. U.S., 295 U.S. 495.

[1] National Labor Relations Board v. Jones & Laughlin Steel Corp. (April 12, 1937), U.S. 75th Cong. 1st Sess. Sen. Doc. No. 51.

[2] 1 Cranch 137.

[3] 6 Wheaton 264.

ford was designed to allay sectional antipathies,[4] that the
Milligan case was a declaration against political radicalism [5] and the Pollock decision was directed against the
rising tide of socialism,[6] and we may suspect that recent
decisions on New Deal legislation were not announced in
a judicial void nor uninfluenced by the threat of judicial
reform.

It is equally obvious that the intellectual air which
judges have breathed is conditioned; every judicial invali-
dation of a legislative act proves that the air of the court
room is not the same as the air of the legislative chamber.
It is not sufficient, then, that we discover the explanation
for *Chicago, Milwaukee and St. Paul* v. *Minnesota* or
Smythe v. *Ames* or *in re Jacobs* or *Lochner* v. *New York*
or *People* v. *Williams* or *Adair* v. *United States* or *Ives* v.
South Buffalo or *Hitchman Coal Co.* v. *Mitchell* or *Ham-
mer* v. *Dagenhart* or *Adkins* v. *Children's Hospital* [7] and
scores of similar decisions in general ideas of *laissez
faire*. Legislators who voted affirmatively for the acts
invalidated by these decisions were equally exposed to
ideas of *laissez faire*, and rejected them.

The historian has to recognize that in tracing the formulation and application of the higher law he is concerned with a body of philosophy which has been cherished especially by the judiciary. For, as Dean Pound
observed, "We must admit the divergence between legal
thought . . . and economic and sociological thought.
. . . Hence we have not merely to ask, what is the legal
idea of justice? It is of no less moment to know why this
idea differs from the economic and sociological idea of

[4] 19 Howard 393.
[5] 4 Wallace 2.
[6] 158 U.S. 601.
[7] 134 U.S. 418; 169 U.S. 466; 98 N.Y. 98; 198 U.S. 45; 189 N.Y.
131; 208 U.S. 161; 201 N.Y. 271; 245 U.S. 229; 247 U.S. 251; 261
U.S. 525.

justice. We have to ask, why did the legal idea come to be what it is, and why does it so persistently remain such?" [8]

There is a preliminary observation which must be made if we are to understand why the judicial differs from the political atmosphere, even in a democracy. We must realize that the law, like other faiths, lives by symbols,[9] and that two symbols most passionately cherished are those of reason and of consistency.[1] We demand of law that it should be both philosophy and science, and we call it jurisprudence; [2] we sternly require of judges that they justify their pronouncements upon more than opportunistic grounds. And it follows from this popular image of the law as a science that we demand consistency; it is indeed a common observation that certainty in law is more important than justice.[3]

We expect our judges, then, to be both scientific and consistent, but we do not expect our legislators to be either scientific or consistent, and we rejected President Hoover when he tried to be an engineer and elected enthusiastically a successor who avowed the opportunistic policy of the football quarterback.

Now there is nothing either scientific or consistent about the higher law, in actual experience; and the words due process, reasonable, and liberty lack precision. Yet

[8] "The End of Law as Developed in Legal Rules and Doctrines," *Harvard Law Review,* XXVII, 195, at 198.

[9] T. Arnold: *Symbols of Government* (New Haven, 1935), esp. pp. 49 ff. and 67 ff.

[1] "The truth is," wrote Holmes, "that the law is always approaching and never reaching consistency. It is forever adopting new principles from life at one end, and it always retains old ones from history at the other. . . . It will become entirely consistent only when it ceases to grow." *Common Law,* p. 36. Arnold has some shrewd comments on the necessity of the appearance of consistency in *Symbols of Government,* p. 49.

[2] T. Arnold: "Apologia for Jurisprudence," *Yale Law Journal,* XLIX, 729.

[3] Even Justice Holmes subscribed to this doctrine. See "The Path of the Law," *Collected Legal Papers.*

when judges fall back upon the higher law, they appear to be conforming to the ideal of a law of nature, and thus satisfy the demand for reason and consistency in law.[4] Actually judicial higher law, as we have seen, is moral law, and when judges invoke it they speak of the conscience of political society.[5] But moral attitudes are determined, in large part, by intellectual inheritance and environment, and the moral attitudes of judges, as expressed in the higher law, reflect an individual or a professional philosophy of life. "The words of the Constitution," as Justice Frankfurter has said, "leave the individual justice free, if they do not compel him, to gather meaning not from reading the Constitution but from reading life. . . . The process of constitutional interpretation compels the translation of policy into judgment, and the controlling conceptions of justices are their 'idealized political picture' of the existing social order. Only the conscious recognition of the nature of this exercise of the judicial process will protect policy from being narrowly construed as the reflex of discredited assumptions or the abstract formulation of unconscious bias." [6]

In the last analysis, then, history, in so far as it takes cognizance of the legislative character of higher law pronouncements, comes back to judicial inheritance and en-

[4] See T. Arnold: *Symbols of Government*, Ch. iii, "The Mystery of Jurisprudence."

[5] "We must begin by ourselves understanding that the constitutional provisions which are contained in our bill of rights in the state and federal constitutions are moral principles, as weighty in moral authority and as vital to the safety of society as any that have ever been promulgated, not even excepting the golden rule. After that we must teach the people. We must make them understand that constitutional rights are moral rights, and . . . that they must never try any experiments which will imperil those moral rights." *Report* of Special Committee . . . to Consider the Question of an Amendment to the Constitution of the State of New York Empowering the Legislature to Enact a Workmen's Compensation Law, p. 17.

[6] "The Supreme Court," *Encyclopaedia of the Social Sciences* (1937), VIII, 479–80.

vironment, and to judges individually and collectively. Judges are in society, but insulated from it. They are students and scholars, but concerned daily with practical problems of the most complex and urgent nature. They are recruited from and servants of a capitalist economy, but barred from personal participation in that economy. They are part of a democratic political system, but aloof from it. Their function is to pronounce law as immutable justice and to interpret the law as the will of the sovereign. Needless to remark, they cannot meet these contradictory specifications, perform these contradictory functions. But what determines the choices which are made?

We may suggest here a few of the more obvious factors which require consideration: the rôle of the bar, and of arguments of counsel; the nature of professional training; the influence of the great commentators and textwriters; and the character of the judges themselves. We must begin with the bar, rather than the bench, and this not only because our jurists are trained first to professional life, but because the interaction of bar and bench is continuous. Most of our justices have been recruited from the bar; it is not inconceivable that the tendency of the bar, in the last half century, to become an adjunct to corporate business, has had some influence upon the judicial view of economic questions. Nor can we ignore the fact that the psychology of the bar is transferred, imperceptibly, to the bench; that partisanship cannot become impartiality overnight, or alertness to technicalities become sublimated to anxiety for principles.[7]

Mr. Gustavus Myers attempted to discover, in a realistic way, the professional training and interests of the members of the highest bench,[8] but even Mr. Myers failed

<hr />

[7] See M. Cohen, "Legal Theories and Social Science," New York State Bar Association *Proceedings*, XXXVIII, 192 ff.

[8] Gustavus Myers, *History of the Supreme Court* (Chicago, 1918).

to appreciate the influence of the bar on the bench through arguments of counsel, and historians have largely ignored this factor, until it might be supposed that judicial information was acquired by inspiration.[9] We are reminded, to be sure, of the impassioned appeal of Webster in the Dartmouth case, the eloquent argument of Pinkney in the McCulloch case, the surprising gesture of Conkling in the San Mateo case, the perfervid demagoguery of Choate in the Pollock case, and the famous Brandeis brief in the Muller case, but these exceptional instances have been noted rather for their dramatic qualities than for their constitutional significance. Yet the economic and sociological complexities of modern cases make the Court in large measure dependent upon the facts and briefs presented by counsel.[1] There is, of course, the important reservation that the choice which judges make from opposing briefs will depend in part upon the prepossessions of the judges themselves. Yet it is not quite true, as Mr. Justice Sutherland acrimoniously remarked of the minimum wage legislation, that "the elucidation of that question cannot be aided by counting heads." [2] Quantitative as well as qualitative considerations do weigh with judges, and it is well to recall Justice Cardozo's observation, apropos social security legislation, that "it is too late today for the argument to be heard with tolerance that in a crisis so extreme the use of moneys of the nation to relieve the unemployed . . . is a use for any purpose narrower than the promotion of the general welfare." [3] However much, or little, confidence

[9] Cardozo: *Nature of the Judicial Process, passim;* E. S. Robinson: *Law and the Lawyers* (New York, 1935); C. A. Beard: "Little Alice Looks at the Constitution," in *Jefferson, Corporations, and the Constitution* (Washington, 1936).

[1] Frankfurter: "Hours of Labor and Realism in Constitutional Law," *Harvard Law Review*, XXIX, 371.

[2] Adkins v. Children's Hospital, 261 U.S. 525.

[3] C. C. Steward Machine Co. v. Davis, 57 Supreme Court Reporter, 883.

judges may place in counsel, it remains true that they are
dependent upon counsel for facts; when the history of
constitutional decisions is written without reference to
this source of information, it is written in a vacuum.

Equally important is a consideration of the professional training and equipment of judges. It may be observed, for example, that one explanation for the popularity of the higher law in the early years of the Republic
was that no other law was available; lacking collections
of cases, precedents, judges were forced to fall back upon
their own conceptions of law.[4] The reason has disappeared, but the habit has continued. Or, to look to modern conditions, it is suggestive that deans of law schools
and editors of law journals complain with monotonous
regularity of the inadequacy of the teaching of constitutional law and history; it is no less significant that until
recently, and except in a very few schools, the economic
and sociological aspects of jurisprudence have been neglected. For every Brandeis familiar with economics, for
every Holmes versed in literature, for every Cardozo
learned in philosophy, there are a dozen judges who regard such learning as irrelevant.

Nor has the decisive influence of great expounders of
the law upon our constitutional system been appreciated
by the historian. The most nearly classical constitutional
history of the United States [5] does not think it necessary
to mention Judge Cooley or his constitutional limitations,

[4] When Kent became Chancellor of New York State, in 1814, he
was able to say, "For the nine years I was in that office (court of
equity) there was not a single decision, opinion, or dictum of
either of my predecessors . . . from 1777 to 1814 cited to me or
even suggested." Quoted in Pound: "Judge Story and the Making
of American Law," *American Law Review*, XLVIII, 676, at 683.
See also J. Goebel: "The Courts and the Law in Colonial New
York," *History of the State of New York*, Vol. III.

[5] A. C. McLaughlin: *Constitutional History of the United States*
(New York, 1935).

though the author once edited Cooley's own *Principles of Constitutional Law in the United States.*[6] We lack studies of bar associations, law schools, professors, and text-writers whose teachings have molded American judicial thought from the days of Wilson, Story, and Kent to those of Gray, Thayer, and Cooley.[7]

Finally, we come to the judges themselves. If law is fixed and immutable, and if the function of judges is *jus dicere* only, and *jus dare* belongs to God,[8] then there is logic in judicial anonymity. But few now subscribe to this phonographic theory of the law, and the opposition to the appointment of Mr. Brandeis or of Senator Black to the highest court indicated that the rôle of the judges in making law is acknowledged.[9] Yet we know shockingly little about our judges. Of some four score judges who have sat upon the Supreme Court we have biographies of perhaps a dozen,[1] and acceptable biographies of half that number. If we look to the state courts, the situation is even more scandalous. Kent, Shaw, Gibson, Ruffin, Doe, Cooley, Dillon, Clarke, to mention only some of the more eminent, all want biographies. Nor can it be alleged that those studies vouchsafed us illuminate the rôle of the judges in reading higher law into the Constitution. The parts played by Marshall, Taney, Field, Lamar, Harlan, Brandeis, and Holmes have been, after a fashion, revealed, but constitutional biography, like constitutional

---

[6] *The General Principles of Constitutional Law,* 1880, ed. 1898.

[7] See comments by Pound: *American Law Review,* XLVIII, 676. Three of these teachers are subjects of old-fashioned Memoirs, but there is no critical analysis of the contribution of any one of them.

[8] Otis: *Rights of the British Colonies,* p. 70.

[9] See C. G. Haines: "General Observations on the Effects of Personal, Political and Economic Influences in the Decisions of Judges," *Illinois Law Review,* XVII, 96; and G. Everson: "Human Element in Justice," *Journal of Criminal Law,* X, 98 ff.

[1] See above, p. 44 footnote 3.

history, has evaded the crucial question of the nature of the judicial process and the creation and re-creation of the higher law.

If much of this is obvious, we can find refuge in Justice Holmes's observation that "we need education in the obvious more than investigation of the obscure." [2] I have suggested that the higher law is intuitive, personal law, and that it persists down to the present. Used originally as a substitute for written law, it came to be embodied in written law, but continued an independent existence. In the hands of the mid-century reformers it became a weapon on behalf of human and against property rights, but the individualist approach of the transcendentalists prevented at this time the formulation of a higher-law concept of police power that would command the approval of the courts and commend itself to society. With the Fourteenth Amendment began a new and increasingly important chapter in the history of the higher law. Largely through interpretation of due process, higher law was imported into the Constitution, and generally as a limitation upon legislative control of property. This interpretation, taken collectively, constituted judicial legislation and constitution-making upon subjects of utmost importance; and the character of the new legislative and constitutional provisions was determined by the judicial view of the nature of society, the function of government, the relative importance of personal and property rights, and similar considerations. We can discover, more particularly, the nature of that legislation by an inquiry into those factors which have conditioned it: the symbolic rôle played by judges and courts, public opinion, political considerations, the judicial climate of opinion, the influence of the bar, of professional training and scholarship,

[2] "Law and the Court," *Collected Legal Papers,* p. 292.

and the character and career of the judges themselves. When we have achieved a codification of natural law and an appreciation of the nature of the judicial process, we shall be in a position to record our constitutional history in more realistic terms.

THE ECONOMIC
INTERPRETATION OF THE
CONSTITUTION RECONSIDERED

BY June 26, 1787, tempers in the Federal Convention were already growing short, for gentlemen had come to the explosive question of representation in the upper chamber. Two days later Franklin moved to invoke divine guidance, and his motion was shunted aside only because there was no money with which to pay a chaplain and the members were unprepared to appeal to Heaven without an intermediary. It was not surprising that when James Madison spoke to the question of representation in the proposed legislature, he was conscious of the solemnity of the occasion. We are, he said, framing a system "which we wish to last for ages" and one that might "decide forever the fate of Republican Government."

It was an awful thought, and when, a few days later, Gouverneur Morris spoke to the same subject he felt the occasion a most solemn one; even the irrepressible Morris

Source: Originally published as "The Constitution: Was it an Economic Document?" in *American Heritage* (December 1958). Copyright © 1958 by Henry Steele Commager.

could be solemn. "He came here," he observed (so Madison noted),

> as a Representative of America; he flattered himself he came here in some degree as a Representative of the whole human race; for the whole human race will be affected by the proceedings of this Convention. He wished gentlemen to extend their views beyond the present moment of time; beyond the narrow limits . . . from which they derive their political origin. . . .
>
> Much has been said of the sentiments of the people. They were unknown. They could not be known. All that we can infer is that if the plan we recommend be reasonable & right; all who have reasonable minds and sound intentions will embrace it. . . .

These were by no means occasional sentiments only. They were sentiments that occurred again and again throughout the whole of that long hot summer, until they received their final, eloquent expression from the aged Franklin in that comment on the rising, not the setting, sun. Even during the most acrimonious debates members were aware that they were framing a constitution for ages to come, that they were creating a model for people everywhere on the globe; there was a lively sense of responsibility and even of destiny. Nor can we now, as we contemplate that Constitution which is the oldest written national constitution, and that federal system which is one of the oldest and the most successful in history, regard these appeals to posterity as merely rhetorical.

That men are not always conscious either of what they do or of the motives that animate them is a familiar rather than a cynical observation. Some 45 years ago Charles A. Beard propounded an economic interpretation of the Constitution—an interpretation which submitted that the Constitution was *essentially* (that is a crucial word) an economic document—and that it was carried through the Convention and the state ratifying conven-

tions by interested economic groups for economic reasons. "The Constitution," Mr. Beard concluded, "was essentially an economic document based upon the concept
that the fundamental private rights of property are anterior to government and morally beyond the reach of popular majorities."

At the time it was pronounced, that interpretation
caused something of a sensation, and Mr. Beard was
himself eventually to comment with justifiable indignation on the meanness and the vehemence of the attacks
upon it—and him. Yet the remarkable thing about the
economic interpretation is not the criticism it inspired
but the support it commanded. For within a few years it
had established itself as the new orthodoxy, and those
who took exception to it were stamped either as professional patriots—perhaps secret Sons or Daughters of the
Revolution—or naïve academicians who had never
learned the facts of economic life.

The attraction that the economic interpretation had
for the generation of the twenties and thirties, and that
it still exerts a generation later, is one of the curiosities
of our cultural history, but it is by no means an inexpli-
cable one. To a generation of materialists Beard's thesis
made clear that the stuff of history was material. To a
generation disillusioned by the exploitations of big business it discovered that the past, too, had been ravaged by
economic exploiters. To a generation that looked with
skeptical eyes upon the claims of Wilsonian idealism and
all but rejoiced in their frustration, it suggested that all
earlier idealisms and patriotisms—even the idealism and
patriotism of the framers—had been similarly flawed by
selfishness and hypocrisy.

Yet may it not be said of *An Economic Interpretation
of the Constitution* that it is not a conclusion but a point
of departure? It explains a great deal about the forces
that went into the making of the Constitution, and a

great deal, too, about the men who assembled in Philadelphia in 1787, but it tells us extraordinarily little about the document itself. And it tells us even less about the historical meaning of that document.

What were the objects of the Federal Convention? The immediate objects were to restore order; to strengthen the public credit; to enable the United States to make satisfactory commercial treaties and agreements; to provide conditions in which trade and commerce could flourish; to facilitate management of the western lands and of Indian affairs. All familiar enough. But what, in the light of history, were the grand objects of the Convention? What was it that gave Madison and Morris and Wilson and King and Washington himself a sense of destiny?

There were two grand objects—objects inextricably interrelated. The first was to solve the problem of federalism, that is, the problem of the distribution of powers among governments. Upon the wisdom with which members of the Convention distinguished between powers of a general and powers of a local nature, and assigned these to their appropriate governments, would depend the success or failure of the new experiment.

But it was impossible for the children of the eighteenth century to talk or think of powers without thinking of power, and this was a healthy realism. No less troublesome—and more fundamental—than the problem of the distribution of powers, was the problem of sanctions. How were they to enforce the terms of the distribution and impose limits upon all the governments involved? It was one thing to work out the most ideal distribution of general and local powers. It was another thing to see to it that the states abided by their obligations under the Articles of Union and that the national government respected the autonomy of the states and the liberty of individuals.

Those familiar with the Revolutionary era know that
the second of these problems was more difficult than the
first. Americans had, indeed, learned how to limit government: the written constitutions, the bills of rights, the
checks and balances, and so forth. They had not yet
learned (nor had anyone) how to "substitute the mild
magistracy of the law for the cruel and violent magistracy of force." The phrase is Madison's.

Let us return to the *Economic Interpretation*. The cor-
rectness of Beard's analysis of the origins and back-
grounds of the membership of the Convention, of the
arguments in the Convention, and of the methods of
assuring ratification, need not be debated. But these considerations are, in a sense, irrelevant and immaterial. For
though they are designed to illuminate the document
itself, in fact they illuminate only the processes of its
manufacture.

The idea that property considerations were paramount
in the minds of those assembled in Philadelphia is misleading and unsound and is borne out neither by the
evidence of the debates in the Convention nor by the
Constitution itself. The Constitution was not *essentially*
an economic document. It was, and is, *essentially* a political document. It addresses itself to the great and fundamental question of the distribution of powers between
governments. The Constitution was—and is—a document that attempts to provide sanctions behind that
distribution; a document that sets up, through law, a
standing rule to live by and provides legal machinery for
the enforcement of that rule. These are political, not economic functions.

Not only were the principles that animated the framers political rather than economic; the solutions that they
contrived for the great questions that confronted them
were dictated by political, not by economic considerations.

Here are two fundamental challenges to the Beard interpretation: first, the Constitution is primarily a document in federalism; and second, the Constitution does not in fact confess or display the controlling influence of those who held that "the fundamental private rights of property are anterior to government and morally beyond the reach of popular majorities."

Let us look more closely at these two contentions. The first requires little elaboration or vindication, for it is clear to all students of the Revolutionary era that the one pervasive and overbranching problem of that generation was the problem of imperial organization. How to get the various parts of any empire to work together for common purposes? How to get central control—over war, for example, or commerce or money—without impairing local autonomy? How, on the other hand, preserve personal liberty and local self-government without impairing the effectiveness of the central government? This was one of the oldest problems in political science, and it is one of the freshest—as old as the history of the Greek city-states; as new as the debate over Federal aid to education or the Bricker amendment.

The British failed to solve the problem of imperial order; when pushed to the wall they had recourse to the hopelessly doctrinaire Declaratory Act, which was, in fact, a declaration of political bankruptcy; as Edmund Burke observed, no people is going to be argued into slavery. The Americans then took up the vexatious problem. The Articles of Confederation were satisfactory enough as far as the distribution of powers was concerned, but wholly wanting in sanctions. The absence of sanctions spelled the failure of the Articles—and this failure led to the Philadelphia Convention.

Now it will be readily conceded that many, if not most of the questions connected with federalism were economic in character. Involved were such practical matters as taxation, the regulation of commerce, coinage, western lands, slavery, and so forth. Yet the problem that presented itself to the framers was not whether government should exercise authority over such matters as these; it was *which* government should exercise such authority—and how should it be exercised?

There were, after all, no anarchists at the Federal Convention. Everyone agreed that *some* government had to have authority to tax, raise armies, regulate commerce, coin money, control contracts, enact bankruptcy legislation, regulate western territories, make treaties, and do all the things that government must do. But where should these authorities be lodged—with the state governments or with the national government they were about to erect, or with both?

This question was a political, not an economic, one. And the solution at which the framers arrived was based upon a sound understanding of politics, and need not be explained by reference to class attachments or security interests.

Certainly if the framers were concerned primarily or even largely with protecting property against popular majorities, they failed signally to carry out their purposes. It is at this point in our consideration of the *Economic Interpretation of the Constitution* that we need to employ what our literary friends call *explication du texte*. For the weakest link in the Beard interpretation is precisely the crucial one—the document itself. Mr. Beard makes amply clear that those who wrote the Constitution were members of the propertied classes,[1] and that many of

[1] "A majority of the members were lawyers by profession.

"Most of the members came from towns, on or near the coast, that is, from the regions in which personalty was largely concentrated.

"Not one member represented in his immediate personal economic interests the small farming or mechanic classes.

"The overwhelming majority of members, at least five-sixths, were immediately, directly, and personally interested in the out-

them were personally involved in the outcome of what they were about to do; he makes out a persuasive case that the division over the Constitution was along economic lines. What he does not make clear is how or where the Constitution itself reflects all these economic influences.

Much is made of the contract clause and the paper money clause of the Constitution. No state may impair the obligations of a contract—whatever those words mean, and they apparently did not mean to the framers quite what Chief Justice Marshall later said they meant in *Fletcher* v. *Peck* or *Dartmouth College* v. *Woodward.* No state may emit bills of credit or make anything but gold and silver coin legal tender in payment of debts.

These are formidable prohibitions, and clearly reflect the impatience of men of property with the malpractices of the states during the Confederation. Yet quite aside from what the states may or may not have done, who can doubt that these limitations upon the states followed a sound principle—the principle that control of coinage and money belonged to the central, not the local governments, and the principle that local jurisdictions should not be able to modify or overthrow contracts recognized throughout the Union?

What is most interesting in this connection is what is so often overlooked: that the framers did not write any comparable prohibitions upon the United States Government. The United States was not forbidden to impair the obligation of its contracts, not at least in the Constitution as it came from the hands of its property-conscious framers. Possibly the Fifth Amendment may have squinted toward such a prohibition; we need not determine that now, for the Fifth Amendment was added by the *states*

---

come of their labors at Philadelphia, and were to a greater or less extent economic beneficiaries from the adoption of the Constitution." — Beard, *An Economic Interpretation of the Constitution.*

after the Constitution had been ratified. So, too, the emission of bills of credit and the making other than gold and silver legal tender were limitations on the states, but not on the national government. There was, in fact, a lively debate over the question of limiting the authority of the national government in the matter of bills of credit. When the question came up on August 16, Gouverneur Morris threatened that "The Monied interest will oppose the plan of Government, if paper emissions be not prohibited." In the end the Convention dropped out a specific authorization to emit bills of credit, but pointedly did not prohibit such action. Just where this left the situation troubled Chief Justice Chase's Court briefly three-quarters of a century later; the Court recovered its balance, and the sovereign power of the government over money was not again successfully challenged.

Nor were there other specific limitations of an economic character upon the powers of the new government that was being erected on the ruins of the old. The framers properly gave the Congress power to regulate commerce with foreign nations and among the states. The term commerce—as Hamilton and Adair (and Crosskey, too) have made clear—was broadly meant, and the grant of authority, too, was broad. The framers gave Congress the power to levy taxes and, again, wrote no limitations into the Constitution except as to the apportionment of direct taxes; it remained for the most conservative of Courts to reverse itself, and common sense, and discover that the framers had intended to forbid an income tax! Today, organizations that invoke the very term "constitutional" are agitating for an amendment placing a quantitative limit upon income taxes that may be levied; fortunately, Madison's generation understood better the true nature of governmental power.

The framers gave Congress—in ambiguous terms, to be sure—authority to make "all needful Rules and Regulations respecting the Territory or other Property" of the United States, and provided that "new states may be admitted." These evasive phrases gave little hint of the heated debates in the Convention over western lands. Those who delight to find narrow and undemocratic sentiments in the breasts of the framers never cease to quote a Gouverneur Morris or an Elbridge Gerry on the dangers of the West, and it is possible to compile a horrid catalogue of such statements. But what is significant is not what framers said, but what they did. They did not place any limits upon the disposition of western territory, or establish any barriers against the admission of western states.

The fact is that we look in vain in the Constitution itself for any really effective guarantee for property or any effective barriers against what Beard calls "the reach of popular majorities."

It will be argued, however, that what the framers feared was the states, and that the specific prohibitions against state action, together with the broad transfer of economic powers from state to nation, were designed as guarantee against state attacks upon property. As for the national government, care was taken to make that sufficiently aristocratic, sufficiently the representative of the propertied classes, and sufficiently checked and limited so that it would not threaten basic property interests.

It is at this juncture that the familiar principle of limitation on governmental authority commands our attention. Granted the wisest distribution of powers among governments, what guarantee was there that power would be properly exercised? What guarantees were there against the abuse of power? What assurance was there that the large states would not ride roughshod over the small, that majorities would not crush minorities or

minorities abuse majorities? What protection was there
against mobs, demagogues, dangerous combinations of
interests or of states? What protection was there for the
commercial interest, the planter interest, the slave interest, the securities interests, the land speculator interests?

It was Madison who most clearly saw the real character of this problem and who formulated its solution. It
was not that the people as such were dangerous; the
truth was, he said on July 11, "that all men having
power ought to be distrusted to a certain degree." Long
before Lord Acton coined his aphorism, the Revolutionary leaders had discovered that power corrupts. They
understood, too, the drive for power on the part of individuals and groups. All this is familiar to students of *The
Federalist,* No. 10. It should be familiar to students of the
debates in Philadelphia, for there, too, Madison set forth
his theory and supported it with a wealth of argument.
Listen to him on one of the early days of the Convention,
June 6, when he is discussing the way to avoid abuses of
republican liberty—abuses which "prevailed in the largest as well as the smallest [states]."

> . . . And were we not thence admonished [he con-
> tinued] to enlarge the sphere as far as the nature of the
> Government would admit. This was the only defence
> against the inconveniences of democracy *consistent
> with the democratic form of Government* [our italics].
> All civilized Societies would be divided into different
> Sects, Factions & interests, as they happened to consist
> of rich & poor, debtors and creditors, the landed, the
> manufacturing, the commercial interests, the inhabit-
> ants of this district or that district, the followers of this
> political leader or that political leader, the disciples of
> this religious Sect or that religious Sect. In all cases
> where a majority are united by a common interest or
> passion, the rights of the minority are in danger. . . .
> In a Republican Govt. the Majority if united have
> always an opportunity [to oppress the minority. What is
> the remedy?] The only remedy is to enlarge the sphere,

& thereby divide the community into so great a number of interests & parties, that in the first place a majority will not be likely at the same moment to have a common interest separate from that of the whole or of the minority; and in the second place, that in case they should have such an interest, they may not be apt to unite in the pursuit of it. It was incumbent on us then to try this remedy, and . . . to frame a republican system on such a scale & in such a form as will controul all the evils which have been experienced.

This long quotation is wonderfully eloquent of the attitude of the most sagacious of the framers. Madison, Wilson, Mason, Franklin, as well as Gerry, Morris, Pinckney, and Hamilton feared power. They feared power whether exercised by a monarch, an aristocracy, an army, or a majority, and they were one in their determination to write into fundamental law limitations on the arbitrary exercise of that power. To assume, as Beard so commonly does, that the fear of the misuse of power by majorities was either peculiar to the Federalists or more ardent with them than with their opponents, is mistaken. Indeed it was rather the anti-Federalists who were most deeply disturbed by the prospect of majority rule; they, rather than the Federalists, were the "men of little faith." Thus it was John Lansing, Jr., of New York (he who left the Convention rather than have any part in its dangerous work) who said that "all free constitutions are formed with two views—to deter the governed from crime, and the governors from tyranny." And the ardent Patrick Henry, who led the attack on the Constitution in the Virginia Convention—and almost defeated it—complained not of too little democracy in that document, but too much.

The framers, to be sure, feared the powers of the majority, as they feared all power unless controlled. But they were insistent that, in the last analysis, there must be government by majority; even conservatives like Morris

and Hamilton made this clear. Listen to Hamilton, for
example, at the very close of the Convention. Elbridge
Gerry, an opponent of the Constitution, had asked for
a reconsideration of the provision for calling a constitutional convention, alleging that this opened the gate to a
majority that could "bind the union to innovations that
may subvert the State-Constitutions altogether." To this
Hamilton replied that

> There was no greater evil in subjecting the people of the
> U.S. to the major voice than the people of a particular
> State. . . . It was equally desirable now that an easy
> mode should be established for supplying defects which
> will probably appear in the New System. . . . There
> could be no danger in giving this power, as the people
> would finally decide in the case.

And on July 13, James Wilson, another staunch Federalist, observed that "The majority of people wherever
found ought in all questions to govern the minority."

But we need not rely upon what men said; there is too
much of making history by quotation anyway. Let us look
rather at what men did. We can turn again to the Constitution itself. Granted the elaborate system of checks and
balances: the separation of powers, the bicameral legislature, the executive veto, and so forth—checks found in
the state constitutions as well, and in our own democratic
era as in the earlier one—what provision did the framers
make against majority tyranny? What provisions did
they write into the Constitution against what Randolph
called "democratic licentiousness"?

They granted equality of representation in the Senate.
If this meant that conservative Delaware would have the
same representation in the upper chamber as democratic
Pennsylvania, it also meant that democratic Rhode Island would have the same representation as conservative

South Carolina. But the decision for equality of representation was not dictated by considerations either economic or democratic, but rather by the recalcitrance of the small states. Indeed, though it is difficult to generalize here, on the whole it is true that it was the more ardent Federalists who favored proportional representation in both houses.

They elaborated a most complicated method of electing a Chief Executive, a method designed to prevent the easy expression of any majority will. Again the explanation is not simple. The fact was that the framers did not envision the possibility of direct votes for presidential candidates which would not conform to state lines and interests and thus lead to dissension and confusion. Some method, they thought, must be designated to overcome the force of state prejudices (or merely of parochialism) and get an election; the method they anticipated was a preliminary elimination contest by the electoral college and then eventual election by the House. This, said George Mason, was what would occur nineteen times out of twenty.[2] There is no evidence in the debates that the complicated method finally hit upon for electing a President was designed either to frustrate popular majorities or to protect special economic interests; its purpose was to overcome state pride and particularism.

Senators and Presidents, then, would not be the creatures of democracy. But what guarantee was there that senators would be representatives of property interests, or that the President himself would recognize the "priority of property"? Most states had property qualifications for office holding, but there are none in the Federal Constitution. As far as the Constitution is concerned, the President, congressmen, and Supreme Court justices can all be paupers.

[2] It has happened twice: Jefferson *vs.* Burr (1801) and J. Q. Adams *vs.* Clay, Jackson, and Crawford (1825).

Both General Charles Cotesworth Pinckney and his young cousin Charles, of South Carolina, were worried about this. The latter proposed a property qualification of $100,000 (a tidy sum in those days) for the Presidency, half that for the judges, and substantial sums for members of Congress. Franklin rebuked him. He was distressed, he said, to hear anything "that tended to debase the spirit of the common people." More surprising was the rebuke from that stout conservative, John Dickinson. "He doubted," Madison reports, "the policy of interweaving into a Republican constitution a veneration for wealth. He had always understood that a veneration for poverty & virtue were the objects of republican encouragement." Pinckney's proposal was overwhelmingly rejected.

What of the members of the lower house? When Randolph opened "the main business" on May 29 he said the remedy for the crisis that men faced must be "the republican principle," and two days later members were discussing the fourth resolution, which provided for election to the lower house by the people. Roger Sherman of Connecticut thought that "the people should have as little to do as may be about the Government," and Gerry hastened to agree in words now well-worn from enthusiastic quotation that "The evils we experience flow from the excess of democracy." These voices were soon drowned out, however. Mason "argued strongly for an election . . . by the people. It was to be the grand depository of the democratic principle of the Govt." And the learned James Wilson, striking the note to which he was to recur again and again, made clear that he was for "raising the federal pyramid to a considerable altitude, and for that reason wished to give it as broad a basis as possible." He thought that both branches of the legislature—and the President as well, for that matter—should be elected by the people.

"The Legislature," he later observed, "ought to be the most exact transcript of the whole Society."

A further observation is unhappily relevant today. It was a maxim with John Adams that "where annual elections end, there tyranny begins," and the whole Revolutionary generation was committed to a frequent return to the source of authority. But the framers put into the Constitution no limits on the number of terms which Presidents or congressmen could serve. It was not that the question was ignored; it received elaborate attention. It was rather that the generation that wrote the Constitution was better grounded in political principles than is our own; that it did not confuse, as we so often do, quantitative and qualitative limitations; and that—in a curious way—it had more confidence in the intelligence and the good will of the people than we seem to have today. It is, in any event, our own generation that has the dubious distinction of writing into the Constitution the first quantitative limitation on the right of the majority to choose their President. It is not the generation of the framers that was undemocratic; it is our generation that is undemocratic.

It is relevant to note, too, that the Constitution contains no property qualification for voting. Most states, to be sure, had such qualifications—in general a freehold or its equivalent—and the Constitution assimilated such qualifications as states might establish. Yet the framers, whether for reasons practical or philosophical we need not determine, made no serious efforts to write any property qualifications for voting into the Constitution itself.

The question of popular control came up clearly in one other connection as well: the matter of ratification. Should the Constitution be ratified by state legislatures, or by conventions? The practical arguments for the two methods were nicely balanced. The decisive argument was not, however, one of expediency but of principle. "To the people with whom all power remains that has not been given up in the Constitutions derived from them" we must resort, said Mason. Madison put the matter on principle, too. "He considered the difference between a system founded on the Legislatures only, and one founded on the people, to be the true difference between a *league* or *treaty* and a *Constitution*." Ellsworth's motion to refer the Constitution to legislatures was defeated by a vote of eight to two, and the resolution to refer it to conventions passed with only Delaware in the negative.

Was the Constitution designed to place private property beyond the reach of majorities? If so, the framers did a very bad job. They failed to write into it the most elementary safeguards for property. They failed to write into it limitations on the tax power, or prohibitions against the abuse of the money power. They failed to provide for rule by those whom Adams was later to call the wise and the rich and the wellborn. What they did succeed in doing was to create a system of checks and balances and adjustments and accommodations that would effectively prevent the suppression of most minorities by majorities. They took advantage of the complexity, the diversity, the pluralism, of American society and economy to encourage a balance of interests. They worked out sound and lasting political solutions to the problems of class, interest, section, race, religion, party.

Perhaps the most perspicacious comment on this whole question of the threat from turbulent popular majorities against property and order came, *mirabile dictu*, from the dashing young Charles Pinckney of South Carolina—of the "lost" Pinckney Plan. On June 25 Pinckney made a major speech and thought it important enough to write out and give to Madison. The point of departure was the hackneyed one of the character of the second branch of the legislature, but the comments were an anticipation of De Tocqueville and Lord Bryce. We need not, Pinckney asserted, fear the rise of class conflicts in America, nor take precautions against them.

> The genius of the people, their mediocrity of situation & the prospects which are afforded their industry in a Country which must be a new one for centuries are unfavorable to the rapid distinction of ranks. . . . If equality is . . . the leading feature of the U. States [he asked], where then are the riches & wealth whose representation & protection is the peculiar province of this permanent body [the Senate]. Are they in the hands of the few who may be called rich; in the possession of less than a hundred citizens? certainly not. They are in the great body of the people . . . [There was no likelihood that a privileged body would ever develop in the United States, he added, either from the landed interest, the moneyed interest, or the mercantile.] Besides, Sir, I apprehend that on this point the policy of the U. States has been much mistaken. We have unwisely considered ourselves as the inhabitants of an old instead of a new country. We have adopted the maxims of a State full of people . . . The people of this country are not only very different from the inhabitants of any State we are acquainted with in the modern world; but I assert that their situation is distinct from either the people of Greece or of Rome . . . Our true situation appears to me to be this—a new extensive Country containing within itself the materials for forming a Government capable of extending to its citizens all the blessings of civil & religious liberty—capable of making them happy at home. This is the great end of Republican Establishments. . . .

Not a government cunningly contrived to protect the interests of property, but one capable of extending to its citizens the blessings of liberty and happiness—was that not, after all, what the framers created?

JOSEPH STORY: A PORTRAIT

JOSEPH STORY was a child of the eighteenth century, of that age of reason which blended so harmoniously into the age of romance, of the Enlightenment which added so readily the historical to the logical proof of progress. He was confident of the ability of men to reduce law to a system and to create, too, a science of politics. He did not doubt that America, which was the heir not only of England but of the Ages, could systematize the whole of law and produce out of it a coherent and harmonious whole, though sometimes he permitted himself to doubt that Americans could receive and apply these systems. He was sure of his morals as of his law and identified the two as became a disciple of the natural rights school; his legal writings are permeated with moralizing. He spoke hopefully of expounding contracts "upon the eternal principles of right and wrong," and submitted that a proper accommodation to the "law of nature" would insure man not only "permanent happiness" here, but salvation in the hereafter. He knew that man could find the truth—or the

SOURCE: Reprinted by permission of the publishers from *The Gaspar G. Bacon Lectures on the Constitution of the United States, 1940–1950* (Boston, Mass.: Boston University Press). Copyright 1953 by the Trustees of Boston University.

law, which was the same thing—and that it would make him free.

Yet Story was sufficiently the scholar, sufficiently the product of the nineteenth century, to insist upon the inductive as well as the deductive process, upon substantiation as well as logic. He did not, indeed, so much argue as persuade; he did not so much dictate as prove; and if his assumptions had sometimes to be given and his evidence qualified, his arguments were none the less effective, his proof none the less convincing. His learning was immense, and he could find in the treatises of the past and the law of the present evidence to support those conclusions which Justice Holmes has so well denominated the "can't helps" of belief. Marshall, too, rested his conclusions upon assumptions sometimes dubious, but Marshall was sufficiently sure of himself, or sufficiently impatient of the paraphernalia of legal scholarship, largely to dispense with proof and rely on logic.

Everything about Story is consistent with this faith in Reason. His essays, his treatises on special branches of the law, his monumental commentaries, his judicial opinions, even his literary and aesthetic judgments, all confess a desire for system, order, and completeness. He was rarely swept off his feet, and only where fundamental principles of property—and therefore of law—were involved did emotion temper logic. Even in religion he was orderly, a proper Unitarian, distrustful of the emotionalism of the evangelical churches, equally distrustful of the wind-blown heresies of the transcendentalist wing of his own church: he was ready to prove that the Christian religion was part of the common law and to sustain the authenticity of the New Testament on legal evidence. He read Byron, to be sure, and Scott—who, indeed, in that generation did not read Scott?—but confessed his real admiration reserved for Gray and Cowper and Goldsmith, and held Jane Austen supreme among novelists.

And when he tried his own hand at poetry—the *Power of Solitude*—he cast it in conventional couplets in faithful imitation of Pope.

Yet there was in Story a strong strain of the romantic. Not for nothing had he been born in Marblehead, and raised on stories of ghosts and goblins, on superstition and romance, and he recalls this inheritance in the most charming passage of his fragmentary autobiography. He confessed an early interest in Junius and Rousseau and an early sympathy for the French Revolution; as he reached maturity he resolutely put all this behind him— Jeffersonianism, Fourth of July rhetoric, and faith in the common man. In so far as romanticism lingered on, it was in a wistful affection for the past, an occasional and misguided yielding to the impulse for poetry, an excessive fondness for Mount Auburn cemetery. It remained, too, more significantly, in historical-mindedness and a sense of historical continuity that was to be immensely important in the formulation of his legal and political theories.

The sense of history was strong in Story, as in his brother Marshall. His family, for generations, had knit itself into the history of the Bay Colony; his father had been one of the patriots in that Revolution whose glories the son never tired of chanting. In his boyhood and youth he had witnessed some of the most memorable events of modern times, the winning of independence, the making of the Constitution, the creation of the new world Republic, and he followed—with waning sympathy, to be sure —events no less stirring on the other side of the Atlantic. He was proud of the achievements of the Fathers and confident of the glorious destiny of the Republic, and some of his addresses—that on "The History and Influence of the Puritans," for example—have typical Fourth of July magniloquence. His study of the law, too—the wonderful tenacity of the civil law, the slow growth of the common law, the development of equity to which he was to contribute so richly, the rise of the law merchant in response to practical problems—all this brought home to him the sense of continuity, of historical growth and adaptation. No more than Marshall could Story doubt that the men who had fought the Revolution intended to create a nation; no more than Chancellor Kent could he doubt that the common law could adapt itself to the exigencies of the New World. He who had seen men create, by act of will, as it were, and out of the inheritance of the past, a new nation and a new constitutional system knew that they could create, too, and of the same stuff, an American law.

So, too, with Story's devotion to the prerogatives of property. It is easy, now, and even popular to criticize Marshall and Story for their contributions to the protection of property rights, and it may readily be admitted that the zeal which they brought to this task was excessive. Yet it should not be forgotten that the right to property was one of that great trilogy of rights celebrated and defended by the Revolutionary patriots, equally with life and liberty, or that the Lockean theory was equally designed to safeguard this precious right. Jefferson, to be sure, and Mason could substitute happiness for property, but that did not last, not even in the South. To Story—as to the generation that fought the Revolution and made the Constitution—property right was a natural right, and it was fitting that he should have brought law to the support of the institution of property and that to this end he should import the law of Nature into the law of the Constitution.

With his unassailable faith in Reason, his strong sense of history, his zeal for property rights, Story came to the bench and to the study at a critical moment in the history of American law. That law was as yet unformed. It was exposed to the vicissitudes of fortune and misfortune—to

an inherited common law not fully understood and
deeply distrusted by many liberals in the Jeffersonian
camp, to the seductive certainties and liberalisms of
French codes, and to ignorance. It was by no means
certain at the beginning of the century that the United
States would take over English law, and there was no
assurance that if it were taken over, it would be properly
adapted to American circumstances. And though the Revolutionary patriots had spouted Vattel and Pufendorf and
Grotius readily enough, comparative law was practically
unknown. What Story pre-eminently did—he was as-
sisted by others like Kent and Gibson and Ruffin—was to
give form to this inchoate law, to fuse into it ingredients
from continental law, and to cast it into American
molds. In doing this he gave to the law an appearance of
logical symmetry that it did not actually have, but coher-
ence and stability were more important at that time than
was philosophy.

Then, too, it must be remembered that the situation in
the United States was unique in another respect as well.
For in the realm of constitutional law this country did
have written constitutions, designed to embody applicable natural law. It was entirely reasonable for judges to
take these at face value, as statements of first principles,
and to interpret them as their authors doubtless intended
that they should be interpreted—as embracing Natural
Law. And in the realms of civil law, common law, equity,
admiralty, and so forth, Americans were fortunate in
having the whole of the past to draw upon, and it was not
remarkable that they should be confident of their ability
to systematize this great inheritance: who could do so
better? Whatever its failings, this generation of jurists of
which Marshall was the most compelling, Story the most
pervasive influence, performed for the new nation a service as great as that achieved by any succeeding generation.

Story's contributions to these things—to natural law, nationalism, and the preservation of the rights of property, were more varied than those of any other American jurist. They did not have the authority, perhaps, of Marshall's nor the originality of Kent's, but Story alone of the jurists of his generation presented to his countrymen a rounded system. And Story alone had, or made, the opportunity to present his system of law not only through judicial opinions but through systematic treatises and teaching. His approach, then, was three-fold: from the bench, from the study, and from the platform. His judicial opinions, in Circuit and Supreme Court, helped to formulate our constitutional, equity, admiralty, patent, insurance, and copyright law. His commentaries, monumental and symmetrical, did more than those of any other expositor until Cooley to mold popular ideas about the constitutional system and more than any except those of Kent to influence professional ideas about law, while they all but created the study of conflict of laws. And from the great law school which was so largely of his own making, so largely the extension of his shadow, he sent out lawyers and judges and teachers indoctrinated with his concepts of law. Nor did his influence end here: through such disciples as Charles Sumner and Timothy Walker and Francis Lieber he handed on a pervasive tradition.

Dean Pound has reminded us that American law at the beginning of the nineteenth century was exposed to four grave dangers. There was the menace of French law, of debasement of law through an untrained or politically controlled judiciary, of premature and crude codification, and of loss of unity through the development of separate local systems. Story did more, perhaps, than any other American jurist to repel these threats. His familiarity with the civil law and with modern continental law and treatises enabled him to harmonize these with the com-

mon law and with natural law. As a teacher, as the real
founder of the modern law school, he did much to insure
a trained bench and bar. As author of the most formidable series of commentaries that have come from the pen
of any American jurist he imposed unity upon the interpretation of law. And these same commentaries, persuasive and authoritative, made codification largely superfluous.

In this one respect the contribution was an unwitting
one. For Story early ranged himself on the side of the
codifiers. Given his belief in natural rights, his strong
sense for law and order, for property, for administrative
and especially juicial efficiency, and the self-assurance
that flowed from his own vast erudition, this was entirely
natural. As early as 1821 he had insisted that there was
but one remedy for the endless multiplication of laws: "a
gradual digest, under legislative authority, of those portions of our jurisprudence which . . . shall from time to
time acquire scientific accuracy. . . . A general code
which will guide the lawyer, the statesman, and the private citizen." And to his friend Edward Everett he confessed himself "a decided friend to codification." In support of this movement—well under way by the twenties
—he contributed articles to the rising *North American
Review*. As late as 1837 he reported to the governor of
Massachusetts in favor of the codification of the criminal
law—a report which, wrote the sanguine Sumner, "will
make an era in the history of the law of our country,"—
and a qualified recommendation to the same purport for
the common law.

The movement for codification was, as we know, defeated. But, as Dean Pound so well says, "what Story the
judge failed in, Story the text-writer accomplished trium-
phantly." The great series of commentaries were, in
effect, codifications. They furnished alike to lawyers far

from libraries and to judges learned in the law the authority which could be found heretofore in a limited form only in Kent. Some of Story's own disciples—Charles Sumner, for example, or Walker, out in Cincinnati—continued to favor codification even after the publication of the Commentaries, and after the Civil War David Dudley Field threw his great prestige on the side of codification, but it is no exaggeration to say that before this time Story's Commentaries had effectively arrested the movement.

Story, indeed, had entered the legal arena; to contemporaries it must have seemed that he had all but preempted it. Others, to be sure, were to write on the law; Kent left a great and merited reputation, and Nathan Dane a lesser one. Others, too, achieved as much from the bench—the names of Marshall, Gibson, Ruffin, Kent, and Shaw come readily to mind. But for total achievement, judicial and literary, none of these can compare with Story. Indeed, it is possible to be even more dogmatic and to assert that with the possible exceptions of Coke, Blackstone, and Mansfield no English or American jurist exercised an influence on the development of the law greater than that of Story.

It was not genius that accounted for this remarkable achievement, for Story was lacking in genius unless that quality is, indeed, merely the capacity for taking infinite pains. His mind was neither original nor brilliant, and Justice Holmes has deprecated his "simple philosophizing." But more happily than any other jurist in our history Story combined indefatigable industry with vast learning, luminous intelligence, and a high sense of order.

Passion for work and intellectual acquisitiveness had characterized him from his earliest years. Leaving the Marblehead academy at the age of fifteen, Story was not

prepared for admission to Harvard College; by studying
fifteen hours a day he not only made good his deficiencies
but caught up with his class. "I scarcely wasted a single
moment in idleness," he later recalled of these years, and
the observation would hold for the whole of his career. At
graduation he stood, properly enough, just below Channing and was assigned the pleasant responsibility of the
class poem—an assignment which possibly accounts for
the delusions he early entertained about his poetic talents. Studying in the office of Samuel Sewall of Marblehead and then of Samuel Putnam of Salem—both late
justices of the Supreme Court—he was admitted to the
bar at twenty-one, a singularly well equipped young man,
sufficiently learned, intelligent, and personable to overcome the handicap of his own Republicanism and
achieve some degree of professional success. In Salem he
developed a large and lucrative practice, and did not
neglect either his civic duties or his scholarly labors. He
was equally ready to deliver patriotic orations, agitate for
"dressed curbstones", write editorials for the Salem *Register,* meddle in local politics, serve in the legislature, or
edit law books. In 1805 he brought out the first of these—
A Selection of Pleadings in Civil Actions. He undertook
at the same time a digest of the whole of American law
similar to that which Nathan Dane undertook later (and
which enabled Dane to establish the professorship which
Story was to fill) and actually completed three manuscript volumes before he abandoned the task. In 1809
came an edition of *Chitty on Bills of Exchange and Promissory Notes;* the next year a new edition of *Abbott on
Shipping* (which Justice Holmes was to cite as an authority nearly a century later) and of *Lawes on Assumpsit.*
All of this was performed in the midst of an active legal
practice, service in the Massachusetts Legislature and in
Congress, and an almost uninterrupted flow of miscella-

neous essays and addresses, with some poetry thrown in for good measure.

This literary achievement was enough to establish the reputation of any lawyer, yet it was only a faint foreshadowing of what was to come. In the years between Story's appointment to the Supreme Court—at the age of thirty-two—and his acceptance of the Dane Professorship at Harvard, many of his most valuable contributions were anonymous. For Wheaton, the Supreme Court Reporter, he drew up treatises on admiralty and prize law, on patents, on charitable bequests, and on piracies, and for Wheaton's Digest of the decisions of the Supreme Court he prepared the items on fourteen categories of subjects. To his young friend Francis Lieber he was equally generous, contributing to the *Encyclopaedia Americana,* which the young refugee so ambitiously undertook to edit, a long series of articles on legal and constitutional subjects —the whole comprising a substantial volume. His pen was constantly at the serivce, too, of the *North American Review* and the *American Jurist.* And in 1828 he published a compilation of *Public and General Statutes of the United States* in three stout volumes.

But it was the appointment to the Dane Professorship that furnished the impetus for the great scholarly labors of the thirties and the forties upon which Story's reputation chiefly rests. Dane himself, perspicacious in this as in other matters, made Story's incumbency of the chair a condition of the gift and wrote into the bequest specific provision for the publication of lectures on the Law of Nature, the Law of Nations, Commercial and Maritime Law, Federal Law and Federal Equity. It was a formidable program, but Dane was confident that Story could accomplish it, and his confidence was not misplaced. Story turned his lectures into commentaries, and beginning in 1832 almost every year witnessed the realization

of a part of the large plan. Call the roll of the volumes: in
1832 *Commentaries on Bailments;* 1833 the three volume *Commentaries on the Constitution;* 1834 the epoch-
making *Commentaries on Conflict of Laws,* and that
same year a brief *Constitutional Class Book;* 1836 *Commentaries on Equity Jurisprudence;* 1838 *Commentaries
on Equity Pleadings;* 1839 *Commentaries on the Law of
Agency;* 1840 the *Familiar Exposition of the Constitution
of the United States;* 1841 *Commentaries on the Law of
Partnership;* 1843 *Commentaries on Bills of Exchange*
and 1845, the last year of Story's life, *Commentaries on
the Law of Promissory Notes.*

Through these commentaries, Story contributed more
than any other jurist to the crystallization and systema-
tization of American law. The numerous editions which
were called for, the royalties attesting to steady sales,
the frequency of citation by counsel and by bench,
all tend to support this generalization. To three fields,
particularly, Story's contributions were of outstanding
importance. His *Commentaries on the Constitution*
effectively molded constitutional law in the generation before the Civil War; his two volumes on equity,
giving that system, according to an English critic, "a
philosophical character with which it never had been
invested by any preceding author," contributed to the
success of equity in the United States; the *Conflict of
Laws,* which Daniel Webster called "the great book of the
age" and Kent described as "full, clear and perfect"—certainly the most original and learned of all his books—
opened up a new subject and revealed the possibilities of
Continental to American and—what was more remarkable—of American to English and Continental Law.

As we contemplate these achievements, we are re-
minded of that prophecy which Chancellor Kent made on
Story's inauguration to the Dane Professorship: "Your
Professor's chair," he wrote, "will be of itself (without the

aid of Cranch & Gallison & Mason & Wheaton & Peters) a
vehicle to conduct you to immortality."

Much as Story achieved, his ambitions were even
vaster, and we cannot stifle a sense of regret that he was
unable to fulfill them. Yet there is a moral here which is
not irrelevant. As early as 1837 Story had determined to
resign from the bench and devote his remaining years to
teaching and writing. He was in a minority, forced with
embarrassing frequency to dissent; but he knew that if he
could not control the law from the bench, he might from
the study. Yet against his better judgment he clung to his
judicial post. He was sure that any successor appointed
by Van Buren would be bad; he distrusted Tyler and
waited hopefully for the election of his friend Clay. Only
when the election of 1844 proved the futility of this hope
did he prepare to leave the bench and return to his studies
—and then it was too late.

He had published the *Promissory Notes* in 1845 and
planned to turn next to the Law of Shipping and the Law
of Insurance. These would have completed his series on
commercial law. He contemplated, next, volumes on
Prize Law and on Insurance—volumes which, together
with his learned appendices on Admiralty, would have
gone far to cover that subject to which he had so richly
contributed from the bench. To cap all these he planned
a comprehensive study of the Law of Nations. And when
he had thus fulfilled his obligations to scholarship, he
looked forward eagerly to penning his reminiscences.

This is the book which it is perhaps hardest to spare.
For others, in time, wrote the requisite treatises on admiralty and on the law of nations. But for Story's own life
we must be content with a fragment of autobiography
and a bundle of letters—letters which in delightful style
reveal a lively feeling for personalities and an acute wit,
qualities which rarely intrude themselves into the more
formal writings.

What a book Story's reminiscences might have been!
His active career covered the half century from the establishment of the Republic to the eve of the Mexican War,
and he knew, vicariously as it were, the history of the
Revolution. He was familiar with most of the leaders of
American life in his generation—all of the presidents
after Washington, all of the great jurists, most of the
prominent politicians. He had early attached himself to
the party of Jefferson and had watched at close hand the
suicidal folly of the Federalists—wondering, after it was
too late, whether Republicanism had anything better to
offer. He had served in Congress during the stirring days
of the embargo and the Orders in Council and had been
inspired to patriotic ardor by the great deeds of American
seamen during the War of 1812. He had known the
merchant princes of Salem and Boston and had contributed indirectly to their empire, and he had contributed,
too, directly and indirectly to the revolution in New England economy which came with industry, banking, and
railroads. The problem of slavery he knew at first hand,
for it presented itself frequently to the bench. He had
trembled at the Missouri Compromise and rejoiced in the
opportunities to assuage sectional strife vouchsafed the
courts in our constitutional system. His judge's bench
had been no ivory tower: his interest in politics was
insatiable, and he did not conclude his legislative activities when he resigned the speakership of the Massachusetts House but continued throughout his career to formulate needed legislation and maneuver it through
Congress. He had watched all the great lawyers of his day
perform—the gigantic Jeremiah Mason; the oracular
Webster; the eloquent Emmett; the magniloquent
Choate; Pinckney, who had once offered him his twenty-
thousand dollar practice, Hopkinson, who inspired the
phrase "Philadelphia lawyer," and his colleagues Birney
and Sargeant, whose efforts in the Girard College case

brought both of them offers to the Supreme Bench; the legendary Luther Martin; Taney of Maryland, quiet and sagacious; the brilliant Tazewell and the ponderous Legaré; and a host of others. He had watched them all, noting their idiosyncrasies with unerring eye. Thirty-four years on circuit, thirty-four years on the highest bench, and we can but sigh for the vast fund of legal anecdotes stored in that capacious memory but never recorded.

For Story was unconfined and undaunted by the limitations of the bench. Other judges had indulged in occasional extracurricular activities—Jay in London and Wilson at the Pennsylvania Law School come to mind—but no other had maintained an independent career. For fifteen years Story divided his time between the bench and the Harvard Law School, and while no one suggested that he shirked his judicial duties, it seems clear that the school at Cambridge came more and more to occupy first place in his heart. As early as 1832 he wrote from Washington, "I would rather work in the law school than here. He confided to Sumner his desire to "permanently associate my name with it, as a perpetuity," and in one of his last lectures he told his class that "the proudest inscription I would ask upon my tomb would be the fact that while I was professor in the Law School of Harvard College, so many thousands graduated from it." The number was excessive, but the sentiment sincere. With Simon Greenleaf, and with the occasional assistance of young Charles Sumner, he carried the whole weight of the school—teaching, holding moot court, advising students, participating actively in the administration of the institution whose chief glory he was.

It was something to have the most learned of living jurists expound the law, and the students were properly appreciative. Yet there is no evidence that they were overawed by his learning or by his immense prestige, while testimony to the affection with which they regarded him is abundant. He was not a hard taskmaster, and he looked upon his students as his "foster children"; if he furnished more inspiration than Greenleaf, Greenleaf probably taught more law. All the reports which have come down to us agree on the discursive and inspirational quality of Story's lectures. He was, wrote David Cruss, "enthusiastic, demonstrative, at times eloquent, quoting Latin and wandering from the text into themes entirely foreign. . . . His lectures had little to do with the text in the book." Rutherford B. Hayes' first observation on Story refers to his "fondness for jesting." "He is very fond of digressions," wrote the future President, "to introduce amusing anecdotes, high-wrought eulogies of the sages of the law, and fragments of his own experience." In short, Hayes concluded, "as a lecturer he is a very different man from what you would expect of an old and eminent judge; not but that he is great, but he is so interesting and fond of good stories." But it was not all fun; there was a good deal of solid substance and a good deal of solemn sermonizing, too. Sometimes the students would draw Story out on the great statesmen of the past or on contemporary English and European jurists, and he would seize the opportunity to impress upon his foster children the duties of citizenship, the dangers of politics, the morals of law. His closing lectures, too, were usually of an exhortatory character. His son has recorded for us one such valedictory:

> It was the last lecture of the term, on the Constitution, and it was not probable that the whole class would ever again meet. As my father took his seat to commence the exercise, this fact seemed to strike his mind, and he began by alluding to it. Moved, as he proceeded, by the train of thought and feeling thus accidentally set in motion, he slid into a glowing discourse upon the principles and objects of the Constitution; the view of the great men of the Revolution, by whom it was drawn; the position of our country; the dangers to

which it was exposed; and the duty of every citizen to see that the republic sustained no detriment. He spoke, as he went on, of the hopes for freedom with which America was freighted; of the anxious eyes that watched it in its progress; of the voices that called from land to land to inquire of its welfare; closing in an exhortation to the students to labor for the furtherance of justice and free principles; to expand, deepen and liberalize the law; to discard low and ambitious motives in the profession, and to seek in all their public acts to establish the foundations of right and truth.

It is scarcely necessary to recall in detail Story's contributions to legal education in America. There had been a Harvard Law School before Story, but by the close of the twenties it was moribund. It was Story who more than any other recreated it, who more than any other founded that modern Law School that is one of the glories of our educational system. He had already declined the Royall Professorship, and he accepted the Dane Professorship with reluctance and at some personal sacrifice but he did not fail in his obligations to the chair which he graced. Within a few years the student body, which had languished, was flourishing, and before Story's death the pre-eminence of the Harvard Law School was acknowledged and unchallenged. Story had long been an advocate of systematic legal training in the school in preference to the haphazards of the law office, and the success of his own law school did much to discredit the old and justify the new type of training.

Yet even here there are some reservations. In his inaugural address on the "Value and Importance of Legal Studies" Story had called for a broad philosophical training for the lawyers who—he was sure—were to guide the destinies of the nation. "Nothing that concerns human nature or human art," he exclaimed, "is indifferent or useless." The law student should "make the master-spirits of all ages pay contributions to his labors. . . . He

should examine well the precepts of religion. . . . He
should unlock all the treasures of history for illustration
and instruction and admonition. . . . He must drink in
the lessons and the spirit of philosophy." Actually Story
made no provision for such training. The curriculum
which he and Greenleaf set up was strictly professional,
and if the eager student were to familiarize himself with
history, religion, and philosophy, he would have to do so
outside the Harvard Law School. Jefferson's plan for the
study of law had been broader and more humanistic, and
it had been attended with some success. In this, as in the
broader field of politics, Story subscribed to Jefferson's
theories and departed from his practices.

Story's contributions, then, to doctrinal writing and to
the scientific training of lawyers were immensely significant. But his chief business was, of course, on the bench.
He did not neglect it but, both on circuit and on the
Supreme Court, wrote his full share of opinions. He delivered not far from three hundred of these from the Supreme Court, and his circuit court opinions were even
more numerous. These opinions are, many of them, prolix
and diffuse. They embrace not only the point at issue but
other relevant and sometimes irrelevant points; and if at
times we feel that they are designed as much to display
legal learning as to conclude an argument, we should
recall that the law in Story's day was still to be made, and
that he was never unconscious of his responsibility in
this connection. Thus in the great case of *De Lovio* v. *Boit*
—which fills seventy-seven pages of Gallison's Reports—
Story undertook to review, for the edification of his countrymen, the whole history of admiralty. He himself confessed, "When I examine a question I go from headland
to headland, from case to case." Marshall, he added
somewhat ruefully, "has a compass, puts out to sea, and
goes directly to his result." Story's son, too, has remarked
this quality of verbosity in his father's opinions. "The

largeness of his learning," he wrote, thinking perhaps of *Martin* v. *Hunter's Lessee*, 1 Wheaton 304 (1816), *Dartmouth College*, 4 Wheaton 518 (1819), and *Charles River Bridge Co.*, 11 Peters 420 (1837)—or of those exhaustive opinions which he himself reported in the first circuit court—"the largeness of his learning sometimes interfered with the broad annunciation of an unencumbered proposition. . . . the range of his thought necessarily made him full." The faithful reader who works painstakingly through Gallison and Mason and Sumner, through Wheaton and Peters, may be forgiven if he wishes that the great jurist had more often followed his own advice to counsel:

> *Be brief, be pointed, let your matter stand*
> *Lucid in order, solid, and at hand.*
> *Spend not your words on trifles, but condense.*

or that other admonition, inspired by long-winded counsel:

> *O could but lawyers know the great relief*
> *When reasoning comes, close, pointed, clear*
> *   and brief,*
> *When every sentence tells. . . .*

It must be said that with Story every sentence did not tell, and the contrast here with Marshall is striking. With law, history, even philosophy Story seems to have made it a principle always to take the long way.

Yet his opinions do not lack for clarity. At his best—as in *Martin* v. *Mott*, 12 Wheaton 19 (1827), for example, or the *Neriede*, 9 Cranch 388 (1815), or parts of *Martin* v. *Hunter's Lessee*, 1 Wheaton 304 (1816), or the dissent in *Cary* v. *Curtis*, 3 Howard 236 (1845), Story can be as luminous and as pointed as Marshall himself. And the Commentaries are for the most part models of orderly condensation and succinctness. If they are open to criticism, indeed, it is on the ground that they tend to oversimplify what is actually complex, to systematize what is inherently differentiated.

Some aspects of Story's contributions to nationalism and to the protection of property rights we have already examined. It remains to suggest some generalizations about his judicial contributions to other fields of the law. The greatest was, doubtless, to the development of equity jurisprudence, though here he must share honors with the learned Kent. "In its broad doctrines and liberal spirit," writes W. W. Story with pardonable enthusiasm, "he delighted, as the clear noon of the law. Its free, flexible, and yet distinct and practical principles, comported better with the character of his mind . . . than the narrow and more technical doctrines of the common law." He had early urged the creation of equity courts in Massachusetts; near the close of his life he drew up, for the Supreme and the Circuit Courts, rules of Practice in Equity; and his decisions, especially in the circuit court, helped to lay the foundations for this branch of the law. He all but created the American law on copyrights and patents, illuminated Real Law, Partnerships and Trusts, and in Insurance pronounced judgments which—according to his not unbiased son— "may challenge comparison with Mansfield's."

With respect to commercial and prize law the situation is not so clear. Great claims have been made here, not only by the younger Story but by so impartial an authority as Warren. Story's role in the making of admiralty and prize law was in part fortuitous. He came to the bench at a time when the dockets were increasingly crowded with such cases, and the flood—released by the commercial wars of the early years of the century and by the slave trade—did not soon ebb. And Story's circuit—the first— embraced the principal shipping and commercial towns in the Union. It is safe to say that for many years commercial, prize, and admiralty cases constituted fully one half of all those which came to the First Circuit Court. Story was thus in a position to formulate the basic doctrines of law in these departments, and some of his opinions—the *Marianna Flora,* 3 Mason 116, 16 Fed. Cas. 736 (1822), affirmed 11 Wheaton 1 (1826), *De Lovio* v. *Boit,* 2 Gallison 398, 7 Fed. Cas. 418 (1815), the *Santissima Trinidad,* 7 Wheaton 283 (1822), and his dissent in the *Nereide,* 9 Cranch 388 (1815)—commanded international attention. Even Justice Marshall often turned to Story for help on admiralty questions and acknowledged his brother's greater learning in this field. "I wish to consult you," he wrote in 1819, "on a case which to me who am not versed in admiralty proceedings has some difficulty." And again, a decade later, "I have received your two letters . . . and have adopted your opinion respecting the admiralty jurisdiction, though in doing so I have reversed the decrees of my brother Barbour." Yet Marshall did not hesitate on occasion to reverse Story or to override him—the famous slave trade case, the *Antelope,* 10 Wheaton 66 (1825), is in point. And during the years both were on the Supreme bench, Marshall delivered fully as many admiralty and prize opinions as did his more learned brother.

In his judicial opinions as well as in his doctrinal writings Story's outlook was legalistic, and it is difficult to escape the impression that he regarded law not as a means but as an end in itself. His attitude toward the law was, indeed, that of a lover to his mistress, and his most moving eloquence was reserved for this object of his adoration. It is not apparent that he ever concerned himself with questions of legal philosophy except in a most superficial fashion, or that he was aware of the existence of such questions. His reading was confined to law and to belles lettres; if he had ever heard of Kant or Comte or James Mill, he fails to confess it. Even in law his reading, or at least his learning, seemed to lack breadth. He was familiar with Blackstone but not, it would seem, with his mighty opponent Bentham. He was deeply read in the literature of continental Europe, and the French jurist Foelix could assure him that only one lawyer in Paris (could it have been himself?) knew all the French works cited in the *Conflict of Laws,* but nowhere does he mention Beccaria or Savigny or Kant. His structure of law was monumental but lacking in any conscious philosophical foundation; it was elaborate but wanting in social orientation.

Story's philosophical insularity was not literary only. He came to maturity at the time when New England was responding to the first stirrings of romanticism, when transcendentalism had become almost respectable and reform was the order of the day. He had gone to college with Channing and Tuckerman; he lived all his life within a few miles of Boston and Concord, and Cambridge itself was not wholly immune to the epidemic of liberalism that infected her neighbors. During the years that Story lived in Cambridge and rode the New England circuit, Channing paved the way for the liberalization of the Unitarian Church, Emerson published his essay on Nature, Parker preached on the "Transient and the Permanent in Christianity," Ripley founded Brook Farm, Brisbane spread abroad the doctrines of Fourierism, Margaret Fuller edited *The Dial,* Garrison published the *Liberator,* Lydia Maria Child broadcast her "Appeal in Favor of that Class of Americans Called Africans," Phillips denounced the murderers of Lovejoy, Whittier wrote his moving "Massachusetts to Virginia," Bronson Alcott and Elizabeth Peabody taught at the Temple School, Howe took over the Perkins Institution for the Blind, Dorothea Dix dedicated herself to the salvation of society's misfits, Pierpont agitated temperance reform, Ladd issued his stirring appeal for peace, Horace Mann inaugurated his great crusade for the common schools, Robert Dale Owen

pleaded the cause of women's rights and Robert Rantoul
the cause of labor. It was the beginning of the greatest
period of reform in American history, it found its inspiration and its leaders in New England, Boston was the Hub
of the Reform World.

But Story, as far as we can tell, passed through all of
this unscathed. He was not, he could not be, unaware of
it. He had begun life as a Republican, a follower of the
greatest of American liberals; he was a member of the
Unitarian Church and president of the Association; he
was close to Channing and Sumner and Follen and Dana.
But to the ferment of reform he remained loftily
indifferent. To be sure he spoke in eloquent generalizations about penal reform, but it is not recorded that he
gave the movement any effective support. He drafted
enlightened legislation for the protection of seamen, but
Dana had occasion to protest against his interpretation of
that legislation. He paid pretty compliments to the virtue
and intelligence of women and celebrated the beauties of
female literature, but Jane Austen rather than Margaret
Fuller was the beneficiary of the compliments, and to the
struggle for political and legal rights for women he contributed nothing. Slavery, to be sure, aroused his indignation, and it is recorded that his one participation in politics was a protest against the Missouri Compromise,
while his charges to grand juries on the slave trade and
his ruling in the Young Eugenie, *La Jeune Eugenie*, 2
Mason 409, Fed. Cas. 15,551 (1822), and the *Amistad*,
15 Peters 518 (1841), cases are familiar enough. Yet
even here it is difficult to know whether he was more
hostile to slavery or to antislavery, and young Rutherford
Hayes recorded in his diary that Story's denunciation of
the "mad men" who counseled nullification of the Fugitive Slave Act was the most eloquent lecture that he had
ever heard.

No, it was not with the Come-outers that Story aligned

himself, not with the music makers and dreamers of dreams. He preferred the company of substantial citizens: the great merchants, the sound bankers, the capable lawyers, the eloquent statesmen—men like Otis and Biddle, Mason and Pinckney, Webster and Clay and Everett. He was a member of the ruling class and, after his ascension to the bench, never doubted that that was the only class fit to rule.

Yet Story was not lacking in humanity or in the common touch. In all personal relations he was simple and authentic, gregarious and humane, generous and affectionate. He was ever at the service of his friends— ready to give counsel or dash off a letter on the Northeastern Boundary controversy or furnish a learned appendix to the Court reporter or compose a stately obituary at a moment's notice. He bubbled over with kindliness— to American scholars who wanted to go abroad and European scholars who wanted to visit America, to lawyers who were ambitious and visitors who were curious. He loved company—the great lawyers with their inexhaustible fund of anecdotes, the proud statesmen who came to him with their problems, his brothers on the bench who relied on his learning and drew strength from his serenity, his students who cheered him when he came home from Washington with the latest political gossip and bore with him when he repeated his stories, stray companions —farmers who could tell him about the crops, coachmen who regaled him with local tradition, innkeepers who hurried to care for his comfort. His curiosity was insatiable, his sympathies catholic, his mind lively and alert, his spirits vivacious and buoyant.

It was this quality of unquenchable good spirits, especially, that contemporaries remarked. Charles Davies, the Portland lawyer, recalled Story's "untiring and inexhaustible vitality, with a constant flow of good humor, from morning to night and night again almost to morning"; Josiah Quincy remembered his "controversial powers, so extraordinary"—did he mean, perhaps, conversational? English visitors who differed on so many other things were agreed on Story, and on this quality which they thought so curious in a New Englander. Harriet Martineau wrote that "his talk would gush out for hours—so heartfelt, so lively, so various, and his face, all the while . . . showing all the mobility and intentiousness of a child's . . . the quick smiles, the glistening eye, the gleeful tone, with passing touches of sentiment." And Consul Grattan, who knew his Boston so well, found him "eloquent, garrulous, lively, amiable . . . decidedly the gem of this Western World."

His mind was rich and affluent, his intelligence spontaneous. He was no animated encyclopaedia like his contemporary Theodore Parker, nor did he parade his learning like his young friend Charles Sumner—though sometimes his opinions gave an impression of just that. But he knew all that a scholar should know and all that a gentleman needed to know. His pen dripped with legal learning, and his tongue tripped lightly over the couplets of Dryden or the odes of Horace. He was an old-fashioned gentleman and should have dressed in stockings and knee-breeches, and a scarlet coat; his humor even ran to puns, and he was always ready with an aphorism or an appropriate touch of sentiment. For all his amiability and his sentimentality he was not without dignity, and there is a certain stateliness in the prose of his opinions and his commentaries.

He was, above all, a happy man, happy in his work and his friends and his family. He had known tragedy and sorrow—the death of his first wife and of most of his children. But he accepted this with Christian resignation. He was never discouraged and only occasionally faint of heart. Life had been good to him, and he knew that Christ—whose historicity he stood ready to prove by rules of legal evidence in a court of justice—would not fail him.

JEFFERSON AND THE BOOK-BURNERS

WHEN, on the night of August 24–25, 1814, General Robert Ross burned Washington, most, though not all, of the infant congressional library went up in flames. Patrick Magruder, who doubled as clerk of the House and librarian, had betaken himself to Virginia Springs, and the convulsive efforts of his assistants to save the library foundered on the lack of wagons. A subsequent congressional investigation concluded somewhat illogically that the hapless Magruder should have foreseen this embarrassment and provided for it, and accepted his resignation.

The news of the destruction of the library shocked Thomas Jefferson, then in retirement at Monticello. He might with some justice regard the library as his special concern: it had been organized under his auspices, and he had found time, while President, to prepare for it a catalogue of desirable books—carefully leaving out those "for entertainment only"—which fixed for the present its acquisition policy. For some years he had been accumu-

SOURCE: *American Heritage*, IX : 5 (August 1958). Copyright © 1958 by Henry Steele Commager.

lating at Monticello a comprehensive and scholarly library; he himself called it "the choicest collection of books in the United States," and it probably was. He had thought to leave it to his darling University of Virginia, but that institution was still on his ardent drawing board, and the need of the nation was pressing. So on September 21 Jefferson wrote his old friend Samuel Harrison Smith (better known as Silky-Milky Smith or as the husband of the vivacious Margaret Bayard, whose letters, later collected in *The First Forty Years of Washington Society*, were to tell all), offering his library to Congress on whatever terms the Congress might think proper.

> I learn from the newspapers [he wrote] that the vandalism of our enemy has triumphed at Washington over science as well as the arts by the destruction of the public library with the noble edifice in which it was deposited. . . . I presume it will be among the early objects of Congress to recommence their collection. This will be difficult while the war continues, and intercourse with Europe is attended with so much risk. You know my collection, its condition and extent. . . . It is long since I have been sensible it ought not to continue private property, and had provided that at my death, Congress should have the refusal of it at their own price. The loss they have now incurred, makes the present the proper moment for their accommodation, without regard to the small remnant of time and the barren use of my enjoying it. I ask of your friendship, therefore, to make for me the tender of it to the Library Committee of Congress. . . .

This handsome offer excited both enthusiasm and consternation. To some it transformed British vandalism into a benefaction; the congressional library, after all, numbered only some three thousand volumes, while Jefferson estimated his own collection (too generously, as it proved) at between nine and ten thousand. Not only this, but while the congressional library had been assembled almost fortuitously, Jefferson's collection was admirably designed for the needs of scholars and statesmen.

> I have been fifty years making it [wrote Jefferson].
> . . . While residing in Paris, I devoted every afternoon I was disengaged, for a summer or two, in examining all the principal bookstores, turning over every book with my own hand, and putting by everything which related to America. . . . Besides this, I had standing orders during the whole time I was in Europe, on its principal book-marts, particularly Amsterdam, Frankfort, Madrid, and London, for such works relating to America as could not be found in Paris. So that, in that department particularly, such a collection was made as probably can never again be effected, because it is hardly probable that the same opportunities, the same time, industry, perseverance and expense, with the same knowledge of the bibliography of the subject, would again happen to be in concurrence.

Smith replied at once that he could see "no obstacle in the acceptance" of this offer. From the former editor of the Republican *National Intelligencer* this was excessively naïve. Die-hard Federalists—they were still another decade a-dying—would doubtless have fought anything bearing Jefferson's name, but this proposal seemed to them peculiarly offensive, for it combined in a single package a collection of iniquitous ingredients: a library of belles lettres and classics which no self-respecting congressmen would read; an arsenal of Jacobinism, infidelity, and immorality; and a lavish financial subsidy to ex-President Jefferson himself.

But the Republicans controlled both branches of Congress, and the Federalists were forced to resort to obstructive tactics. Thus after the Senate had acted favorably on Jefferson's proposal and returned the bill to the House, Thomas Jackson Oakley of New York (he was later to be chief justice of that state, in which rôle "he was noted for his impartiality") moved to authorize the committee to

buy not Jefferson's library, but any library; this crude
evasion of the issue was summarily rejected. Cyrus King
of Maine (then still a district of Massachusetts) moved
the purchase of such books only as the Congress should
deem suitable; John Reed of Massachusetts supported
this, and added to it an amendment fixing the maximum
price of $25,000. With these and other amendments be-
fore the House, "the debate," observed the editor of the
Annals of Congress, "became rather too animated." In the
end the Republicans swept aside all objections, and sent
the bill on to the Senate for action.

Meantime a committee had counted the actual number
of volumes in Jefferson's library—6,487—and placed a
modest price of $23,950—a sum, be it noted, less than
the maximum which the parsimonious Reed was prepared to pay. A bill to buy the library at this price passed
the Senate without a division and on December 3, 1814,
went to the House. Here, on its final reading the next
month, the Federalists took their last stand.

Oakley of New York, Reed and Timothy Pickering of
Massachusetts, King of Maine, and a freshman representative, Daniel Webster of Portsmouth, New Hampshire,
led the forces of righteousness in the assault on Jeffersonian subversion. "The debate," says Joseph Gales of the
Annals, "although it afforded much amusement to the
auditors, would not interest the feelings or judgment of
any reader." The Washington correspondent of the New
York *Evening Post* thought differently, and happily preserved for us some of the arguments advanced by the
opposition. These were in part financial, in part literary,
in part moral. Twenty-three thousand, nine hundred and
fifty dollars, it was observed, would pay for the enlist-
ment of 210 men for the Regular Army or the purchase of
2,000 stands of arms—an argument that must have
sounded less than convincing to mortified delegates from
the Hartford Convention even then on their way to Wash-

ington. And coming from that party which had long claimed a monopoly on culture and philosophy, the literary arguments were no less startling. It was urged—so the New York *Post* observed—

> that the library was not such as Congress wanted, being almost entirely literary, containing comparatively little of law or history, that it abounded with productions of an atheistical, irreligious and immoral character,—a fourth of the books were in foreign languages, and many in the dead languages, such as romances, tracts on architecture, farriery, cookery and the like. Upon the latter subject, it was mentioned . . . there were no less than ten different works, nine being in foreign languages. . . .

Perhaps the spectacle of nine books of cookery, most of them doubtless in pernicious French, was itself enough to determine New England opposition!

It remained for Cyrus King, however, to argue the case most vehemently on moral grounds. Half brother to the redoubtable Rufus King, a graduate of Phillips Andover and of Columbia College, he made here his one, brief, claim to fame. Though Gales did not think his remarks worth preserving (perhaps his political sentiments colored his judgment), Editor Hezekiah Niles did, and it is to the pages of Niles' *Register* that we must turn for a report of King's motions and speeches:

> Besides opposing the bill on the general ground of the inexpediency of appropriating so large a sum as twenty-three thousand dollars, for this object, at a time of such national embarrassment, and when we had no place of safety for a library when purchased, Mr. King observed, that it appeared from the catalogue, there were many books unnecessary, improper and useless for congress, and that on the contrary, this library was destitute of others, indispensable in the ordinary transactions of our business; with a view to remedy these inconveniences, he moved that the bill be committed to a select

committee, with instructions to report a new section, as follows:

Sec. 2 *And be it further enacted.* That as soon as said library shall be received at Washington, the joint library committee be, and they are hereby authorized and directed to select therefrom, all books not useful and necessary for congress, and to cause the same to be sold, and the proceeds thereof invested in other books for the use of congress.

This motion being negatived, Mr. King observed, that it appeared from the same catalogue, and from the information of intelligent gentlemen, who had seen this library, *and it might be inferred from the character of the man who selected it,* and *from the country* (France) where he says he made the principal collection, and from the time when he made it, that there were in this library many books of an irreligious and immoral tendency, embracing many of the works of the French infidel philosophers, who had caused and inflamed the volcano of the French revolution, which in its progress, had desolated the fairest portions of Europe, and had extended its fatal—its destructive effects, to our once happy country; to prevent a general dissemination of this infidel philosophy, *and of the principles of a man, who had inflicted greater and deeper injuries upon our country,* than any other person, except Mr. Madison, ever did upon any country. Mr. King again moved to recommit the bill to a select committee. . . .

The motion was next attacked by an honourable gentleman from Massachusetts (Mr. Hulbert) who, after advocating the bill on general principles, with his usual ability and perspicuity, observed, as it respects this motion, and the reasons assigned by the mover in favour of it, that these reasons were inconsistent with the motion, as the section provided for the preservation of these books, alleged to be irreligious, by sending them back to Mr. Jefferson, whereas the motive of his colleague was to prevent the contagion which might spread from them; that if he was sincerely desirous of preventing this evil, he ought to amend the section by introducing a provision for the burning of such books.

Mr. King informed the honourable speaker, that he would accept with pleasure of the modification proposed by his colleague: that indeed he had at first drawn his amendment with a provision that these books should be burnt by the library committee, but that it afterwards appeared to him, to comport better with the dignity of the house, to send them back, especially as said committee might be unwilling to perform a task usually allotted to the common hangman. That as the motion now stood, the fears of his colleague as to the ill effects of these books upon the pure minds of Mr. Jefferson and his friends, were certainly groundless, as they were happily secured therefrom by their own depravity. . . .

The amendment was accordingly withdrawn, and the bill passed, putting into the pocket of Thomas Jefferson 23,900 dollars, for about six thousand volumes of books, good, bad and indifferent, old and new, useful and worthless, in all tongues and languages, about one quarter French, and another quarter in languages, dead and living, other than English; many which cannot be read by a single member in either house of Congress, and more which never will nor ever ought to be read by a member—while the library is destitute of other books, absolutely necessary, in doing the public business. This is true Jeffersonian, Madisonian, democratic economy, which has bankrupt the treasury, beggared the people, and disgraced the nation. [*Niles' Weekly Register, 1814–15*, Vol. VII, Supp., pp. 63–5.]

We must not, however, let Niles have the last word, but rather his rival, Robert Walsh, of the short-lived *American Register*. "The next generation," wrote Walsh, "will, we confidently predict, blush at the objections made in Congress to the purchase of Mr. Jefferson's library. Party-spirit, darkling and chafing, spoke the language of an auctioneer or a chapman, and erred egregiously even in its huckstering calculations."

THE BLASPHEMY OF
ABNER KNEELAND

GENTLEMEN, blasphemy is but one part of the system
Fanny Wright has introduced among us. It is but one
step, a fatal one indeed, but still but one step on the
road to ruin. The system is matured and graduated.
Atheism is to dethrone the Judge of heaven and earth; a
future state of rewards and punishments is to be described as a nursery bugbear; moral and religious restraints are to be removed by proclaiming death to be
an eternal sleep; marriage to be denounced as an un-
lawful restraint upon shifting affections . . . ; illicit
sexual intercourse to be encouraged by physiological
checks upon conception; the laws of property are to be
repealed as restrictions upon "the greatest good"; a
community of property to be established; all children to
be supported out of the common fund, that nobody need
fear becoming fathers or mothers, and the horrible experiments of "New Harmony" and "Nashoba" . . . to
be introduced here as fast as possible and pervade the
world. Such are the connected objects combined into
one system by the disciples of Robert Owen and Fanny
Wright.

It was Mr. Parker's closing appeal to the jury in the trial

SOURCE: *The New England Quarterly*, VIII : 1 (March 1935).
Reprinted by permission.

of Abner Kneeland for blasphemy, and it might well have moved stronger men than Mr. Bumstead and Mr. Clapp and Mr. Dimmick and Mr. Finch and the other jurymen who listened with such rapt attention.[1] It was effective, too, effective with all but the recalcitrant Mr. Greene, who stubbornly refused to be convinced by this compound of rhetoric and illogic. And so, despite the eloquence of Mr. Parker and the charge of Judge Putnam, and the zeal of eleven good Christians, the case ended in a mis-trial.

This was the second trial in the case of the *Commonwealth* v. *Abner Kneeland,* and there were two more still to come. For four mortal years this business of the blasphemy of Abner Kneeland dragged its tortuous way through the courts of Massachusetts, until it became a positive nuisance. It inspired torrents of legal eloquence, loosed floods of sermons, and agitated oceans of print. Society was rocked to its foundations, the pillars of morality and religion tottered, and the commonwealth seemed doomed, but in the end the forces of light triumphed over the powers of darkness, immorality was rebuked, and blasphemy silenced.

Abner Kneeland was inoffensive enough, one might

---

[1] The records of the trials of Kneeland have been reprinted in *American State Trials,* John D. Lawson, Editor, xiii, 450–575. The opinions of Justices Shaw and Morton can be found in *Massachusetts Reports,* 20 Pickering, 206 *ff.* Mr. Kneeland's defence, written in jail, was published as the *Review of the Trial, Conviction, and Final Imprisonment* . . . *of Abner Kneeland, Written by Himself* (Boston, n.d.): this pamphlet quotes in full the offensive article on the Virgin Birth, which was not read in court and does not, therefore, appear in the published record. Channing's petition can be found in W. H. Channing: *The Life of William Ellery Channing* (Boston, 1880), 504 *ff.* On Kneeland in Iowa, see Mary R. Whitcomb: "Abner Kneeland: His Relation to Early Iowa History," *Annals of Iowa,* Series iii, vi, 340 *ff.* Brief biographical sketches are in the *Dictionary of American Biography* and J. McCabe: *Biographical Dictionary of Modern Rationalists* (London, 1920).

think, with his kindly blue eyes and his silvery hair and his endearing oddities of manner. He had been a farmer, a carpenter, a legislator, a teacher, a preacher, and an editor, nor did these accomplishments exhaust his versatility. He fancied himself something of a scholar and had translated the New Testament and could cite Greek texts as smartly as Professor Felton; he knew enough law to argue his own case but not enough to win it; he could turn his hand dexterously to a new system of orthography, or to doctoring (he had been married four times and had delivered his wives of twelve children—all by the Thomsonian or vapor bath system!) and he could even chart a utopia if that were required of him.

But first and last he was a preacher, in the pulpit and out. How many pulpits he had graced in his life—in Vermont and New Hampshire, in Boston, Philadelphia, and New York—and always he had been preaching for himself, praying for himself, trying to discover the truth in this welter of dogma and belief. But all to no avail. He had tried the Baptist, the Congregational, and even the Universalist church, but always the consolations of Christianity failed, and even the mighty Hosea Ballou was not able to revive them. With much ado Mr. Kneeland seceded from the church and embraced pantheism.

Mr. Kneeland had spent thirty years in explaining himself and in expounding his gospel, and he had no intention of abandoning the practice just because he had changed the text. The atmosphere of New York proving uncongenial, he betook him to Boston, and there, in 1830, organized the "First Society of Free Enquirers" and established the *Boston Investigator,* the first rationalist journal in the country. The society met at Julien Hall, and when the irate proprietor turned them out, they moved cheerfully to the Federal Street Theatre, which was twice as large—but not before Julien Hall had been placed at the disposal of another disturber of the peace, William Lloyd Garrison.

It was the *Investigator* that got Kneeland into trouble. The origin of the difficulty is somewhat obscure, but Kneeland himself insisted that the whole thing had been instigated by one Lucius Sargent, whose fiction had been cuttingly reviewed in the paper and who was hot for revenge. However this may be, it is clear that the rationalist journal had for some time been a stench in the nostrils of the Boston clergy. When the issue of December 20, 1833, appeared, the authorities felt that patience was no longer a virtue, and the hapless editor was promptly indicted for blasphemy.

This issue of December 20 was to become almost painfully familiar to Boston. It contained three articles, all more than ordinarily offensive: two of them reprinted from the *Free Inquirer* of New York City, one of them by Kneeland himself. The first of these profane articles dealt with the subject of the Virgin Birth, and contained a quotation from Voltaire so indelicate that four successive judges protected four different juries from the embarrassment of listening to it. The second article was filled with irreverent ridicule of prayer, and suggested a comparison of God with General Jackson—unpardonable in Boston. These two articles, to be sure, had been written by a mysterious Ben Krapac, and inserted in the *Investigator* while the editor was out of the city: an extenuating circumstance, perhaps, but not a valid legal plea. Wicked and indecent as these squibs were, it was upon the third article that the state rested its case—an article whose authorship the editor cheerfully confessed.

> 1. Universalists believe in a god which I do not; [so Kneeland had written] but believe that their god, with all his moral attributes, is nothing more than a chimera of their own imagination. 2. Universalists believe in

Christ, which I do not; but believe that the whole story concerning him is as much a fable and fiction, as that of the god Prometheus. . . . 3. Universalists believe in miracles, which I do not; but believe that every pretension to them can either be accounted for on natural principles or else is to be attributed to mere trick and imposture. 4. Universalists believe in the resurrection of the dead, immortality and eternal life, which I do not; but believe that all life is material, that death is an eternal extinction of life to the individual who possesses it, and that no individual life was ever or ever will be eternal.

This was the blasphemy of Abner Kneeland, blasphemy, so the learned counsel argued, which constituted a clear violation of the act of July 3, 1782—An Act against Blasphemy. "If any person"—so read the law—"shall willfully blaspheme the holy name of God, by denying, cursing, or contumeliously reproaching God, his creation, government, or final judging of the world, or by cursing or reproaching Jesus Christ or the Holy Ghost, or by cursing or contumeliously reproaching the holy word of God, that is, the canonical scriptures as contained in the books of the Old and New Testaments, or by exposing them or any part of them to contempt or ridicule, he shall be punished."

The first trial took place in the municipal court of Boston in January, 1834. Counsel for the state, Mr. S. D. Parker, opened with a severe arraignment of the fearful social consequences of infidelity. "There have been other infidels," he thundered, "Hume, Gibbon, Voltaire, Volney, *etc.* but the works of these persons were read only by men of literary habits—necessarily a few. But here is a journal, a newspaper, cheap, and sent into a thousand families. Where one man would be injured by Hume, Gibbon, or Volney, a thousand may be injured by this newspaper, so widely circulated, so easily read, so coarsely expressed, so industriously spread abroad." Mr. Kneeland was not a little surprised to learn that his influence was a thousandfold that of Voltaire and Gibbon, but his natural pleasure in this situation was shortly rebuked, for Mr. Parker hastened to add that "Christianity wanted no protection from the law against the hostility of Abner Kneeland, the conceited, the poor, the weak mortal now on trial at the bar of this court." In the circumstances, it was somewhat difficult to understand why the state had troubled to indict Mr. Kneeland at all, but Mr. Parker waved aside this dilemma and explained that the law forbade blasphemy, and the law must be upheld.

That Mr. Kneeland had committed blasphemy was not to be doubted. He was legally responsible for the articles on the Virgin Birth and on prayer, legally responsible for the unspeakable indecency of the first and the scurrilous and contumelious reproach of the second; and as for the third, if words had any meaning, that, assuredly, was a denial of God, His creation, His government, and His final judging of the world. Squirm as he would, Mr. Kneeland could not deny these evidences of guilt or explain them away.

Yet this was precisely what Mr. Kneeland attempted to do. Through his counsel, Mr. Dunlap, he issued a denial so all-embracing that it might well have confused a judge less astute than the Mr. Thacher who presided with such admirable partiality over the trial. Mr. Dunlap challenged first the constitutionality of the law under which the defendant was indicted, and he gutted the history of the Bay State to prove that the authors of the constitution wished to establish complete religious freedom in that commonwealth. Not satisfied with this he proceeded to deny responsibility for the two articles reprinted from the New York *Inquirer*, and to argue that, in any event, these articles did not come within the alleged law. The piece dealing with the Virgin Birth—Mr. Dunlap blushingly refrained from reading it—was improper and coarse, but after all, the law said nothing about the Virgin. The comparison of God to General Jackson was unfortunate, but it was not blasphemous in character, for its intention was simply to apply reason to the vulgarization of a religious ceremony, and Mr. Dunlap was prepared to prove that worthy clergy had used terms far harsher than these in criticizing the practices of rival denominations.

But what of the troublesome third article—the article which had flowed from Mr. Kneeland's pen? By a careful attention to the laws of grammar and the rules of construction, Mr. Dunlap was prepared to show that this contained neither denial, curse, nor contumelious reproach. Look, said Mr. Dunlap, with the air of a teacher addressing the fourth grade—look at the punctuation of this sentence: "Universalists believe in a god which I do not." Note, there is no comma between the word "god"—spelled with a small and not a capital "g"—and the word "which." Obviously, what Mr. Kneeland intended to say was that he did not believe in the god in which the Universalists believed. It was very simple, if you but read it aright. Never did a comma create such a stir: as learned counsel argued, the fate of civilization and morality seemed to hang on its curl.

But Judge Thacher was quite unmoved either by considerations of grammar or by arguments of law, and in his charge to the jury he remembered that he was a deacon in the Reverend Mr. Lothrop's Brattle Street Church. The law was constitutional, he informed the jury, and it was a good law. "It would be an incredible thing," he pointed out, "if a race of men descended from the Puritan settlers of New England . . . should in the lapse of a century and a half have so far departed from the sentiments of their fathers as to disregard all considerations when they were forming a political compact. . . . We find however, that the framers of the constitution had not degenerated from the character of their ancestors." Nor

was there any doubt in the judge's mind that Mr. Kneeland had committed blasphemy: as for grammatical objections, if Mr. Kneeland had not inserted a comma between "which" and "god," he would do it for him, and
forthwith the comma appeared. Having thus re-
punctuated the sentence, Judge Thacher gravely informed the jury that they were to place upon the words
the common-sense construction. Nor did Mr. Thacher
forbear to emphasize the grave social consequences of
blasphemy unrebuked.

> I cannot omit to repeat [he said] the observation of the
> illustrious Erskine in the trial of Thomas Williams for
> publishing Paine's Age of Reason. . . . Of all human
> beings, he says, the poor stand most in need of the
> consolations of religion, and the country has the deep-
> est stake in their enjoying it, not only from the protec-
> tion which it owes them, but because no man can be
> expected to be faithful to the authority of man, who
> revolts against the government of God.

Finally there was the piece on the Virgin Birth. No
more than the counsel would Judge Thacher assail the
ears of the court with the horrid words, but he would not
fail to point out that "if Mr. Kneeland had meant to say
that Jesus Christ was a mere man like ourselves and that
Joseph was his father, could he not have found language
to express the sentiment with decency without a disgust-
ing reference to those parts of the human frame which
even savages cover with the veil of modesty, and of which
among the civilized it is always deemed indecent to
speak." "It is for you to judge," he concluded illogically,
"whether his language was fitting."

The result was never for a moment in doubt: the jury
brought in a verdict of guilty, and Judge Thacher pronounced sentence. But Massachusetts was not yet done
with the case. Mr. Kneeland promptly appealed, and the
case went to the supreme court, and here it took three

trials to secure a conviction. In the first, as we have seen, Mr. Greene produced a mistrial; in the second Mr. Dunbarr: both names were preserved for immortality by the grateful Kneeland. The third trial in the supreme court was held in November, 1835: Mr. Parker, worn out with repetitions, gave way to Attorney-General Austin, the same who two years later was to say of Lovejoy that "he died as the fool dieth." Mr. Kneeland, emboldened by his good fortune in the earlier trials and perhaps by the stirrings of that tender passion which was shortly to culminate in his fourth marriage, dispensed with the services of Mr. Dunlap and pled his own case.

It was an able and persuasive argument, more elaborate than Mr. Dunlap's and more candid. Mr. Kneeland faced fairly the issue of obscenity in the first and the question of irreverence in the second of Ben Krapac's articles. What was it, after all, that so shocked the sensibilities of men? What were these horrid words that palsied the tongues of judge and counsel? Let us bring this thing out into the open (so he said) and look at it as intelligent, adult men. It was a quotation from Voltaire that had done the mischief: the great French philosopher was discussing a curious custom of the Hottentots of removing, at the time of birth, one testicle from all male children. A horrible practice, Ben Krapac acknowledged, but perhaps no more difficult for us to understand than for the Hottentot to comprehend how any one could have been begotten without aid of the human body at all. This was the sum and substance of the obscenity for which Mr. Kneeland was responsible—the use of a word "which is to be found in all our common school dictionaries, where children of all ages and of both sexes, are not only allowed to see it, but are also there taught its meaning." If this offended gentlemen, all Mr. Kneeland could say was: *Honi soit qui mal y pense.*

As for the piece on prayer, if he should be convicted for

that, it would assuredly be "one of the most cruel cases that has happened since the days of witchcraft." Besides, this ridicule of common forms of prayer referred not to God but to man; it contained neither denial, curse, nor contumelious reproach, except to those who believed that God had nothing to do but answer their prayers for beefsteak and potatoes. If churchmen really worshipped that kind of a god, so much the worse for them. As for the charge that he was an atheist—a charge to which the bench had lent its support—Mr. Kneeland rejected it with indignation. No sane man, he submitted, *could* be an atheist. No, Mr. Kneeland was a pantheist, and his creed had been published long ago in the *Investigator* for anyone to read. "I believe that the whole universe is nature," he had written, "and that the word nature embraces the whole universe, and that God and Nature are perfectly synonymous terms."

But it was all to no avail. Judge Wilde charged the jury that Mr. Kneeland had denied the existence of God, and that such denial constituted a violation of the statute forbidding blasphemy. The jury promptly returned a verdict of guilty, and the judge sentenced the prisoner to sixty days in the common jail. From this decision Mr. Kneeland again appealed, this time to the full supreme court, and in the spring of 1838, four years after the original indictment, the case came up for a final hearing.

Again Mr. Kneeland chose to argue his own case, but this time he altered his tactics. Instead of a candid defence of the articles which he had published and written, he embraced a policy of evasion and obstruction. He refused to acknowledge that he was editor or publisher of the *Investigator*, he refused to acknowledge (though he did not deny) that he had written the confession of faith upon which the indictment principally rested. All these things he left for the state to prove, and the state, caught unaware, was not prepared to prove them. The result was a compromise between Mr. Kneeland and the attorney-general which did credit to neither: the state agreed to drop from the indictment the pieces on the Virgin Birth and on prayer, in return for an admission by Mr. Kneeland, that he had written the third article. But these tactics profited Mr. Kneeland not a whit. The great Chief Justice Shaw presided: he had helped to revise the constitution in the famous convention of 1820 and he might be presumed to know whether its guarantees of religious liberty covered Mr. Kneeland's case. That the law against blasphemy was constitutional Judge Shaw did not for a moment doubt: it had been consistently upheld in numerous decisions of the courts, and similar laws, on the statute-books of sister states, had always been regarded as valid. Judge Shaw ruled that blasphemy consisted in "speaking evil of the Deity with an impious purpose to derogate from the divine majesty, and to alienate the minds of others from the love and reverence of God," and he held that Mr. Kneeland's article had been of this character. Brushing aside as irrelevant those problems of punctuation and construction which had agitated his brethren, he maintained that the whole intent of the article in question was blasphemous in that it tended to alienate the minds of men from reverence of God. Not satisfied with this the judge went out of his way to deplore the conceit which had persuaded Mr. Kneeland to present his own case.

It was not often that Judge Shaw's colleagues differed with him, but Mr. Justice Morton felt moved to file a dissenting opinion. A mere denial of God, he argued, was not blasphemy; even a wilful denial of the Deity could not be held to constitute blasphemy, for "a man may not be punished for wilfully doing what he has a legal right to do." The very essence of blasphemy is intent: it was formerly customary, he pointed out, to insert in a charge of blasphemy the words *falso et maletiose scripsit,* and these words were the very gist of the indictment and absolutely necessary to prove an offence. Now Justice Morton was not convinced that Mr. Kneeland was guilty of any wicked or malicious intent, or that the language which he had used was peculiarly offensive. Not only was there no intent to injure, but there was no evidence that any injury had occurred, and it is "only injury to civil society which can give the civil government jurisdiction over blasphemy." Not only was Judge Morton convinced that the state had no valid case against Mr. Kneeland, but he was persuaded that the zeal with which this case had been prosecuted was misguided and unfortunate.

> To allow and encourage discourses and arguments in proof of the existence of the Deity and in support of the Christian religion, and to prohibit arguments on the other side, would appear to imply a want of confidence in the truth, power, and efficacy of these great doctrines which . . . would lead to scepticism and infidelity. These essential and all-important truths are too deeply rooted, and have too strong a foundation, to need or admit of the dangerous aid of human legislation.

But despite the eloquence of Mr. Morton the decision of the lower court was sustained, and the sentence confirmed. Nor was that martyrdom merely a matter of two months in the common jail. The fourth Mrs. Kneeland was with child, and the shock of the sentence (so Mr. Kneeland alleged) brought on a miscarriage: the mother hovered for some time on the brink of death, but eventually recovered.

The imposition of the sentence aroused protest throughout the state, and editorial writers everywhere resorted gratefully to the never-failing store-house of Puritan intolerance. "This remarkable persecution of an unfortunate individual, for opinion's sake," said the Boston *Advocate*, "which has been persisted in for four years, will stamp another indelible page of shame on the history of

Massachusetts. It will form another chapter to be placed
beside those that relate to the dark superstition, religious
bigotry, and intolerance when four Quakers were hung in
1669 and 19 witches in 1692." The Lowell *Advertiser* was
less restrained. "We cannot speak," it lamented, "of this
outrage upon *human* rights, upon *expediency,* upon the
freedom of the press, and of *speech,* upon *mercy,* upon
truth, upon *Christianity,* and upon the *Spirit of the* AGE
without feelings of the deepest shame and sorrow for the
State."

   Even the saintly Dr. Channing was aroused, Channing
who seldom permitted irrelevant and momentary
depravity to becloud his view of the celestial future of
mankind. At the instance of Mr. Ellis Gray Loring he
drew up a powerful petition for pardon: on twelve counts
it pleaded the cause of the unfortunate defendant and of
the honor of the state. Mr. Kneeland might yet have been
saved, but the petition was circulated among the liberal
clergy, and all was lost. For among the scores of signatures were those of such men as Mr. Emerson, Mr. Ripley,
the Rev. Theodore Parker, Dr. Noyes, and Dr. Follen,
transcendentalists, abolitionists, and come-outers—men
little if any better than Abner Kneeland himself. The
Reverend Samuel Kirkland Lothrop of the Brattle Street
Church promptly circulated a counter-petition; he
regarded himself as peculiarly the guardian of the morals
of Boston, and his forthright mind was impatient of sub-
tleties. The counter-petition was signed by scores of respectable citizens who trembled for society and for the
state, and copies of it, reciting in full the obscenity and
depravity of Mr. Kneeland, were hung in railroad stations
and other public buildings where all who were shocked,
amused, or edified might sign.

   Dr. Channing's petition was in vain, and the
blasphemer was jugged in the common jail. From the
window of his cell he could see the Bunker Hill Monu-

ment: it was still incomplete, and that (thought Mr. Kneeland) was as it should be. From the jail Mr. Kneeland addressed an open letter to his friends and sympathizers.

> Fellow Citizens! Countrymen!! and Lovers of Liberty!!! Sixty-three years ago a battle was fought on Bunker Hill in plain sight of my window where I now am. But what was it all for? LIBERTY! And what am I here for? For the honest exercise of that very *Liberty* for which our fathers fought and bled!!!

What with letter-writing and the composition of an exhaustive, but not impartial, review of the case, and visitors, the sixty days went fast enough, and by mid-summer of 1838 Abner Kneeland was a free man, little the worse for his experience and with reputation vastly enhanced.

But Boston had disappointed him, Boston with its frigid Unitarianism and its smug good manners. He would leave Boston, leave this ingrown New England where men trembled like children at good salty speech and even revolutions had to be conducted with good taste. He would go West. He was sixty-four years old, but full of vigor and, despite his hard life, of faith. He had known Robert Dale Owen and was not unfamiliar with the technique of utopia. If the East was abandoned to religion and sunk in orthodoxy, perhaps there was still hope for pantheism under the liberal skies of the West. So in 1839 Kneeland and the "Society of Free Enquirers" of Boston acquired an extensive tract of land in Van Buren County, Iowa, on the bank of the Des Moines River, and here they established a community dedicated to rationalism and the worship of nature, and they named it Salubria.

But Salubria did not prosper, although Farmington near by, revelling in its godliness, did. Kneeland built himself the handsomest mansion in all Van Buren County, and he even entered politics and ran for the territorial legislature on his own Free Thought ticket, but Democrats and

Republicans sank their secular differences and ganged up to defeat a man whose God was nature and whose Bible, Paine. Politics failing, Kneeland took to the lecture platform, but here too he was thwarted, for the Reverend Harvey Adams led his band of Andover men into the county and plunged it into faith. In desperation Kneeland turned to school teaching, but nature itself turned on him, and his school-house blew down. Rejected by his neighbors and abandoned even by nature, the aged rationalist consoled himself with his books and with the friendship of the last of his faithful followers, Mr. and Mrs. Twombly. They had a child, and Abner Kneeland lived to baptize him Voltaire Paine Twombly.

THE DILEMMA OF
THEODORE PARKER

THEODORE PARKER was, for a brief span of years, one of the most distinguished men in American public life. From his pulpit in the Music Hall, Boston, he addressed his congregation—the famous Twenty-Eighth Congregational Society—of over seven thousand, but his real parish was the entire north. He was the self-appointed conscience to the nation, but never a still, small voice. Sumner, Chase, and Hale he advised, encouraged, and scolded; Webster, Choate, and Douglas he lashed with scorpions. Wherever he went in his ceaseless traveling, men and women thronged to hear him pass in review the great moral questions of the day, and from the Penobscot to the Mississippi his short, stocky, ungainly figure with the great Socrates-like head, prematurely bald, was a familiar, though not always a welcome sight. Only Greeley and Beecher exceeded him in popular fame, and he disdained the eccentricity of the one and avoided the pompousness of the other. Emerson counted him one of the four great men of his generation, and the gallant Samuel Grid-

SOURCE: *The New England Quarterly*, VI : 2 (January 1933). Reprinted by permission.

ley Howe named him "the foremost man of this continent"; [1] he himself confessed with unnecessary frequency
to the distinction of being the best-hated man in the country. His was the most liberal and humane voice in the
American church, and thousands, revolting from an op-
pressive Calvinism, heard him gladly. He was the leader in
that movement which has come to be known as the sociali-
zation of Christianity, and he grappled with the problems
of society, of labor and poverty, crime and vice, with a
realism strikingly modern. His scholarship was monumental; Thomas Wentworth Higginson, who knew every
one, called him "the most variously learned of living
Americans," [2] while Wendell Phillips remembered that
the lordly *Tribune*, when it would not publish even his
speeches "bent low before the most thorough scholarship
of New England." [3] He was, with Garrison and Phillips,
the most active and ardent of the anti-slavery agitators;
like these, he excited passion and furnished social statistics, but his peculiar contribution was to throw over the
movement a well-knit mantle of transcendental philosophy.

On the church, on society, and on the state he impressed his powerful intellect, but it was a progressive
church, a fluid society, and a state about to be revolution-
ized, and in the heat of the Civil War his impression
disappeared as in melted wax. His personality remains,
vivid, robust, and gallant, but his actual contributions
suffer from two limitations paralyzing to historical immortality. On their practical side they were so largely in
the spirit of the times that they have been incorporated
into the body of American life and thought; the contri-

[1] Samuel Gridley Howe: *Letters and Journals* (Boston, 1909),
II, 463.
[2] Thomas Wentworth Higginson: *Contemporaries* (Boston,
1899), 38.
[3] Wendell Phillips: *Speeches, Lectures and Letters*, Second Series (Boston, 1891), 426.

butions of learning, when they are successful, are necessarily suicidal. On their philosophical side they present a division, a duality, that crippled their contemporary effectiveness and insured their subsequent rejection. It is this philosophical dilemma that I wish to examine more particularly, a dilemma peculiarly interesting because it was the dilemma implicit in transcendentalism generally.

Transcendentalism is the philosophy which holds that ultimate and absolute truths are to be apprehended by the mind rather than through the senses, that these truths transcend experimental proof, and are *a priori*. It asserts that all things are first an idea in the mind, are known intuitively and absolutely, are not susceptible to nor affected by sensational experience, nor subject to any authority but a subjective one. Santayana calls it a systematic subjectivism,[4] but the emphasis upon system is misleading. Few philosophies, not excepting pragmatism, have been so informal, so unsystematized. Transcendentalism, in its American character, was indeed rather an attitude of mind than a logical dogma: it was by its own logic utterly individualistic and unorganized. It was, on its negative side, a revolt from the sensationalism of Locke and Hume and Priestley; on its positive side a re-affirmation of the ultimate authority and dignity of the human spirit. Though its philosophic origins were distinctly German and it was carried to America through English literary channels, it was peculiarly American: it had, indeed, in its political character, made its appearance at the time of the American Revolution, for the doctrines of natural law, liberty, equality, democracy, are necessarily transcendental.

But what was an attitude of mind in Emerson and Thoreau, and an emotion in Bronson Alcott and Walt Whitman, became with Theodore Parker an organized

[4] George Santayana: "The Genteel Tradition in American Philosophy," *Winds of Doctrine* (New York, 1926), 194.

intellectual method. The most succinct statement of transcendentalism is to be found in Parker's essay by that
name, delivered in 1855:[5] it is as clear-cut and definite
as Emerson's essay on transcendentalism is vague and
irrelevant, but Santayana insists that it is the peculiar
glory of Emerson that he refrained from confining his
philosophy in the frame of a system.[6] What Parker con-
densed in the essay on transcendentalism he expanded in
the learned *Discourse of Matters Pertaining to Religion,*
and it was implicit in all of his voluminous writing. No
American transcendentalist elaborated his idealism in
more detail, embroidered it with richer scholarship, formulated it with greater precision, applied it more widely
or more vigorously. Having discovered and established a
system of intuitive truths, Parker rigorously reviewed not
only sensational philosophy but orthodox religion, conventional society, and organized government. With relentless logic he reduced complex problems of church and
state and society to first principles and judged them by
his absolute and transcendental standards. Was it a stubborn Calvinism that exercised its ancient tyranny over
the minds of men? That Calvinism was a result of a false
philosophy of man, a sensational philosophy that
accepted the authority of the written word or of the authenticated miracle instead of the intuitive authority of
the individual spirit. Did hunkerism rear its evil head in
the land and demand obedience to man-made laws? That
demand was based on the wicked fallacy that there is no
higher law, no absolute right. Did man exploit his
fellow-men, did wealth accumulate and men decay? It
was because a sensational philosophy had distorted
values, impaired the dignity of the human spirit and
enhanced the significance of material things. Did slave-

[5] *Transcendentalism. A Lecture by Theodore Parker* (Boston,
1876), Free Religious Tracts No. 4.
[6] Santayana: *Winds of Doctrine,* 197.

owners plead the justification of the Bible or of history, or the complex and difficult character of the problem? The apology was based on a denial of absolute right, absolute justice, it took refuge in historical precedents and justified itself by an appeal to experience rather than to *a priori* truth.

But it was to the problem of religion that Parker first and most rigorously applied his idealistic philosophy, it was as a religious reformer that he became nationally known, and it was as the foremost representative of the higher criticism that he made his chief contributions to scholarship. His intuition assured him that man was instinctively religious, and instinctively reverenced a God, that mankind might attain to divinity, and that there was an after life. It affirmed for him the infinite perfection of God and the adequacy of man for all his functions.[7] These grand truths, it must be repeated, were "laid in human nature, there spontaneously given by the great primal instincts of mankind." Their application to the religion, the theology, the church, of the 1830's, first in the *Levi Blodgett Letter* (1840), then in the explosive *Discourse of the Transient and the Permanent in Christianity* (1841), and finally in the elaborate *Discourse of Religion* (1842), created a furore which reverberated through the length of the land. The character of these successive pronouncements is illuminating: Parker began with criticism, advanced to an announcement of general principles, and then developed these principles by an exhaustive argument from facts of necessity and facts of demonstration. The remaining eighteen years of Parker's life were given over to the elaboration of these philosophical principles, their application to a wide variety of social

[7] For a concise statement of Parker's religious philosophy, see "Letter from Santa Cruz called Theodore Parker's Experience as a Minister," in the appendix to John Weiss: *Life and Correspondence of Theodore Parker* (New York, 1864), II, 470 ff.

problems, and their substantiation by factual proof. This was a natural development: how utterly illogical it was in its methods and its results, and to what inconsistencies it led, will appear upon closer examination.

It is unnecessary to remark that Parker was not the first in this conflict between orthodox Unitarianism and transcendentalism. The historical-minded will recall Channing's "Baltimore Discourse" of 1819 as the opening skirmish;[8] the scholarly will remember Furness's "Remarks on the Four Gospels," of 1836. Whatever the importance of these, and of the writings of Walker, and Noyes, and Kneeland,[9] it was, of course, with Emerson's "Divinity School Address" that the battle was joined. And the conflict once precipitated, it raged with ever-increasing intensity all along the line of philosophy, theology, and society. Heady with the wine of new ideas, militant theologians rushed out into the arena of public affairs, into the market-place, the legislative chambers, the school-rooms, and even the home, challenging institutions, defying custom, and demanding reform. Emerson has described it, not without malice, in his *New England Reformers;* his explanation of the new critical spirit in *Man the Reformer* is more illuminating:

> We are to revise the whole of our social structure, the state, the school, religion, marriage, trade, science, and explore their foundations in our own nature; we are to see that the world not only fitted the former men, but fits us, and to clear ourselves of every usage which has not its roots in our own mind. What is a man born for but to be a Reformer, a Remaker of what man has made, a renouncer of lies; a restorer of truth and good, imitating that great Nature which embosoms us all, and

[8] "Unitarian Christianity: A Discourse at the Ordination of the Rev. Jared Sparks," *Works of William E. Channing, D.D.* (Boston, 1841), III, 59.
[9] On the early stages of the Unitarian controversy, see especially William C. Gannett: *Ezra Stiles Gannett. A Memoir by his Son* (Boston, 1875), Ch. vii.

which sleeps no moment on an old past, but every hour
repairs herself, yielding us every morning a new day,
and with every pulsation a new life? . . . The power
which is at once spring and regulator in all efforts of
reform is the conviction that there is an infinite worthiness in man, which will appear at the call of worth, and
that all particular reforms are the removing of some
impediment.[1]

What a ferment was there is New England of the
thirties and the forties! The atmosphere was charged
with new ideas, filled with the din of new names. German
idealism, Hellenism, the French enlightenment, Sweden-
borgian mysticism, Oriental pantheism, clamored for
naturalization, for translation into the American vernacular. Never was the American scholar so thoroughly
American, so indigenous, so conscious of the homely
phrase, of the native application; never was he so cosmopolitan, so catholic, so sensitive to the thought and the
literature of other nations and other times. It was a motley but magnificent crew that came sailing into Boston
harbor in the eighteen-thirties, bringing a precious cargo:
Kant and Goethe, Herder and Hegel, Schelling and Schil-
ler, Strauss and Schleiermacher, Vatke and De Wette,
Baur and Ewald, Jacobi and Fichte, from German ports;
Cousin and Fourier, Jouffrey, Constant, and Comte, from
France; Coleridge and Carlyle, from England and Scotland. "The wharves," wrote John Weiss, "were littered
with the spoils of a century. . . . We all rushed in and
helped ourselves." [2] We can picture the throng of omnivorous transcendentalists hurrying down to the docks: the
energetic Ripley and the aggressive Margaret Fuller,
fickle Brownson and timid Convers Francis, Olympian
Emerson and keen-eyed Thoreau, the poetic Dwight, re-
bellious young Frothingham, awkward George Bancroft,

[1] Ralph Waldo Emerson: *Nature, Addresses and Lectures* (Boston, 1892), 236–7.
[2] Weiss: *Theodore Parker*, I, 161.

gallant Sam Howe, dilettante William Henry Channing
and lovable but tiresome Bronson Alcott. The self-
appointed chairman of the reception committee was,
inevitably, Theodore Parker.

Even as a student in the Divinity School he had aston-
ished his contemporaries by the breadth of his learning
and the catholicity of his interests. He was satisfied with
nothing less than omniscience: he wished to master all
languages, to read all books, to be familiar with all
thought. His energy was inexhaustible, his industry indefatigable, his memory unfailing. He hurled himself on
knowledge with tigerish ferocity; he belabored his opponents, Lowell says, "with the whole tree of knowledge torn
up by the roots." He undertook to familiarize his countrymen with the progress of theological studies in Germany,
and to establish here the scientific and historical study of
theology. He introduced Strauss, advertised the Tübingen
school of Ewald and Baur, reviewed Oldhausen and Dorner, and prepared a translation of De Wette's *Introduction to the Old Testament* that was a monument of labor
and a marvel of erudition.[3] It can scarcely be doubted that
the *Discourse of Religion* of 1842—published when the
author was scarcely thirty years of age—was the most
learned contribution to theological scholarship of this
period, not excepting even the mighty Norton's *Evidences
of the Genuineness of the Gospels*. He planned a "History
of the Reformation," he collected material for a "History
of Religious Thought since the Reformation," he
projected an enormous work on the "Historical Development of Religion." [4] His energy was equalled only by his
ambition, and they were both surpassed by his knowl-

---

[3] *A Critical and Historical Introduction to the Canonical Scriptures of the Old Testament. From the German of De Wette.* Translated and Enlarged by Theodore Parker (Boston, 1843).

[4] Some 270 pages in manuscript contain all that Parker left of
this ambitious plan. Fragments are printed in Weiss: *Theodore
Parker*, II, 49 ff.

edge. The ever-delightful Thomas Wentworth Higginson tells us that a projected series of volumes on various aspects of religious history and philosophy was abandoned because nothing was proposed but that Parker had already accumulated material for just such a volume.[5] The latest scholarly books would be noticed in the *Christian Examiner,* or perhaps in *The Dial,* or the *Massachusetts Quarterly*—that *Dial* with a beard which Parker edited single-handed;[6] and every incoming ship brought the treasures of European bookshops to create the richest private library in Boston.[7]

It was, indeed, his scholarship that betrayed him. Not content with asserting truths of intuition, he spent himself in substantiating them by facts of demonstration. His love of learning was an appetite, it came to be a passion, it may have grown into a vice. His learning was the most massive, perhaps, in all America—more varied than thorough, if you will, more ambitious than profound—it was acquired not in the uninterrupted leisure of the study but in a lifetime tragically brief, crowded with the duties of an enormous parish, hot with the insistent duties of anti-slavery work. His information was as encyclopaedic as it was exact: he could fling a thundering bibliography at the scholarly Professor Francis in response to a cry for aid;[8] he could cite the very page of an obscure monograph on Salic Law when Sumner turned to him in desperation; he was the one man, so the classicist John King

[5] Higginson: *Contemporaries,* 41.
[6] The *Massachusetts Quarterly Review* was published from 1847 to 1850. R. W. Emerson, J. E. Cabot, and Parker composed the original board of editors. Cabot himself is authority for the statement that Parker was actually sole editor: *Memoir of Ralph Waldo Emerson* (Boston, 1887), 498.
[7] Parker's library, now housed in the Boston Public Library, contained some 16,000 volumes. For a detailed description, see T. W. Higginson: "Report on the Parker Library," *Annual Report Boston Public Library* (Boston, 1883), 19 ff.
[8] See, for example, the letters to Francis in Weiss: *Theodore Parker,* I, 358, 360, 361.

of Salem records, with whom it was possible to discuss intelligently a disputed reading in a Greek play.[9] He took Buckle severely to task for bibliographical omissions in the *History of Civilization,* corrected Hildreth in detail, and administered to Prescott the most severe scholarly lacing that that historian was to receive.[1] His knowledge of legal institutions and history excited the admiration of the learned Sumner (who was not given to admiring others), and when indicted for violation of the fugitive slave law, he prepared for his own defence a masterly treatise on the history of English and American law.[2] His appetite for languages was insatiable: Greek, Latin, Hebrew, French, German, Italian, and Spanish he acquired in student days; Syriac, Arabic, Coptic, Bohemian, Russian, Icelandic, Danish, Finnish, Lithuanian (and a score more) came later; at the end, he was wrestling with native African dialects. He confessed a curiosity for the occult sciences, and collected an imposing library on folk-lore and balladry, and on travel and geography. His knowledge of science was more superficial, but he dared to jeer at Agassiz, anticipated the doctrine of evolution,[3] participated in geological expeditions, had an astonishing familiarity with the flora and fauna of New England, brought geological specimens to Thoreau, and read avidly the transactions of German and French scientific societies. "His mind," remarks Weiss, "was like the

[9] Higginson: *Contemporaries,* 43–5.
[1] The essay on Buckle is in the *Collected Works of Theodore Parker,* ed. Frances Power Cobbe (London, 1863–5), XI; the essay on Hildreth and the two essays on Prescott are to be found in Vol. X.
[2] *The Trial of Theodore Parker . . . with the Defence,* by Theodore Parker (Boston, 1855).
[3] See the "Sermon on Christian Advancement," "Sermon on Natural Religion," "Sermon to Progressive Friends," No. 3, the *Five Sermons on the Testimony of Matter and Mind to the Existence of God.* In his scientific views and his attitude toward Agassiz, Parker was influenced by his close friend, the Swiss geologist Desor.

republican idea itself; it could afford to be hospitable but could not afford to be exclusive."

It is clear that Parker was fascinated by knowledge for its own sake; it is possible that he came, quite unconsciously, to make a fetish of facts. He read, to borrow a neat phrase from Santayana, not transcendentally, but historically, not to find out what he himself felt but to discover what others had felt.[4] His friend John Dwight warned him of this danger. "Don't you often," he wrote, "turn aside from your own reflections from the fear of losing what another has said or written on the subject? Have you not too much of a mania for all printed things,—as if books were more than the symbols of that truth to which the student aspires? You write, you read, you talk, you think in a hurry for fear of not getting all." [5] There speaks the transcendentalist, and he speaks as if to the most stubborn sensationalist. But Parker would not be warned: his vice grew on him with the passing years— his respect for facts, his use of the historical and the inductive method.

He had begun by announcing *a priori* truths which might be clarified by reference to some facts of demonstration; he ended by burying his intuitive argument under a veritable avalanche of facts. It was a shift in method, and a gradual one, but here method and emphasis were everything. It was a substitution, or at least a confusion, of means and end that the transcendentalist, of all philosophers, could not afford to make. The method was increasingly the method of science; the emphasis was increasingly on the authenticating facts. And though Parker professed scorn for the formal and deliberate application of the scientific method to philosophy, he confessed nevertheless the ultimate admiration for that

---

[4] Santayana: *Winds of Doctrine,* 192.
[5] John White Chadwick: *Theodore Parker, Preacher and Reformer* (Boston, 1900), 154.

method—imitation. He was, indeed, naïve enough to believe that if he only stated his conclusions first instead of last he had preserved the idealistic philosophy, and the picture of this ardent transcendentalist systematically ransacking the facts of history with the tools of science in order to prove his intuitive truths is not without its comic character. Three examples will suffice: one from the realm of theological scholarship, one from the field of political reform, and one from the struggle against slavery.

Few of Parker's essays were more learned, more incisive, than the lengthy review of Dorner's *Entwicklungsgeschichte der Lehre von der Person Christi*, which appeared in *The Dial* in 1842. Here Parker scored the low state of theological studies in America and England and ridiculed the preconceptions and superstitions with which the subject was commonly approached. In theology, he charges:

> Common Sense rarely shows his honest face; Reason seldom comes. It is a land shadowy with the wings of Ignorance, Superstition, Bigotry, Fanaticism, the brood of clawed and beaked and hungry Chaos and most ancient Night. . . . In science we ask first What are the facts of observation whence we shall start? . . . The first work is to find the facts, then their law and meaning.[6]

If theology is to be rescued from its shameful state, he continued, it must be approached historically and scientifically: we must create a science of theology comparable to the science of geology, or of medicine. And even as he was penning this essay, he was confiding to his friend, Francis:

> All study of theology must be abandoned, or it must be studied in a method and with a thoroughness and to an extent which bears some resemblance to the state of

[6] *Works*, ed. Cobbe, IX, 214–15.

other sciences. Theology is contemptible at present in comparison with astronomy, geology, or even the pretended science of phrenology.[7]

Yet, in the same essay in which these laudable sentiments appear, Parker turned aside to denounce the application of sensationalism to religion and philosophy and to charge as inevitable results materialism, selfishness, scepticism, and atheism.

> No skill of the artist [he thundered], no excellence of heart, can counteract the defects of the *Novum Organum* when applied to morals, metaphysics or theology. . . . We are not surprised that no one, following Bacon's scheme, has ever succeeded in driving materialism, selfishness and scepticism from the field of philosophy, morals and religion. The answer to these systems must come from men who adopt a different method.[8]

It would be difficult to find a clearer example of trying to have philosophical cake and eat it too.

Let us look next to the tremendous sermons on the Mexican War.[9] Parker's attitude toward that conflict was that of most of his transcendentalist friends, but he found occasion to express it more frequently and more publicly, perhaps, than any other. In the sermons on the war he takes the position of a Christian moralist. "War," he asserts, "is an utter violation of Christianity. If war be right, then Christianity is wrong, false, a lie. But if Christianity be true, if reason, conscience, the religious sense, the highest faculties of man, are to be trusted, then war is the wrong, the falsehood, the lie." The precepts of brotherhood, of peace and of love are not only those of Christianity, but are "the dictates of man's nature, only developed

[7] Weiss: *Theodore Parker*, I, 186.
[8] *Works*, ed. Cobbe, IX, 220-1.
[9] *Discourses of Politics* (*Works*, IV), "A Sermon of War," June 7, 1846; "Speech Delivered at the Anti-War Meeting," February 4, 1847; "Sermon of the Mexican War," June 25, 1848.

and active; a part of God's universal revelation; His law writ on the soul of man true after all experience and true before all experience." [1] This is lofty ground; it is distinctly transcendental ground. These truths are intuitive truths—true "before all experience." If this is truth, it is absolute truth; if it is true before all experience, the lessons of experience are irrelevant and impertinent. Yet read further in the great "Sermon of War" of 1846, and what do we find? Parker is authenticating these *a priori* truths by facts of demonstration. Here are pages and pages of bewildering statistics—the cost of war in money, in hours of labor, in misapplied energy, in social demoralization, in lives. Here are figures on the effect of the war on the fisheries of Massachusetts, on the annual expenditures for docks, arsenals, forts, on the daily cost of subsistence for a soldier. Here we can read comparisons between the appropriations for military purposes and for public education, appropriations to West Point and to the colleges of New England. Here are appeals to the lessons of history, to the cost in money and lives of past wars, to the experience of other nations. It is all most effective, but, like "the flowers that bloom in the spring," it has nothing to do with the thing of absolute truth. The appeal from the deductive to the inductive seems safe enough, but suppose it could be demonstrated that war actually developed the economic energies of a people, increased wealth, regenerated society? Would the transcendentalist be forced from his high ground? If intuitive truth transcends experience, what is the value of an appeal to experience; if *a priori* truth is not susceptible to factual proof, what is to be gained by citing statistics?

It was to the struggle against slavery that Parker devoted the energy and eloquence of the last decade of his life, and it is as a radical abolitionist that he is, perhaps, best remembered. His attitude toward the institution was

[1] "Sermon of War"; *Works,* ed. Cobbe, IV, 4.

grounded in his philosophy. Slavery, he insisted, was an absolute wrong, an evil, a sin, a crime against humanity, a violation of nature. Its maintenance was possible only by dependence on a false philosophy of life—the sensational one. Historian though he was, Parker deliberately closed his eyes to the historical evolution of the institution; sociologist though he was, he refused to recognize its complex social character. Like Garrison, he held that slavery must fall, regardless of consequences. "There is something in man," he wrote, "which scoffs at expediency, which will do right, justice, truth, though Hell itself should gape and bid him hold his peace; the morality which *anticipates* history loves the right for itself." [2] Granting the *a priori* premises, the conclusions followed logically enough. But for all his ardent transcendentalism Parker was not content to rest his case on absolute right. On the contrary, his two volumes of *Discourses of Slavery* [3] read like Helper's *Impending Crisis*. The discourses reek with statistics, they spill over with historical references. Here are comparisons of land values, population growth, school attendance, crime, newspaper circulation, commercial activities: all that body of unanalyzed data which (even in hands more skilful than Parker's) lends itself readily to misinterpretation. Government reports, historical documents, papers and journals, all hurried their tribute to this transcendental statistician, all went to prove a principle by its very nature not susceptible to proof.

This, precisely, was the dilemma of Theodore Parker. His love of learning, his intellectual acquisitiveness, his

[2] *Transcendentalism, a Lecture.*
[3] *Works*, ed. Cobbe, V and VI. See especially "A Letter to the People of the United States touching the Matter of Slavery," December 1847; "An Address on the Condition of America," May 12, 1854; "Some Thoughts on the Progress of America and the Influence of Her Diverse Institutions," May 31, 1854; "The Present Crisis in American Affairs," May 7, 1856.

respect for facts, proved his undoing. He never abandoned his original intuitional philosophy, but every new
accumulation of proof represented a vote of no confidence. He remained to the end as transcendental as
Whitman, and as experimental as Spencer, as intuitive as
Jefferson, and as sensational as Franklin. He maintained
the complete and unique validity of facts of consciousness and then proved them by facts of demonstration. He
elaborated the absolute and submitted first principles to
laboratory tests. Others noted this dualism, but it was so
instinctive with Parker that he was never aware of it. He
jumped to and fro between the deductive and the inductive, the *a priori* and the *a posteriori,* with an acrobatic
agility. "Transcendentalism," he wrote, "has a work to do
to show that physics, politics, ethics, religion, rest on
facts of necessity and have their witness and confirma-
tion in facts of observation." [4] But as John Dewey points
out, "the claim to formulate *a priori* the legislative constitution of the universe is by its nature a claim that may
lead to elaborate dialectic developments. But it is also one
that removes these very conclusions from subjection to
experimental test, for by definition, these results make no
difference." [5]

The most persistent and most glaring example of Parker's philosophic dualism was his habit of judging the tree
by its fruit, judging men, institutions, philosophies, by
their results. Sensationalism was rejected because it resulted in hunkerism, orthodox Calvinism because it
brought fear and unhappiness, slavery because it led to
poverty and degeneration. Actually, Parker was
interested in results rather than in first principles. Thus
he subjected his whole philosophy to the vicissitudes of
fortune, to the vagaries of human chance. But this was

[4] *Transcendentalism, a Lecture.*
[5] John Dewey: *The Influence of Darwinism Upon Philosophy*
(New York, 1910), 17.

the measuring-rod of sensationalism, of pragmatism, even. "Our great difference," wrote William James in contrasting the philosophy of the scholastic spirit with that of the pragmatist:

> Our great difference lies in the way we face. . . . The strength of his system lies in the principles, the origin, the *terminus a quo* of his thought; for us the strength is in the outcome, the upshot, the *terminus ad quem.* Not where it comes from but where it leads to is to decide.

Parker's mind was not metaphysical. He was naturally a man of action rather than a contemplative philosopher. It is illuminating to remember that he reserved his greatest admiration for Benjamin Franklin rather than for Jefferson. He was the Luther rather than the Melanchthon of the new religious reformation. Vigor, breadth, energy, simplicity, ruggedness, homeliness, enthusiasm characterized his thought rather than depth, subtlety, refinement, or serenity.[6] Philosophical problems he was inclined to overwhelm with learning rather than to penetrate with understanding. Nice metaphysical points he ignored or muddled. He accumulated facts more readily than he matured ideas, and he seldom probed ideas to their depths. His interpretation of the crucial problem of evil, for example, is puerile and undignified—puerile because, as Josiah Royce points out, it justifies evil as necessary to avoid other greater but unexplained evils; undignified because, as Ludwig Lewisohn has observed, its doctrine of compensation robs life of its tragic significance.

This confusion of intuition and experience was not so much a personal idiosyncrasy as a social characteristic. Parker's dualism was to an extent the dualism of that entire group of ardent New England reformers who would recreate society in the name of first principles, who

---

[6] Chadwick, Parker's ablest biographer, brings this out clearly. See his *Theodore Parker,* VII and XIV, *passim.*

glorified individualism in Fourierist phalanxes; perhaps it was implicit in the conflict between the possibilities of a New World environment and Old World institutions. Those fathers whose wisdom Parker loved to celebrate had justified a Declaration of Independence on intuitive principles and established a new form of government on experimental precepts, and indeed a large part of American history may be interpreted as an attempt to vindicate by facts of demonstration the transcendental ideas of democracy and equality and liberty. Not until half a century after Parker did pragmatism resolve the apparent paradox by announcing that transcendental ideals might and should be progressively realized by experience—by the "Will to Believe"; in our own day Professor Thomas Vernor Smith has applied the instrumentalist philosophy specifically to this problem and in his *American Philosophy of Equality*[7] discovered that the ultimate justification of the ideal of equality is precisely its functional value.

When Parker was a young man, just installed in his West Roxbury parish, he went one day to visit the already venerable Dr. Channing. They discussed conscience. "I asked him," Parker recorded in his journal, "if conscience were not an *infallible* guide. He seemed to doubt it, but is going to think of the question. To me it seems that conscience will always decide right, if the case is fairly put and old habits have not obscured the vision."[8] Conscience—and the clear vision, that was it; the triumph of the right when the mind is educated and all the facts are in. Over twenty years later he was in Rome, fighting a hopeless fight against consumption. See him as he

[7] Thomas Vernor Smith: *American Philosophy of Equality* (Chicago, 1927). See also his *Democratic Way of Life* (Chicago, 1926).
[8] Weiss: *Theodore Parker,* I, 108–9.

trudges patiently down three flights of stairs out into the cold drizzle of a February day. Darwin's *Principles of Selection in Natural History* had just come to hand, and he had been writing his friend, George Ripley, reaffirming his intuitive faith in God and immortality. He is hurrying off now to a bookstall: he has heard that an obscure book by a Dutchman, Nieuwendt, on the existence of God, can be found there, and he has been hunting for it for years. Death stalks him as he hastens through the gathering dusk of the late afternoon, but his eye is alight with excitement, and his brain is burning with enthusiasm, and the tenderest of smiles turns up the corners of his mouth as he thinks of old George Ripley back there in New York, and remembers Brook Farm days.

THEODORE PARKER, INTELLECTUAL GOURMAND

"DR. FÜSTER is well, but schlimmer—poor soul—he has only one scholar who pays, and that is myself, studying Polish. I learned Russian, Illyrian, and Bohemian a little with him, long ago." It is Theodore Parker writing to his good friend Desor, the Swiss geologist, and he has been indulging his monstrous appetite for knowledge. Indulgence it indubitably was, an indulgence that led to weakness but never to satiety. For Parker's appetite was as omnivorous as it was incessant: Polish, Illyrian, and Bohemian (he mastered none of them, to be sure) were but incidents in the study of philology, and philology itself was but one of many subordinate interests. Languages were a fascinating game, and it was fun to see how many of them he could play with, and not a little flattering to be known as a prodigy of learning.

And the reputation was not undeserved. He was probably the most variously learned man in America, this short, stocky, mild-eyed preacher with his bucolic ways who each Sunday fired the hearts and lifted the spirits of

SOURCE: *The American Scholar*, III : 3 (May 28, 1934). Copyright 1934 by Henry Steele Commager.

the thousands who packed the great Music Hall in Boston. To look at him, as he stood there, awkward and with still uncertain gestures—quite without the polished grace of an Everett or the proud assurance of a Sumner or the serene nobility of an Emerson—to look at him one would scarcely suspect that the richness and abundance of his learning was the envy and the despair of all his contemporaries. His sermons, to be sure, had a solidity and a substance that suggested the school-room rather than the pulpit, but they were no parade of scholarship, no boastful show of erudition. Couched in the homely language that Parker loved—Anglo-Saxon words, most of them— and borrowing their imagery and their analogies from the simple, every-day life of the people, they dealt not with abstruse doctrinal problems but with the great moral issues of the day. For Parker's learning was a democratic learning, as native as Lexington Common and as utilitarian—despite the Polish and the Illyrian and the Bohemian—as an encyclopedia. There was an ever-present danger, to be sure, that he might come to regard scholarship as an end in itself, that he might become an antiquarian, and his passion for the sheer accumulation of knowledge grew on him until it became something of a vice. But the roaring current of public affairs never permitted him to cultivate the fields of scholarship without an earnest regard to the harvest, and he found a use for even the most exotic information. He attempted to master the whole field of theology and church history, and then turned his scholarly batteries on the entire façade of Calvinistic theology and did more than any other American to shatter it and to liberate those whose spirits had been imprisoned behind its barricade. He surveyed the entire field of ancient and modern history and drew from that survey moral lessons on questions of slavery, of war, and of democracy that he drove home to his contemporaries with compelling logic. He read deeply and wisely in philosophy and erected on the basis of that study the most cogent rationalization of transcendentalism and the most eloquent attack on sensationalism that was to come out of New England. He immersed himself in the history of the law, from Justinian to Blackstone, and when he was indicted for attempting to rescue a fugitive slave took charge of his own defence, forced the court to quash the indictment, and prepared a written *Defence* that is a marvel of legal learning. His study of languages led him to an appreciation of comparative religion that anticipated the work of James Freeman Clarke, and his extensive dabblings in geology and biology prepared him to accept the Darwinian theory of evolution. And the magnificent library which he accumulatd lovingly through the years, searching the bookstalls and auction rooms of Europe, tracking down incunabula, adding rare sets of the reports of learned societies, was built up with the avowed purpose of presenting it to the people of Boston as a testimonial of his faith in democratic education.

It had been no part of Parker's purpose, originally, to be a tribune of the people, to guide them along paths of righteousness with the torch of learning. He had anticipated, this broad-shouldered Lexington farm-boy with six generations of Yankee blood in his veins, cloistered life in the study and in the pulpit of a small New England parish. His youth had been passed in wearisome toil on a stubborn farm, his schooling had been meager, and poverty denied him the boon of four years at Harvard. These obstacles he surmounted, and studying with a passionate perseverance that shattered his health, he prepared himself for Divinity School and a life of scholarship. If the Harvard Divinity School of the 1830's was not vibrating to the new currents of scholarship, there was at least a proper respect for learning, of a restricted kind. Professor Andrews Norton was a veritable paragon of biblical erudi-

tion; John G. Palfrey of anti-slavery fame may have inspired Parker with a love of history; and gentle Convers
Francis in near-by Watertown opened his own library and
his hospitable mind to the young neophyte. Soon Parker,
trudging across the campus with an armful of books from
Francis' library, was a familiar figure; and when he was
not following the academic routine he was translating the
letters of LaFayette for Dr. Sparks, teaching Dr. Palfrey's
class in Hebrew, editing the *Christian Interpreter,* tutor-
ing students in Greek, German, and Hebrew, or working
on the monumental translation of De Wette's *Einleitung
in das Alte Testament.* In a short time he had graduated,
"candidated" at Barnstable and at Concord, and accepted
a call from the quiet little parish of West Roxbury, not yet
the scene of the hopeful experiment in plain living and
high thinking that was Brook Farm.

It was peaceful there in the white parsonage set back
from the white picket fence and shaded by great elm and
maple trees, and from his study Parker could look out
over the lovely garden of his friend and parishioner,
George Russell. He could sit up there twelve or fifteen
hours a day, plugging away at De Wette, studying the
classics anew, toying with an edition of Shakespeare's
sonnets which was never to be completed, and working
his way doggedly through the new theological literature
coming out of Germany. It was this, indeed, that proved
his undoing, for the more deeply he read in De Wette and
Schleiermacher, Vatke and Baur, Ewald and Strauss, the
greater was his discontent with conservative Unitarianism and the sensational philosophy which it accepted.
And then Emerson delivered his memorable Divinity
School Address, and Professor Norton charged him with
the "latest form of Infidelity" and the great struggle between conservative and liberal Unitarianism was on.
Parker watched it with a growing dissatisfaction. "There
is a higher word to be said," he wrote in his Journal, and

he determined to say it. The long peaceful days were over—never to return—and Parker entered the theological arena on behalf of transcendentalism.

We cannot follow here the heated controversy that ensued—the publication of the "Levi Blodgett Letter" and the notorious South Boston sermon that shocked so many good Christians, and the ill-advised attempt to force the upstart Parker out of the Boston Association of Unitarian Ministers. What came out of it all was not only a clearly formulated philosophy of transcendentalism in the realm of religion but the introduction, under the compelling stress of controversy, of new standards of theological scholarship, and a new concept of the function of scholarship in the field of religion. And Parker's chief contribution was not the erudite *Discourse of Religion* with its massive learning and its eloquent persuasiveness, but rather his insistence upon the scientific study of theology. "All study of theology must be abandoned," he confided to his old friend Francis, "or it must be studied in a method and with a thoroughness and to an extent which bears some resemblance to the state of other sciences." His own contributions, aside from the great *Discourse*, were mostly of a critical nature. He introduced and popularized the "higher criticism," reviewing Strauss's *Life of Christ* and Dorner's *Christology* and Ackerman's *Christianity in Plato*, celebrating the achievements of the Tübingen school, and publishing his learned edition of De Wette. His influence spread throughout the church: young James Freeman Clarke, who was to popularize comparative religion, felt it; so did Octavius Frothingham reading heavy German books in Parker's study, and ardent inquisitive Daniel Conway up from Virginia, and brilliant versatile Thomas Wentworth Higginson. He furnished much of the inspiration for the critical study of religion, but his own far-sown scholarly plans were never brought to fruition—plans for a History of the Reformation which he

wanted to write, and the History of Religious Thought
Since the Reformation for which he collected material,
and the all too ambitious Historical Development of Religion of which we have only some fragmentary but
impressive notes.

Meantime Parker was turning his attention to secular
scholarship. *The Dial* had come into existence, that
seasonable quintessence of the New England mind
of the forties, sponsored by Emerson and high-flying Margaret Fuller and young George Ripley. Parker distrusted
Margaret, but Emerson he venerated, and George Ripley
he counted his dearest friend: it was inevitable that he
should contribute to the new journal and just as inevitable that, once enlisted, he should become the most frequent and the most popular contributor. And later, when
The Dial came to its lamented end, Parker promptly established a successor, *The Massachusetts Quarterly,* the
"*Dial* with a beard." Some of his best scholarly work was
done for these quarterlies—the learned essays on German literature and on German theology, the warm eulogy
of Dr. Follen, the slashing attacks on Prescott, the fine
critical estimate of John Quincy Adams, and the somewhat less satisfactory appreciation of Emerson. These
essays, with some contributions to the *Christian
Examiner* of the same years, indicate better than anything else the scope and depth of Parker's scholarship and
the theories of historical and literary criticism which he
entertained.

The essays were patterned on the Macaulay model: if
they lacked the coruscating brilliance of the Chatham
and the Clive they possessed the same qualities of learning and partisanship. For Parker studied and wrote with a
view to proving a point: scholarship was for him a
weapon rather than a luxury, and he was no more able to
avoid moralizing than was Macaulay himself. But though
he did not subscribe to later theories of scientific and

impartial history, he was surprisingly modern both in his
methods and in his conception of the proper scope of
history. In nothing that he wrote are these various, even
contradictory, principles better illustrated than in the essays on Prescott.

Prescott's *Ferdinand and Isabella, Conquest of Mexico,*
and *Conquest of Peru* had been greeted with a chorus of
approval in two hemispheres, and it was a bold thing to
file a dissenting opinion. Before passing judgment on the
volumes Parker attempted to read everything available
that Prescott himself had read, and when he turned from
the sources to Prescott's own account he found it unsatisfactory on counts of accuracy, organization, scope, and
philosophy; even the style he set down as "commonplace." The principal objections to Prescott's histories
were two: the concept of history was narrow, unilluminating, and aristocratic, and the histories failed to record
moral judgments where such judgments were called for
("Isabella," Parker wrote didactically, "deserves the censure of every historian"). The second complaint we can
dismiss as a mistaken though thoroughly characteristic
one, but the first anticipated a concept of history later
celebrated by Green, Lamprecht, and McMaster. Parker
asserted:

> The historian is to describe the industrial condition
> of the people—the state of agriculture, commerce, and
> the arts, both the useful and the beautiful; to inform us
> of the means of internal communication, of the inter-
> course with other nations—military, commercial mili-
> tary, or religious. He must tell of the social state of the
> people, the relation of the cultivator to the soil, the
> relation of class to class. . . . It is well to know what
> songs the peasant sung; what prayers he prayed; what
> food he ate; what tools he wrought with; what tax he
> paid; how he stood connected with the soil; how he was
> brought to war, and what weapons armed him for the
> fight.

Prescott, Parker observed, gives none of this. His Histories are unsatisfactory precisely because they are not only aristocratic but essentially frivolous. They are so largely concerned with the pomp and pageantry of the court and the battlefield that they ignore the things of the mind and of the spirit which gave to life its significance. Quite aside from the justice of these animadversions it is obvious that Parker here presents a theory of history thoroughly democratic and that he reveals a mind not only critical but philosophic and richly informed.

No less astonishing was the learning displayed in the other essays. They ranged from an analysis of the "American Scholar" as unconventional in substance as it was conventional in theme, to an erudite study of St. Bernard of Clairvaux; from a detailed criticism of Hildreth's "History" to a sympathetic appreciation of ballad literature. They embraced the fields of economics and sociology as well as of philosophy and theology, history and literature. As the years passed they became increasingly concerned with the great social problems of the day, and they took on increasingly a journalistic flavor relieved only by the solidity of their information and the eloquence of their phrasing. They are marked, indeed—the later ones—by profuseness rather than discrimination, by passion rather than philosophy, yet even in the most timely of the studies, such as those on the Mexican War and on Webster, the historical learning that went into their preparation is remarkable, and the preparation was as thorough and as massive as for the more academic essays.

But the real monument to Parker's learning, and the one from which he derived the deepest satisfaction, was not his essays or his edition of De Wette or his correspondence with scholars throughout the world, but his library. It was not large, as libraries go now (some 16,000 volumes perhaps) but that it was the richest private library in Boston if not in the entire country can scarcely be doubted. Young Theodore had bought his first book with money earned selling blueberries in Boston; it was Ainsworth's *Latin Dictionary* and he always felt for it a peculiar affection. The choice of the dictionary was prophetic, for the library came to be particularly rich in dictionaries and glossaries—even the African dialects were represented—and in fine editions of the Greek and Latin writers. There were sets of Pindar and Juvenal, Appularius and Suetonius, Dionysius and Polybius, as well as the more obvious Plutarch and Plato, Herodotus and Homer, Aristotle and Aeschylus. There were numerous works of the Church Fathers such as Migne's *Patrologia*, the *Maxima Bibliotheca veterum patrum*, the *Annales Eccleciastici* of 1597, the *Martyrologum Romanum*, Mabillon's *Annales ordinis S. Benedicti*, the rare *Alsatia illustrata Celtica Romana Franca*, and the rarer *Monumenta S. Patrum Orthodoxographica* published at Basle in 1569. Some of these we might perhaps expect in the library of a student of church history, but it is startling to find in a private library the tremendous *Monumenta Germanica Historica*, the *Allgemeine Deutsche Bibliothek*, the *Encyclopaedie des Wissenschaft und Kunst*, the *Bibliothek des Literarischen Vereins in Stuttgart* and the *Heidelberger Jarhbücher der Literatur*, the *Biographie Universelle* and the *Corpus Scriptorum Historiae Byzantiae*. There was an extensive collection of geographies and travels, subjects in which Parker had an abiding curiosity: Rauwolf's *Aigentliche Beschreibung der Raisz*, sixteen volumes of *Mémoires concernant des Chinois*, *Grönlands Mindesmaerker*, Malt-Brun's *Universal-Geography*, the *Historie Générale des Voyages*, Münster's *Cosmographia* from 1554, and some twenty volumes of the *Allgemeine Historie des Reisen*. Almost every important historian, English, French, Italian, Spanish, was represented, and the imposing collection of legal works testified to Parker's unflagging interest in jurisprudence. Here was Savigny's *Zeitschrift,* the *Corpus Juris Germanici Publici ac Privati* from 1766, the works of Puffendorf and Grotius, Eichorn and Spangenberg, and even the Danish Paul Ancher, and more extensive sets such as Howell's *State Trials,* the *English State Trials,* and Campbell's *Lives of the Chief Justices.*

Many of the volumes bear Parker's comments, and some of them have full marginal annotations. In a copy of Alexander Murray's *History of the European Languages* Parker has written, "I had long been looking for a copy of this curious book, which I borrowed years ago and studied, when I found it advertised in a newspaper published in Charlestown, S. C., and [had it] sent to me that I might profit from a violent and abusive article against me. *Fas est et ab hoste doceri";* and in the fly leaf of a copy of *Claudii Ptolemaei Alexandrini Geographicae Enarrationis, Libri Octo,* of 1535, we read, "I received this long-sought volume on the seventy-ninth anniversary of the Battle of Lexington. It is the edition of Michael Servetus, whereon see Mosheim Gesch. M. S. s.xviii p. 60 et seq." A copy of the *Indian Good Book* contains the interesting note, "This is the only literary monument of the language of the Abenaki Tribe. T. P." Parker's copies of Locke's Treatises on Human Understanding, of many of the classics, of his large collection of anti-slavery pamphlets, of the writings of Cousin and Comte, and the works of John Adams and Franklin and Jefferson, are richly embroidered with marginal comments, while his Journal records from day to day his critical reaction to his astonishingly variegated reading.

Few things are more unilluminating than bibliographical lists, but even this string of titles, fragmentary and inadequate as it is, suggests something of the scope of Parker's intellectual interests, and the eagerness and patience with which he pursued them. And the library, notwithstanding its ultimate destination, was emphatically not a collector's library. Each book had its place and its purpose and each earned its keep. There were, of course, concessions to antiquarianism, but the footnotes of the *Discourse of Religion* or of the *Defence,* the Journals and the correspondence, all bear abundant witness to the intimacy with which Parker knew and used his great collection.

But at the same time the library indicates something of the defects of Theodore Parker's mind as a scholarly instrument. Obviously Parker tried to absorb too much: catholicity of mind was a virtue but attempted omniscience became a vice. He was a gourmand rather than a gourmet of intellectual food, and suffered the fate common to gluttons. It cannot be said of the author of the *Discourse* or of the essays on Prescott that he was superficial, but it can be said that his own intellectual curiosity together with the pressure of public affairs never permitted him to develop his thought as a whole. His intellectual ambition and his mental restlessness drove him to ever new fields, and his incessant service as a tribune of the people did not allow him time to cultivate the soil deeply enough. He read widely in philosophy but his philosophic writings are suggestive rather than profound; his hospitable mind embraced the whole of history but he never elaborated a philosophy of history; he was one of the best-informed classical scholars of his time, but his criticisms consist of brilliantly disjointed jottings in his Journal. His passion for the accumulation of books led him to such an exaggerated estimate of their value that his friend John Dwight rebuked him for his "mania for all printed things," while Lowell hit him off neatly in the *Fable for Critics:*

> *His sermons with satire are plenteously*
> * verjuiced,*
> *And he talks in one breath of Confutzee, Cass,*
> * Zerduscht . . .*

You may add for yourselves, for I find it a bore,
All the names you have ever, or not, heard before,
And when you've done that, why, invent a few more.

Yet this alone does not account for Parker's limitations
as a scholar. Insistent as the distractions were he might
have denied some of them, such as the incessant lecturing, had he been so inclined. But Parker's real ambitions
were not so much scholarly as they were journalistic; his
mind was moralistic rather than metaphysical; and he
had a passion for the accumulation of facts rather than
for the formulation of ideas. He did not move easily in the
realm of philosophy nor was he at home with abstract
ideas. For all of his elaborate justification of transcendentalism he was closer to Franklin than to Emerson. He was
a great popularizer—in no vulgar sense of the word—
rather than an original thinker. He furnished the
scholarly rationale to the great moral crusades of the
day—religious liberalism, humanitarianism, and abolitionism, and Wendell Phillips said truly of him, "He
brought us, as no one else could, the loftiest stature of
New England culture. He brought us a disciplined intellect, whose statement was evidence, whose affirmation
the most gifted student hesitated long before he ventured
to doubt or to contradict." It would be difficult to find any
other figure in our history who accepted so fully the
responsibilities of learning, or revealed so admirably the
function of the Scholar in the Republic.

THE SIGNIFICANCE OF
THE DIAL

EVERYTHING seemed to happen in New England, in the eighteen-forties; it was a day of hope and of beginnings and even of fulfillment. "All things," said Emerson, "hear the trumpet and must rush to judgment—Christianity, the laws, commerce, schools, the farm, the laboratory; and not a kingdom, town statute, rite, calling, man or woman but is threatened by the new spirit." Horace Mann had just opened the first Normal School, in Lexington; out in West Roxbury George Ripley was building the Brook Farm community, and Bronson Alcott, father of the little women, was setting up a private utopia at Fruitlands, and Adin Ballou another and different Utopia at Hopedale. Theodore Parker broke with the church, and everyone thought of Luther and the theses; Dorothea Dix embarked upon her crusade to save the victims of man's inhumanity; in Rhode Island a Harvard graduate, Thomas Dorr, led a rebellion. And in Boston itself a group of Transcendentalists launched a new magazine, *The Dial.*

SOURCE: Originally published as "All Star Cast of Editors and Writers," in *Books* (December 31, 1961). © 1961 New York Herald Tribune, Inc. Reprinted by permission.

Nothing more exciting than *The Dial;* never before had there been such a magazine and there was not to be its like again. Born of that discontent that animated the minds and spirits of so many New Englanders—particularly those who lived in Concord or visited there—it perfectly expressed their spiritual yearnings, their religious and moral philosophy, their wide-ranging literary interests, their mysticism and their romanticism, their passion for the rebirth of the individual and the reformation of society. "Hearts beat so high, they must be full of something," said Margaret Fuller, whose heart was always spilling over with sentiment and fervor; and Emerson, in his "Address to the Readers," sounded the same romantic note: the stuff of the new magazine was to come, he said

> from the beautiful recesses of private thought; from the experience and hope of spirits which are withdrawing from all old forms, and seeking in all that is new somewhat to meet their inappeasable longings; from the secret confession of genius afraid to trust itself to aught but sympathy; from the conversation of fervid and mystical pietists; from the tear-stained diaries of sorrow and passion; from the manuscripts of young poets . . . we hope to draw thoughts and feelings which can impart life.

That *The Dial* was the very epitome of Transcendentalism was indisputable. But what was Transcendentalism? A dozen of its spokesmen tried to answer that question, Emerson and Parker and Christopher Cranch among them, but perhaps the simplest definition is that Transcendentalism is what emerged from the pages of *The Dial!*

It all started, late in the thirties, with meetings of an informal club that was sometimes called the Symposium, sometimes the Transcendental Club and sometimes the Hedge Club, after the Rev. Frederic Hedge, because it met when he came down from Bangor, Maine. In time it came to be understood that the members should have a journal of their own: the *North American Review* was far too official; the *Christian Examiner* was pretty well closed to them because they were heretics; and Brownson's *Boston Quarterly Review* was altogether too Brownsonian for their tastes. Emerson provided the inspiration and the leadership, and his friends and disciples rallied around: George Ripley, his head full of new worlds; young Theodore Parker, who was already making a name for himself in many fields; the mystical Jones Very; and Margaret Fuller, of course, and Elizabeth Peabody, one of the wonderful Peabody girls from Salem; and Bronson Alcott, and Emerson's young friend Henry Thoreau. Margaret—she was always called that—agreed to take on the editorship, with help from Ripley, and she carried it for two years. Poor Margaret—how she toiled, how she pled for contributions—and then reworked them, how she labored to fill in all the empty pages; and all of it out of devotion; there was no money for her or for anyone else. After two years she had to quit, and Emerson took over, reluctantly but bravely enough, and carried it for another two years.

What a galaxy of contributors these two managed to round up! The very first number—no one thought well of it, not even the editors—included contributions from Emerson himself, from Thoreau, Ripley, Parker, Christopher Cranch, John Sullivan Dwight, Bronson Alcott, and Margaret Fuller. Imagine! Would it be possible for any magazine to duplicate that today, with all our vast population and our limitless resources?

These carried the burden, these and a handful of friends, through the sixteen numbers that were published. There were contributions from Theodore Parker, of course, the self-appointed conscience of Boston—its Savonarola and its Erasmus, too, for that matter: his

essays were as learned as they were vigorous. Bronson
Alcott contributed his "Orphic Sayings"—nobody quite
understood them, but almost everybody thought them
fine; and Thoreau submitted some chapters from *A Week
on the Concord and Merrimac Rivers* and a good many
poems as well—some of them Margaret rejected!—and
Jones Very added some poems that hardly anyone but
Emerson appreciated; Dwight wrote about music, and the
indefatigable Margaret herself celebrated Goethe and
championed the rights of women, while Emerson gave
the struggling magazine half a dozen of his best essays.
Poor Emerson—in the end he had to take it over. "I wish
it to live," he wrote, "but I do not wish to be its life.
Neither do I like to put it in the hands of the Humanity
and Reform Men, nor in the hands of the Scholars." So he
struggled along as best he could, doing many of the
things Margaret had done, with Thoreau to help him
now. All very slipshod and unsatisfactory, but what other
magazine ever had such an editor and subeditor?

Years later, looking back on this chapter of his life,
Emerson recalled that the agitation which led to the creation of *The Dial* "had perhaps the fault of being too
secondary or bookish in its origin, or caught not from
primary instincts, but from England and still more from
German books." True enough: there was something from
England here and more from Germany, for this was the
age of the discovery of Germany, as exciting as the discovery of a new world in Elizabethan days. Everybody
was studying German, translating German works, reading
Goethe, reading Kant, reading Schleiermacher, rushing
off to study theology or pedagogy at German universities. Yet *The Dial* was not just a reflection—not even a
reflection of the "sunshine hours," as Emerson had pre-
dicted; it had a character of its own. It was not precisely
the Yankee character, though there was much of that; it
was the character of American as distinct from German

romanticism, or American as distinct from German idealism. Thus where in the Old World romanticism looked
wistfully to the past, in the New it looked to the future;
thus where in the Old World idealism was highly individualistic and for the most part conservative, in the New it
was cooperative and mostly radical. It was not intended
as an organ of reform, and Emerson was determined to
keep it out of the control of men like Theodore Parker
who would make it that. Yet Emerson himself contributed
"Man the Reformer" to its pages, and Margaret Fuller,
who was all spirit, made it a vehicle for Woman's Rights.

What was the peculiar character of *The Dial*? Its editors, wrote Emerson, "have obeyed the strong current of
thought and feeling which . . . has led many sincere
persons in New England to make new demands on literature, and to reprobate that rigor of our conventions of
religion and education which is turning us to stone,
which renounces hope, which looks only backward,
which asks only such a future as the past, which suspects
improvement and holds nothing so much in horror as
new views, and the dreams of youth." This was all on the
negative side, but the positive program was implied. *The
Dial* did make new demands on literature and religion,
did reject the conventions of education, did look forward
rather than backward and celebrate new views and
indulge the dreams of youth. It provided a place for religion without the Church, for education without the University, for law without the State, for culture without the
Academy, for art without the Salon, for new views without organized Reform.

Alas, no one read it, none but the Transcendentalists;
its circulation lapped the three hundred mark but never
quite reached it. Margaret had kept it up two years, and
Emerson kept it going another two years and then gave
up the struggle. Parker might have carried it on, but some
of the Transcendentalists distrusted him, and soon he

was editing—and writing—his own magazine, the *Massachusetts Quarterly Review*—the *"Dial* with a beard," as he said. The country wasn't ready for *The Dial* yet, not even for Transcendentalism: we forget how local the movement was at this time and how generally disparaged. In the end piles of the unwanted magazine were burned.

THE SECOND WAR OF AMERICAN INDEPENDENCE

IT IS a sobering consideration that those wars which the United States indubitably won—the Spanish-American War, for instance, and the two World Wars—created far more problems than they solved, while the War of 1812, which the United States most decidedly did not win (and neither did the enemy), left no heritage of unsolved problems or vexatious issues, no aftermath of disillusionment or bitterness, but rewards, satisfactions, heroes and respect.

That war lacks even a name. We call it the War of 1812, which is not a name but a date: no other war is so shabbily treated. The older name, now out of favor, was much more satisfactory and should be revived: the Second War of American Independence. For that, in fact, is what it was.

The American Revolution brought political independence from the Mother Country, but it did not end America's colonial position, or its long involvement in the rival-

SOURCE: *The New York Times* (June 17, 1962). © 1962 by The New York Times Company. Reprinted by permission.

ries, the politics and the wars of the Old World. Those
rivalries began with the discovery and exploration of the
continent in the sixteenth century; all through the seventeenth and eighteenth centuries they exploded into a series of wars—wars to which we have given the collective
name, the Struggle for the Continent.

The first grand climacteric of that struggle came in
1763 when Britain drove France from the American continent—and, for good measure, took the Floridas from
Spain. The second climacteric came just twenty years
later when, humbled now by a new coalition of the American states, France, Spain and other marginal allies, Britain was forced under the Treaty of Paris to recognize the
independence of her former colonies and to give up large
portions of her American territory.

From the point of view of the Americans, the first War
of Independence was a central fact in history: it ended
one era and inaugurated another. In a sense they were, of
course, right; in the perspective of almost two centuries,
1776 seems a more important date than 1789 or 1815.
But from the point of view of Europe the American war
was rather the end of a chapter than of a volume; clearly
there were more chapters to come.

We do not realize, now, how precarious was the life of
the infant United States and how generally unfavorable
the prognosis. She was born the largest of Western nations, but the great Montesquieu had made clear that, for
a republic, size was weakness, not strength, and that a
people who had taken a century and a half to reach the
Appalachians could not expect to colonize and hold the
tramontane West. She was born a democracy, but as
Gouverneur Morris pointed out, history told them that it
was "almost as vain to expect permanency from
democracy as to construct a palace on the surface of the
sea." She was—or seemed—weak and disunited, without
an army or a navy, without a Church or a ruling class,

without those institutions that everywhere in the Old World provided firmness and continuity.

And she was almost without friends. From all sides powers that were hostile or fearful glared upon her. Britain refused to give up the Northwest posts, or the Indian alliances, and awaited, with satisfaction, the eventual fragmentation of this upstart. Along the northern boundary, English Canadians frowned upon the new nation with its equalitarian and lawless ways.

Spain, incomparably the largest of world powers, encircled the United States south and west; her vast empire ran from the Saint Johns River in Florida (which she had recovered under the treaty of 1783) across the Caribbean and embraced the whole of the American continent north of Panama and west of the Mississippi. Fearful of the American pioneer, the Spaniards intrigued ceaselessly with the southern Indians to interpose a barrier to the American advance, and intrigued, too, with the pioneers themselves, to detach them from their American allegiance.

France seemed to be out of the picture, but she was far from reconciled to her exclusion, and Napoleon, who disposed of continents the way other rulers disposed of towns, envisioned the restoration of a French empire in America and prepared to translate that vision into reality.

The struggle for the continent, suspended after Yorktown, was renewed in the 1790's and gathered force. The French Revolution was a European war; with the ascendancy of Napoleon it became a world war, fought out in Egypt and Silesia, on the Mediterranean, the Caribbean and the Indian seas, and catching up neutrals as well as belligerents in its violent embrace.

In vain did Americans attempt to remain aloof from all of this. In vain did Washington fashion a neutrality policy, and warn against "the wiles of foreign influence" and against entangling our fate "in the toils of European ambition, rivalship, humor or caprice." In vain did John Adams break with his own party in order to assuage the French and keep the peace. In vain did Jefferson try to repel those "billows" which "reach even this distant and peaceful shore" and to insist that "every difference of opinion is not a difference of principle."

Willy-nilly, Americans were caught up, once again, in the age-old struggles of the European world. They were subjected to Orders and Counter-Orders that violated their rights, their dignity and their interests; their ships were harassed and hundreds of them confiscated; their sailors impressed by the thousand.

A war with Britain was put off by the unpopular Jay Treaty; an open war with France was disguised as a "quasi-war" (that is still its official name); the pacific Jefferson launched a war with the Tripoli pirates. Spain cut off free use of the Mississippi River; soon Napoleon wrested Louisiana from the feeble grasp of Madrid and launched a massive attack on Santo Domingo as a preliminary to the re-creation of a French empire along the Mississippi. When Jefferson solved the problem by the purchase of Louisiana ("The day that France takes possession of New Orleans," he wrote, "we must marry ourselves to the British fleet and nation"), the Federalists denounced the action as so outrageous that it justified dissolving the Union!

For, Jefferson to the contrary, differences of opinion became differences of principle; the French Revolution and Napoleonic wars divided Americans in politics and in sentiment. It formed parties and furnished party issues for almost twenty years: the Jay Treaty, the XYZ affair, the Alien and Sedition Acts and the Virginia and Kentucky Resolutions, the Louisiana Purchase, the Embargo, West Florida—these were the embroilments against which Washington had warned; these were the entanglements which Jefferson had feared.

The climax of all this was the War of 1812. It was, in a sense, a needless war; the British Orders in Council, which excluded American ships not only from Napoleonic Europe but from every port in the world from which British ships were excluded, were repealed just as Congress declared war. It was, in a way, a mistaken war; Napoleon was, perhaps, the real enemy, and certainly a Napoleonic victory would have been far more serious for the United States than a British victory. It was, most certainly, an unpopular war, and one for which both the Government and the people were woefully unprepared. New England voted against the war; so deep was her opposition that she all but withdrew into neutrality during the contest.

Yet, in a larger sense, it can be said that the war was not only justified but necessary. The legal provocation was beyond dispute, for the British (and the French, too) had played fast and loose with American rights, and made arrogantly clear that they had no intention of changing their policy or their attitude or of making any concessions to a nation they despised. The psychological justification for the war was strong: failure to assert independence against the giant powers of Europe might mean that independence would be frittered away, and that the new nation would return to a quasi-colonial status, or disintegrate into impotent factions.

The war itself was one that Americans have, mostly, been glad to forget; the British never pretended to remember it, and to this day British histories ignore it or relegate it to a footnote. It was badly planned, badly managed and, for the most part, badly fought. The nation went into the war deeply divided, and the divisions deepened.

True, there were famous victories at sea and hundreds of tiny privateers made the oceans unsafe for the British flag. At Put-in-Bay, Captain Perry met the enemy and made them ours and on Lake Champlain Captain Macdonough destroyed a British flotilla and repelled an invasion.

But on the whole the military record was one of failure. The British invaded at Detroit, Niagara, and down the Champlain; they conquered—and reannexed—the Maine coast from the Penobscot to Passamaquoddy Bay; they ravaged the coast of Virginia, attacked Baltimore, captured and burned Washington. In the end they swept the American Navy from the seas, and the merchant marine too.

The national Treasury was empty, and had it not been for the patriotism of three foreign-born financiers— Stephen Girard, John Jacob Astor and David Parish—the war loans would have failed and the Government would have been forced into bankruptcy.

It seemed as though the Government would collapse, as if the nation itself would collapse. Neither happened. Quite the contrary; the fall of Washington brought a turn in the tide. News of the outrage went through the nation like an electric shock; thousands hurried to enlist, and the Administration itself found new courage—and new leaders.

New generals emerged, who could hold their own against the British. Chippewa and Lundy's Lane could be counted as victories, the attack on Baltimore failed, and the whole nation rejoiced that the flag was still there. Even New England began to recover something of her Revolutionary spirit, and the Hartford Convention, originally designed to bring about peace or to threaten secession, ended on a note of compromise. While the most skillful diplomats who have ever represented the United States abroad—John Quincy Adams, Albert Gallatin and Henry Clay—ran rings around their dull-witted British adversaries at the peace conference in Ghent, news of the stunning defeat of the British General Prevost at Lake Champlain and of increasing tensions between Britain and her allies at the Congress in Vienna brought a change of heart.

In the end, American diplomats came home with a treaty that settled nothing, but really settled everything. Not a word about the causes of the war, not a word about impressment of American seamen. The treaty simply wiped the war off the books. It had been a mistake and the British promptly proceeded to forget that it had ever happened.

But Americans persuaded themselves that it was a victory, and the Senate ratified the treaty by unanimous vote. For it came just as America had given itself over to a delirium of joy. "Glorious Victory," ran the headlines of the newspapers—"Unparalleled Victory," "The Rising Glory of America." It was, indeed. On Jan. 8, 1815, General Jackson and his Kentucky riflemen had met the veterans of Wellington's armies at New Orleans and inflicted on them the worst defeat in the history of British arms.

A great surge of strength and of pride poured through the nation. All the humiliations and defeats were forgotten, the divisions and dissensions. Pride in the little navy that had given such a good account of itself: "I do not know that the naval history of the world furnishes an example of a more splendid action," wrote Jefferson. Pride in the heroes of Chippewa and Lundy's Lane, and in Jackson who became, overnight, a symbol. Pride in the nation that had challenged the most powerful army and navy in the world, and held its own.

And, fearful though the contest seemed, in the end the cost was not high. Total casualties were only 5,000. Eighty million dollars had been added to the debt, but it was still smaller, per capita, than it had been in 1791, and a great wave of prosperity swept over the nation. The material damage was easily repaired; the spiritual damage was ignored or forgotten.

The war marked the end of two centuries of colonialism, two centuries of involvement in the affairs of the Old World. It marked the beginning of America as a truly independent power, a continental power, a hemispheric power. Now Americans looked westward, not east. Louisiana was theirs; West Florida was taken, East Florida was commandeered, as it were, from a reluctant Spain; and already Americans were casting covetous eyes on the Spanish lands in the South and the West.

State after state was added to the Union—two of them across the Mississippi. The British and Canadians cheerfully accepted the Rush-Bagot Agreement on an unfortified boundary between Canada and the United States which, in effect, put an end to British pretentions and intrigues in the West. The United States became the champion of the South American republics, and within a few years announced it would consider any attempt by the nations of the Old World "to extend their system to any portion of this hemisphere as dangerous to our peace and safety."

It was the end, too, of old party divisions. Not again for more than a hundred years would American parties form along lines laid down by foreign powers. The Federalist party, which had opposed the war and sponsored the Hartford Convention, quietly disappeared, and there ensued an Era of Good Feeling. At last Jefferson was vindicated; differences of opinion were not differences of principle, and parties did not know what to differ about, so they differed about personalities.

The new nationalism came on with a flood. The national bank, which had been allowed to lapse during the war, was rechartered. Congress enacted a tariff which contemporaries, at least, thought protective. The new peacetime Army was fixed at 10,000—compare that with the establishment of 1,000 in 1789—and the Navy launched a war against the Dey of Algiers, and forced him to accept American terms.

Madison blew hot and cold on internal improvements, but that did not matter; the Erie Canal was under way, the greatest enterprise of its day, and soon a network of canals linked up the Atlantic coast with the great interior; soon, too, steamboats were conquering the Western waters, linking the Mississippi with Europe as well as with the Eastern seaboard.

Nationalism found eloquent spokesmen in every realm. John Marshall dominated the Supreme Court with Joseph Story at his right hand; between them they wrote nationalist principles into the Constitution in one great decision after another—*Gibbons* v. *Ogden, McCulloch* v. *Maryland,* the Dartmouth College Case, the Fairfax Land Case, the *Cohens* v. *Virginia, Martin* v. *Mott.*

Noah Webster's generation had yearned for cultural independence, but had not achieved it. Now there was a beginning, even in the cultural realm. *The North American Review* was as respectable as the British quarterlies, and aggressively American. Washington Irving celebrated the folklore of the Hudson Valley; Fenimore Cooper peopled the continent with Indian heroes, and for good measure compiled a history of the American Navy; if Bryant was not all that different from Wordsworth he was something more than an imitation.

American historians became conscious of the nation: Jared Sparks reared pious monuments to the Founding Fathers, Peter Force collected and edited the documents, and soon George Bancroft was busily at work on his great history—which was to prove what every American knew in his bones, that America was the climax of man's story. There was even a school of American painting—an American romanticism that painted the beauties of the

Hudson River and the Delaware, and of the plains and prairies and mountains too.

"Never," wrote Joseph Story exultantly, "did a country occupy more lofty ground. We have stood the contest, single-handed, against the conqueror of Europe; and we are at peace, with all our blushing victories thick crowding on us. If I do not mistake, we shall attain to a very high character abroad as well as crush domestic faction." Let us then, he added, "create great national interests which shall bind us in an indissoluble chain."

"Indissoluble" was the word that tempted Providence. But when the chain was broken, in 1861, it was Americans who broke it, not Europeans; it was Americans who welded it together again. And when, a century after the Treaty of Ghent, Americans did "interweave their destiny with Europe," they did that on their own terms, too. The war of 1812 had made the nation truly independent.

THE ERA OF REFORM

"IT WAS now the day of ideals in every camp. The
general restlessness was as intense among reflecting Conservatives as among reflecting Liberals; and those who
looked to the past agreed with those who looked to the
future, in energetic dissatisfaction with a sterile
present. . . . A great wave of humanity, of benevolence,
of desire for improvement . . . poured itself among all
who had the faculty for large and disinterested thinking."
John Morley was describing Richard Cobden's England
(and his own, as well) but what he wrote applied with
even greater force to the America of the middle period of
the nineteenth century. It was a day of universal reform—a day when almost every man you met might
draw a plan for a new society or a new government from
his pocket; a day of infinite hope and infinite discontent.
Every institution was called before the bar of reason, and
of sentiment, too: the church, the state, the law, the
army, the family, property—and required to justify itself.
Nothing was immune, nothing was sacred, nothing was
taken for granted, nothing but the right of inquiry. "A

SOURCE: Originally published as the introduction to *The Age of
Reform* by Henry Steele Commager. Copyright © 1960, D. Van
Nostrand Company, Inc., Princeton, N.J. Reprinted by permission.

restless, prying, conscientious criticism broke out in the most unexpected quarters. . . . Am I not a too protected person? Is there not a wide disparity between the lot of me and the lot of thee, my poor brother, my poor sister?" So asked Emerson, the cow from which they all drew their milk. "In the history of the world the doctrine of reform never had such scope as at the present hour." It is Emerson, again—"We are to revise the whole of our social structure—the state, the school, religion, marriage, trade, science, and explore the foundations in our own nature." It is this moral fundamentalism, this radical comprehensiveness, that most sharply distinguishes the reform era of the Middle Period from the other major reform eras of our history—the Revolution, the Populist-Progressive period, and the New Deal. These were, for the most part, political and constitutional; they were nationalistic and even parochial; they were secular and practical; the last two of them, at least, were opportunistic and almost without benefit of philosophy. But the reform movement of the generation of Emerson and Theodore Parker, Horace Mann and Margaret Fuller, had a very different character. Let us examine that character.

First, this reform movement was, to an astonishing degree, the product of philosophy—or at least of a dominant and pervasive view of the nature of Man and the relation of Man to Nature and to God. That philosophy we call Transcendentalism. It assumed that there were great moral truths that are *a priori*, and that *transcend* mere sensational proof. The most important of these—if there can be a hierarchy of truth—were that God is benevolent, Nature beneficent, and Man divine. These were not new ideas—after all they had been widely accepted during the Enlightenment; what was new was their subjective and *a priori* authentication. And if these moral principles were, in reality, true, then it followed that any secular departure from them was contrary to God's pur-

pose with man. If Man was divine, and mankind per-
fectable, then it was unspeakably wicked that a man's
body should be confined in slavery, his mind clouded by
ignorance, his soul corrupted by superstition or by sin.
Let there be light! Let us restore men to that divinity with
which God endowed them. Let us bring freedom to the
slave, learning to the ignorant, enlightenment to the su-
perstitious, prosperity to the poor, health to the sick and
the crippled; let us give to women, to children, to workingmen, to the perishing and the dangerous classes, all of
those rights and privileges and opportunities and bene-
factions that God and Nature intended they should enjoy!
As Emerson so well put it: "The power which is at once
spring and regulator in all efforts of reform is the conviction that there is an infinite worthiness in man, which
appears at the call of worth, and that all particular reforms are the removing of some impediment."

"The removing of some impediment!" What is man
born for but to be a re-former—to remove impediments,
to recast institutions, to make over man himself? God
would not have made Nature benevolent and Man divine
if He had not intended perfection. It could be achieved—
it would be achieved, now.

The reform movement, then, was designed to harmonize man with the moral order, and it quickly took on the
character of a moral crusade. More, it took on the character of a religious crusade; it is the only one of our major
reform movements that had this character, and the only
one where the clergy provided not only inspiration but
leadership. The Revolutionary leaders were moral, but
rarely pious; they distrusted organized religion and invoked God as they invoked Nature, as an impersonal part
of a cosmic system with which they wished to be in
harmony. And as for the New Deal, even its most high-
minded architects did not argue the Divinity of Man, or
look to moral regeneration. And who was the Channing

of the Revolutionary era, who the Parker of the Roosevelt Revolution? But what would the reform movement of this middle period be without its phalanxes of clergy: Emerson, Channing, Parker, Ripley, Pierpont, Hedge, Higginson, Brownson, Weld, Sam Jo May and James Freeman Clark, and a score of others? And what would it have been without their disciples, without Bronson Alcott and Margaret Fuller who looked to Emerson; and Dorothea Dix and Wendell Phillips who depended on Channing; and S. G. Howe and Horace Mann who drew strength from Parker; without the evangelical fervor of a Theodore Weld and the piety of the Tappan brothers, and the moral fervor of the daughter of the Reverend Lyman Beecher and the wife of the Reverend Calvin Stowe!

We are so familiar with the Transcendentalist philosophy of this reform movement, with its religious impetus and its clerical leadership, that we are tempted to take it for granted. But it is important to note that Transcendentalism did not sponsor reform in Germany, or in England or, for that matter, among the Kantian idealists of Vermont: James Marsh, who has some right to speak for them, dismissed "the whole of Boston Transcendentalism" as "a superficial affair." In Britain, indeed, it was the Utilitarians and the Rationalists—the heirs of John Locke —who were the reformers. Perhaps the simplest explanation of the otherwise mysterious failure of Utilitarianism to play any significant role in America is that in America Utilitarianism was called Transcendentalism. Never was the resourcefulness of the American better revealed than in his ability, in one generation, to work a revolution out of the philosophy of Locke and, in the next, out of a philosophy that repudiated Locke.

A third characteristic of the reform movement of this era is its comprehensiveness. *Every* institution was called upon to show its credentials, and to justify its course of conduct—the great and the trivial alike, the institution of

172 The Search for a Usable Past

the State or the practice of shaving, the institution of the
Church or the eating of meat, the institution of marriage
or the wearing of beards! In our day most reformers are
content with a single crusade, but the reformers of the
'thirties were, most of them, "universal" reformers. Bronson Alcott proposed a Club for the Study and Diffusion of
Ideas and Tendencies Proper to the Nineteenth Century;
Robert Owen called a World Convention to Emancipate
the Human Race from Ignorance, Poverty, Division, and
Misery; Garrison proclaimed that the world was his
country and his countrymen all mankind; and John
Humphrey Noyes—another of the universal reformers—
reported that Garrison's mind "was heaving with the
subject of Holiness and the Kingdom of God, and he
would devote himself to them as soon as he could get
anti-slavery off his hands." As soon as he came to Boston,
young Theodore Parker issued a call for a "council of
Reformers" to discuss "the General Principles of Reform"
and the means of promoting them, and when the Council
duly met it spent six hours discussing "All the Holy Principles of Reform." Nor was this universality verbal only.
Parker championed religious freedom, woman's rights,
the cause of labor, penal and prison reform, peace, and
abolition. Wendell Phillips took on antislavery, woman's
rights, labor reform, and money reform. Horace Greeley
was interested in Fourierism, free land, the rights of
labor and of women, purity in politics, peace, penal reform, temperance, and at least a hearing for spiritualism,
Grahamism, and phrenology. The New York philanthro-
pist Gerrit Smith began as an anti-Mason, took up vegetar-
ianism and dress reform and temperance, championed
the cause of the Greeks and the Irish, settled poor whites
and Negroes on his Adirondack lands, advocated woman
suffrage, and in the end concentrated on antislavery and
helped finance the Kansas crusade and John Brown.

With all this there was, inevitably, an interlocking directorate of reformers. One good cause always led to another, and each of the reformers had to help out all the others if he expected their help in his particular crusade. Besides, all the reforms were interrelated, all part of a larger moral pattern; neither salvation nor divinity was divisible.

Fourth, this reform crusade, again in contrast to the Revolution and to the great reforms of the twentieth century, was highly individualistic. Given its original philosophy, that was inevitable, for Transcendentalism, after all, vindicated private truth and private salvation. The characteristic figure of this era was the Come-Outer, who had always in mind the admonition by Lowell:

> They are slaves who dare not be
> In the right with two or three

And if it was impossible to get two or three, one would do. Thoreau was no Come-Outer, not consciously anyway, but Walden Pond was nevertheless something of a symbol for his generation of New England intellectuals. Yet for all their individualism, these reformers were always organizing and holding meetings—across state boundaries, even across the ocean. What a passion they had for Conventions—Antislavery and Woman's Rights, and Peace, and Temperance, and a dozen others. They organized Utopian communities, too, though few of these worked, and fewer still survived. But no one was asked, or expected, to subordinate his mind (or to still his voice) to the common will; there was unlimited discussion and an unlimited right of secession. It is a wonder that they ever got anything done, what with all the societies to organize and letters to write and conventions to attend and speeches to deliver, and what with the whole of society to reform, and that overnight! But they did. They had the Victorian capacity for work, which we have lost; they worked prodigiously; they wrote voluminously; they talked incessantly; they accomplished twice as much as any subsequent generation.

Fifth, the obverse side of this passionate individualism and voluntarism is that this reform movement, in marked contrast with the other major reforms, and with the contemporary English reform activity, was nonpolitical. It did not boast a Jefferson or a Hamilton, a Bryan or a Theodore Roosevelt, a Franklin D. Roosevelt or a Henry Wallace; it did not even have anyone in public life of the stature of Lord Brougham. This indifference to, or positive repudiation of, politics was rooted in philosophy; after all, if you are going to obey Higher Law you must be prepared (like Thoreau, like Garrison, like Parker) to get along without mere secular law. Besides, of what use to rely on government? It was like expecting a criminal to dispense justice! Was not government itself leagued with the forces of unrighteousness? It was the State that fought wars; it was the State that supported slavery; it was the State that subjected women to monstrous subordination and exploited little children. As Lowell told them it was a case of

> Right forever on the scaffold,
> Wrong forever on the throne.

So, Thoreau proclaimed the moral duty of civil disobedience; Garrison publicly burned the Constitution; Parker and Higginson attacked the Court House; Emerson read the Fugitive Slave law and wrote in his Journal, "This filthy enactment was made in the nineteenth century, by men who could read and write. I will not obey it, by God!"; and Lowell—and others—seceded from the Mexican War.

There were, to be sure, exceptions to this repudiation of politics. Robert Owen and Frances Wright helped organize a Workingman's Party; George Bancroft was ceaselessly active in politics, and Horace Greeley, too. It says much for the futility of reliance on party that the Workingman's Party petered out in a year or so, and that Bancroft could be an ardent Democrat and Greeley an ardent Whig, and neither have anything much to show for their party ardors. Some of the reformers, to be sure, had to work through the machinery of the State: Horace Mann and his colleagues who fought for public schools; the gallant Dorothea Dix who enlisted the sympathy of state legislators on behalf of the desperate and the perishing classes of society; even the land reformers, who finally pushed a Homestead Act through Congress. But on the whole, reform was not political, and politics was not reformist.

A sixth characteristic of this reform movement is that it was fanatical without being violent, and radical without being revolutionary. Notwithstanding agitation as extreme as any on the European continent, and attacks on established institutions as vehement, the United States (like England) escaped the uprisings so widespread on the European continent in the 'forties. No governments were toppled, not even in Rhode Island; no tyrants were unhorsed; there were no barricades in the streets, and no soldiers to ride down desperate mobs. If the American reform was a revolution, it was the most sedate of revolutions, conducted with weapons that were all moral and intellectual, wielded by the most dignified group of agitators in history. Those who were not clergymen were men of letters; one sometimes feels that a degree from Harvard or a clerical collar was a prerequisite to admission to the ranks of the insurgents. There were, to be sure, isolated instances of violence: Thoreau defied a taxcollector; Garrison burned the Constitution; Parker excited forcible nullification of the Fugitive Slave Act; the long-suffering tenants of Rensselaerwyck killed a sheriff; and poor Thomas Dorr led a popgun rebellion. All this furnished rich material for poems and sermons and tracts by the hundred, but it adds up to less violence than any self-respecting metropolis boasts in a single year in our own day. Yet there is this to be said of the reformers—the Phillipses and Parkers, the Tappans and Welds, the Howes, and the Dorrs—that peaceable as they were, they meant business.

The fate of Thomas Dorr, who was given a life sentence for treason and released the next year, suggests a parallel characteristic: as the reformers did not themselves use violence, they were not the victims of violence. They kept—most of them—their jobs, their pulpits, their college posts, their editorial chairs, their popularity on the lyceum circuit. Nobody boycotted Emerson; Parker preached to three thousand parishioners on a Sunday; Greeley managed to sell a few copies of the *Tribune;* Horace Mann went to Congress, and so did Gerrit Smith; Samuel Gridley Howe married a New York heiress, and the Tappans kept their social position and their money. Harriet Martineau could write on *The Martyr Age in the United States,* and many of the reformers longed for martyrdom, but few achieved it. Again there were exceptions, especially among the Abolitionists: the gallant Elijah Lovejoy comes to mind, and perhaps John Brown, and some others, reckless agitators who openly defied public opinion, headstrong abolitionists who invaded the South, or fugitive slaves who were caught and sent back to slavery. Yet the interesting fact is that while there was a radical movement, and a radical philosophy, there was no counter conservative movement or conservative philosophy. What Horace Mann and Wendell Phillips and Margaret Fuller had to deal with was inertia rather than resistance; certainly it was not counterrevolution.

An eighth characteristic of the reform movement was its regional and sectional character. Like the literature of the day, it was, to an extraordinary degree, a flowering of New England. It is true that New York made important contributions, especially the "burnt-over" region, and that Ohio, especially the Western Reserve, was not without influence. But no one who studies either the philosophy or the leadership of the movement can mistake its sharp New England flavor. Call the roll of the leaders: Emerson, its philosopher; Channing and Parker, its theologians; Horace Mann, its educator, and with him Henry Barnard and John Carter; Catherine Beecher and Margaret Fuller and Mary Lyons and Emma Willard, champions of woman's rights; William Ladd and Elihu Burritt, workers in the vineyards of peace; the Chevalier Howe and Dorothea Dix and Charles Loring Brace in humanitarian reform; the abolitionists Garrison and Phillips, Theodore Weld and Horace Greeley, and even Lovejoy himself. The literary spokesmen, too, almost all bore the New England stamp: Emerson and Thoreau, Lowell and Whittier, Bryant and Greeley; it is suggestive that the other major literary figures of that day—Irving and Cooper, Poe and Simms, and Melville—were for the most part indifferent to the appeal of reform.

What is equally impressive, but not equally puzzling, is that the South was almost wholly untouched by reform, not only by the currents of antislavery—that was to be expected—but even by those of education and humanitarianism. The explanation is not difficult. To Southerners, painfully sensitive to attacks on their peculiar institution, all "isms" were alike, and all obnoxious: abolitionism, feminism, Utopianism, Unitarianism, Republicanism, equalitarianism, humanitarianism. Thus the Richmond *Enquirer* wrote of the campaign of 1856 that if the Republicans had their way the "isms" of "free society, lectures against marriage, licentious philansteries, free love saloons, Mormon states and Quaker villages" would spread all over the South. Or, as one writer in *De Bow's Review* put it in urging exclusive reliance on the Bible and Aristotle: "Books written in the whole range of moral

science, if not written by Southern authors, within the
last twenty or thirty years, inculcate abolition either directly or indirectly. If written before that time, even by
Southern authors, they are likely to be as absurd and as
dangerous as the Declaration of Independence, or the
Virginia Bill of Rights." In short the Southern attitude
was not unlike that of some of our professional red-bait-
ers today: whatever Northern liberals said or did was
pernicious, because it was contaminated at its source.
And, given their assumptions about the necessity and the
sanctity of slavery, Southerners were, of course, right, for
slavery could not stand the open mind, and education
and humanitarian reform threatened to open minds.

Ninth, along with regionalism, went cosmopolitanism.
The currents of reform did not seep below the Mason-
Dixon line, but they flowed across the Atlantic like some
Gulf Stream, and provided a common climate for the
United States and Britain. The reform movement of this
generation was, in fact, Anglo-American, it was even
international. Quakers and Unitarians, in their determination to do good, ignored national boundaries; labor
leaders and land reformers carried on their agitation with
equal fervor in Manchester and in New York. The anti-
slavery movement had its real beginnings in England, and
its greatest triumphs. The struggle for woman's rights,
for temperance, for peace, were all joint enterprises. Penal reform owed more to Bentham and Romilly and Elizabeth Fry than to any American, and Bentham could
write to President Jackson that "I am more of a United
States man than an Englishman." Educational reform
had its real origins in Swiss cantons and German states
where Pestalozzi and Fellenberg and Wehrli and Froebel
fixed the patterns that Horace Mann and Henry Barnard
and Calvin Stowe tried to copy. The Utopian movement,
originally inspired by an America which seemed Nature's
Utopia, had its formal origins in England and France,

and many of the leaders of American Utopianism—
"Mother" Ann Lee, founder of the Shakers, and Robert
Owen of New Harmony and Frances Wright of Nashoba
—were from the British Isles, while phalanxes were mod-
elled on the plans of Charles Fourier, and Icaria on
those drawn by Etienne Cabet, and the romantic Oleana
sprang from the musical bow of Ole Bull.

Finally, reform was one aspect of romanticism, as was
Transcendentalism for that matter, for what is more romantic than the cultivation of individual truth and individual salvation? Romanticism did not so much prescribe
particular reforms as infuse the spirit of reform. It found
expression in a sentimental, and philosophical, attitude
toward Nature—we can see it in the paintings of Bier-
stadt or Church, in Emerson's famous Address, and in
Thoreau's Walden; and in the sentimental attitude toward women and children, and primitive peoples as well.
It is possible that the sentimentalizing of the slave by
Stephen Foster or Harriet Beecher Stowe made more converts to abolition than the arguments of a Garrison or a
Parker. Romanticism was intimately connected with the
new humanitarianism—the attack on capital punishment, the reform of the penal code, the tender concern
for the blind and the deaf, the sick and the feeble-
minded, the more compassionate treatment of animals,
children, felons, and sailors. It informed alike the anti-
slavery poems of Whittier, the annual reports on education by Horace Mann, and Herman Melville's *Mardi.*

Yet it is important to note that romanticism did not
necessarily inspire or encourage reform. In much of Europe it had just the contrary effect, and in the American
South, too, where it nourished the myth that slavery was
a blessing to the blacks and that the plantation system
was but an improvement on medieval chivalry. It is
proper to inquire why romanticism worked one way in
Germany or England or the American South, and another

way in New England and Ohio and New York. Is this just
another example of the resourcefulness of Americans,
like their ability to make Transcendentalism do the work
of Utilitarianism? To some extent it is. But there is more
to it than that. For it can be argued that Yankees read the
meaning of romanticism more accurately than Carlyle or
Hegel or Viollet-le-Duc or, for that matter, John Pendle-
ton Kennedy or George Fitzhugh. Where European and
Southern reactionaries read into it the picturesque, the
Gothic, the aristocratic, and the traditional, northern
Americans read into it the goodness of Nature, the divinity of man, and the infinite promise of the future. James
Fenimore Cooper put it well in an observation by his
"traveling bachelor":

> The moral feeling with which a man of sentiment and
> knowledge looks upon the plains of your (Eastern)
> hemisphere, is connected with recollections; here it
> should be mingled with his hopes. The same effort of
> the mind is as equal to the one as to the other. . . .
> But the speculator on moral things can enjoy a satisfac-
> tion here that he who wanders over the plains of Greece
> will seek in vain. The pleasure of the latter . . . is
> unavoidably tinged with melancholy regrets, while here
> all that reason allows may be hoped on behalf of man.

That might indeed be the epitaph of the great reform
movement of the Middle Period, all the more appropriate
because wrung, as it were, from one of the few major
literary figures who had no use for reform or reformers:
"All that reason allows may be hoped on behalf of man."

"DEMOCRACY IN AMERICA"

I

FOR over three centuries the New World has been an object of curiosity to the Old, and for half that time the United States, particularly, has been called upon to point a moral or adorn a tale. Literally thousands of travelers —British, French, and German predominating—have visited here and rushed home to transcribe their impressions: sometimes they have not waited to return but have given a palpitating world their conclusions in advance, as it were. The roll call of British commentators is long and distinguished: it includes, to name only a few of the more prominent, the Trollopes, mother and son, Harriet Martineau, Dickens, Lyell, Grattan, Marryat, Freeman, Spencer, Bryce, and, in our own day, Wells, Bennett, Joad, Chesterton, and Belloc. French visitors and interpreters are less familiar but scarcely less numerous: one bibliography lists some 1500 volumes by French travelers, and the list includes books by Crèvecœur, Talleyrand, Barbe-Marbois, Chastellux, Chateaubriand, Brissot de Warville, Tocqueville, Considérant, Chevalier, Clem-

SOURCE: Originally published as the introduction to the edition of *Democracy in America* by Alexis de Tocqueville published in 1947 by The Oxford University Press as part of their series "World's Classics." Reprinted by permission.

enceau, Jusserand, Tardieu, and Siegfried. No other nation, assuredly, has been subjected to such a literary
barrage, exposed to so many million words of praise,
blame, and admonition. Only a tough people could have
survived.

What is the explanation of this persistent and passionate curiosity about America?—a curiosity whose only
parallel in modern history is the eighteenth-century
Continental interest in England. Americans are beginning to realize, now, that their country has never been
isolated, but Europeans have always known this, for
throughout its history America has troubled the Old
World. In the sixteenth and seventeenth centuries it was
El Dorado, and the nations of Europe fought for the rich
prize. In the eighteenth century it became something new
under the sun, a republic, a democracy, a federal union,
the hope (as Turgot put it) of the human race. Throughout the nineteenth it was a blessing and a menace—and
a curiosity. To the poor and oppressed it was the promised land; to the rich and privileged a standing threat;
while diplomats everywhere had to reckon with it in their
plans and intrigues. Its vast distances and shaggy beauty
fired the imagination; its youthful vitality and convulsive
growth inspired wonder and respect; its democracy was a
challenge, its social equality a rebuke, its toleration a
model. If laws of history or of the evolution of society
were to be formulated, they must be based in large part
upon the American experiment; if new political institutions were to be fashioned, they must be modeled in part
upon those of the United States. No statesman could be
indifferent to the new nation on the western shores of the
Atlantic; no economist could omit it from his calculations; even philosophers and moralists were required to
accommodate their speculations to its experience.

Everything about America was astonishing: its broad
prairies and majestic rivers; its native peoples, so roman-

tic in prospect, so malevolent in reality; its restless frontier, sweeping across the continent like the tides at St.
Michael; the villages that mushroomed overnight into
cities; the babel of languages; the Negroes who, slave or
free, molded society into their own pattern; the farms
large as Old World counties; the democracy of manners
so often mistaken for vulgarity; the spectacle of Catholics
and Protestants living amicably side by side, and of
scores and hundreds of queer sects; the singular notion of
free public education and the confusion of schools and
colleges; the disconcerting freedom of women and the
purity of morals; the town meeting, the state legislature,
the political party, the popular election of a chief magis-
trate; the disparity of wealth and the blurring of class
distinctions; the fabulous prosperity, the buoyant confidence, the latent power. No wonder it took a thousand
essays to penetrate to the truth about America.

Americans themselves gave little help. Notwithstanding that nervous boastfulness which impressed so many
visitors, Americans, on the whole, gave but a poor account of themselves—certainly a confusing one. Their
newspapers played up the sensational and the eccentric;
their literature reflected an unfamiliar local color or,
more recently, mirrored a society incredibly violent and
rude; their politicians indulged in antics that seemed,
and often were, preposterous; and that somehow the political machine worked smoothly enough seemed rather a
dispensation of Providence than a tribute to common
sense. And, in our own day, the moving pictures, easily
the most influential of interpreters, gave a fabulous picture of wealth, crime, vulgarity, speed, excitement, sala-
city, and abnormality. In Britain nature seemed to conform to art, and from the days of Fielding and Smollett to
those of Wells and Bennett, the library was a not unsatisfactory substitute for travel, but it was inconceivable that
America could be what, on her many surfaces, she ap-

peared to be. The picture was diverse and contradictory, and the least perspicacious foreigner could confidently predict that America would be unpredictable.

It must be admitted that European visitors did little to resolve the confusion. Most of the literature of description and interpretation, English as well as continental, is pretty shoddy stuff. The interpretation of national character is difficult enough in the most auspicious of circumstances: the circumstances attending the lucubrations of European visitors were rarely auspicious. Of all the thousands of books on America, perhaps less than two score are of lasting value.

Why is the average so low, why is so much of the stuff mediocre or worse? Why, especially, have men and women otherwise thoughtful, learned, and observant, failed so signally to understand and interpret the United States? The question is not relevant to the works of a Grattan, a Münsterberg, a Bryce, but it is properly directed to the overwhelming majority of the commentators, British and continental. Only a partial explanation can be submitted here. Many, if not most, of those who wrote about America, came here with a closed mind, came not to learn but to confirm preconceived notions. They assumed—naturally enough—that the Old World was the norm and interpreted every deviation from that norm as quaint, vulgar, or eccentric. That Americans, who had inherited admirable political, legal, religious, and social institutions, preferred to fashion new ones appeared to them quite perverse. Few of those who wrote so glibly on America saw the whole of it, or saw any part of it thoroughly: altogether too many got their impressions of the American countryside from the windows of a train, their impression of cities from hotel lobbies or dining rooms. Others, overwhelmed with the vastness and variety of American life, took refuge in anecdotes or in exclamatory descriptions of the picturesque and the exceptional. Some visitors were inspired by purely business considerations—the search for land, for business openings, for investment opportunities. Still others, with their eye on royalties, made a book the excuse for their visit rather than the visit the justification for their book; what they wrote, therefore, was designed to titillate or flatter a British or European audience—an audience notoriously uncritical and credulous in everything concerning America. And, finally, of all those who attempted to interpret America, only a handful were intellectually competent to the task: of most of them it could be said, as the sage Franklin said in another connection, "their poor noddles were distracted."

These observations apply with less force, perhaps, to French than to British visitors and commentators. The French had, to be sure, a clearer field, an easier task. There was no tradition of enmity to embarrass relations between Americans and French, but one of friendship: Lafayette proved as immortal as George III. From America, France had neither so much to fear nor so much to hope as Britain. Its relation was avuncular rather than maternal, and it could regard the new nation with an objectivity scarcely possible to the mother country. Then, too, France had had her Revolution, and needed neither to borrow nor to resist American radicalism; nor was America draining France of her population, or threatening her supremacy in commerce, manufacturing, or business. Nor were the two peoples divided—to adapt Shaw's hackneyed phrase—by the barrier of a common language and common institutions. The British were inclined to regard any departure from English ways as a reflection upon themselves, and, at the same time, to resent imitations as the possessors of the genuine commonly resent those who urge the merits of the counterfeit: the French, who were not looking for a New France, were not outraged when they failed to find a New Britain.

To most of these melancholy generalizations, as well
as to their Gallic qualifications, Alexis de Tocqueville is
an exception. He was thorough and indefatigable in his
search for facts, patient and skillful in their organization,
sympathetic and perspicacious in their interpretation, luminous in their presentation. His purpose was lofty, his
earning solid, his understanding profound. By common
consent his *Democracy in America* is the most illuminating commentary on American character and institutions
ever penned by a foreigner, the one which, a century
after its appearance, seems best assured of immortality.

I I

"I confess that in America, I saw more than America; I
sought the image of democracy itself, with its inclina-
tions, its character, its prejudices, and its passions, in
order to learn what we have to fear or to hope from its
progress." So wrote Tocqueville, and the confession is
basic to an understanding of his work. America, in short,
was not the primary object of his investigation, but
rather democracy—a word which Tocqueville used much
as we use it today to embrace social and economic as well
as political practices and institutions. The inspiration of
the inquiry was not so much curiosity about America as
concern for France especially, and for the Old World in
general. America was, it seemed, merely the laboratory;
the findings were designed for application abroad.

For democracy, Tocqueville was persuaded, was inevitable and irresistible, its doctrines and practices destined
to spread over the Western World. The invasion of England was already under way: Tocqueville's brief visit
there had persuaded him of that, and every letter from J.
S. Mill or from Nassau Senior strengthened the persuasion. France could not escape, France whose tradition of

liberty and equality made her peculiarly susceptible; before long the ferment of democracy would be at work in all the nations of Europe. "The question here discussed," said Tocqueville, "is interesting not only to the United States, but to the whole world; it concerns not a nation, but all mankind."

Yet if democracy was inevitable, would not mere description suffice? And here we come to the heart of Tocqueville's thought. Democracy was, indeed, inevitable. Democracy however was no simple thing but infinitely complex, not a rigid system or an implacable doctrine but an attitude of mind and a habit of conduct. It was a mixture of good and evil—Tocqueville was not always sure which was predominant—but it was possible to separate the good from the evil. It was possible, above all, to separate the natural from the artificial, the universal from the particular, to accommodate democracy to its various environments.

Tocqueville was one of the first students of politics to discern the truth—so often ignored or contemned in our own day—that the great forces of history do not operate uniformly and automatically in every society, but are naturalized, as it were, wherever they appear. He proposed, for France, a reconciliation of fatalism and free will, of the iron forces of history and the genius of the nation. "The more I study the former condition of the world," he wrote, "and see the world of our own day in greater detail, the more I consider the prodigious variety to be met with, not only in laws, but in the principles of law, the more I am tempted to believe that what we call necessary institutions are often no more than institutions to which we have grown accustomed, and that in matters of social constitution the field of possibilities is much more extensive than men living in their various societies are ready to imagine."

The field of possibilities was more extensive than men

imagined! Here was the real justification for the study of democracy in America. Democracy was on the march, but the manner in which it was to come, the form it was to take, the consequences it was to have, were all matters over which men might exercise control. And for everything that concerned democracy America was not only the most convenient but the most elaborate laboratory. It held the answer to the questions that were bound to trouble the Old World. Can men govern themselves? Is it possible to reconcile liberty and order, the individual and the state? Does democracy but substitute the tyranny of the majority for the tyranny of the few? Can any government tolerate free speech and a free press, or will liberty inevitably degenerate into license? Can men of different races, tongues, and faiths live amicably side by side? Will the melting pot, with its fusing of peoples, produce an inferior race? Will universal education be accompanied by a vulgarization of culture? Can art, literature, and philosophy flourish in a society that substitutes the verdict of the majority for the judgment of training and tradition? Is democracy synonymous with mediocrity, and is the well-being of the many worth the sacrifice of beauty and grace? Will democracy so depreciate the military virtues as to expose itself to enervation from within and destruction from without?

No scholar could hope to find conclusive answers to questions so profound and so complex, but that the American experience might illuminate the problem was apparent, for America was the proving ground of history. Here, as James Russell Lowell was shortly to observe, "the elements are all in solution, and we have only to look to see how they will combine. History, which every day makes less account of governors and more of man, must find here the compendious key to all that picture writing of the Past."

It was, to be sure, the key to the future rather than to

the past that Tocqueville sought, but that America held
the key to this, too, was clear. It was clear, at least, to
young Tocqueville—who was the first to appreciate the
scientific possibilities of the New World—and *Democracy in America* vindicated his judgment and his vision.

III

It is just over one hundred years, now, since young
Tocqueville—he was barely thirty—brought out the first
two volumes of *Democracy in America*. He was filled
with misgivings—and so was his publisher, M. Gosselin.
But soon the book was acclaimed in two continents and
crowned by the French Academy, and M. Gosselin was
delighted. "So it appears that your book is a masterpiece,"
he boasted, rubbing his hands together. It was the comment of a tradesman, said Tocqueville with a sneer. But
it was, too, the verdict of posterity.

What explains the fame, the longevity, of *Democracy
in America*? No other book of its kind has weathered so
well, or been so frequently reprinted, and without misgivings even by publishers. The book, certainly, is not
without faults. It is, for all its sharpness and spareness,
over-long—two more volumes appeared in 1840, making
four in all. It makes no concessions to the reader, either
in analysis or in interpretation, it has no narrative
quality, it is devoid of humor. It includes much that is
merely descriptive; it omits much that is important.

It is no difficult task to draw up a general indictment
and itemize a bill of particulars. Tocqueville came not to
observe America as a whole, but to observe the operations
of democracy; and democracy rather than America, it
must never be forgotten, was his primary concern. He
tended to substitute his own reflections for facts, or,
where the facts were stubborn, to force them into his own
preconceived pattern. When he wrote the second—and

best—part of *Democracy in America* the sharp impact of
personal experience was fading, the pressure of France
was strong, and Tocqueville indulged himself more readily in rationalization, yielded increasingly to the temptations of *a priori* reasoning. He did not sufficiently check
what he felt was bound to happen with what actually was
happening, and where history ran counter to his predic-
tions he was inclined to give the impression that history
was somehow at fault. Thus he could write at length, and
ominously, of the tyranny of the majority without once
citing a convincing example of such tyranny; thus he
could insist upon the inherent weakness of the executive
authority at a time when the strongest of American Presidents occupied the White House. His acquaintance with
America was limited; he knew the East better than the
West, the North better than the South. His investigations
were haphazard rather than systematic, his sources of
information inadequate and often misleading. He made
it a point to meet the best people, and the best people,
then as now, were inclined to deprecate democracy: Justice Story complained, with reason, that Tocqueville had
borrowed liberally from his Commentaries, and Story was
a high federalist. An aristocrat, Tocqueville exaggerated
the importance of manners, and was capable of the observation that "nothing is more prejudicial to democracy
than its outward forms of behavior; many men would
willingly endure its vices who cannot support its manners." He was not sufficiently familiar with the English
background of American institutions, and frequently
mistook for peculiarly American or peculiarly democratic what was merely Anglo-American. He missed many
things that less perspicacious observers saw, possibly because the obvious did not always accommodate itself to
his philosophical pattern; in his anxiety to get below the
surface he failed to appreciate things that were on the

surface. Thus he could argue the ultimate disintegration of the Union because he failed to notice economic developments or to comprehend the nationalizing effect of the industrial revolution. He missed the abolition movement, and transcendentalism, and his interest in penal and prison reform—the ostensible ground for his visit to America—did not persuade him to study the reform movement in general. For all his concern with democracy, he seemed singularly uninterested in its immediate political manifestations, and the casual reader of his book would scarcely realize that while Tocqueville was traversing America, Andrew Jackson was President.

These are serious defects, defects that would guarantee oblivion to most volumes of description or interpretation. Yet *Democracy in America* has not only survived oblivion; it has earned for itself a place as a classic. For the faults of the book are, after all, superficial rather than fundamental; they are grievous only with reference to the standards Tocqueville himself set, and those standards were incomparably high. The omissions, the inadequacies, the misconceptions of the book can easily be supplied or corrected by other books; for its shining merits there is no substitute.

What are these merits? First, it can be said, Tocqueville chose a great and noble theme and handled it with dignity. That theme was the adjustment of the civilizations of Western Christendom to democracy. Others had written about America; Tocqueville undertook to relate American to world history, to fix the significance of America in history. His subject, he wrote in all humility, "is interesting . . . to the whole world; it concerns not a nation, but all mankind." His purpose was to prepare men everywhere for the "providential fact" of equality; to dissipate fears, quiet excessive hopes, encourage accommodation; to lift men above narrow and selfish views and

persuade them to broad and generous views. There is
almost a Periclean quality about his own statement of his
grand design:

> I have sought to show what a democratic people is in
> our days, and by this delineation, executed with rigor-
> ous accuracy, my design has been to produce a twofold
> effect on my contemporaries. To those who make to
> themselves an ideal democracy, a brilliant vision which
> they think it easy to realize, I undertake to show that
> they have arrayed their future in false colors; that the
> democratic government they advocate, if it be of real
> advantage to those who can support it, has not the lofty
> features they ascribe to it; and moreover, that this
> government can only be maintained on certain condi-
> tions of intelligence, private morality, and religious
> faith, which we do not possess; and that its political
> results are not to be obtained without labor.
>
> To those for whom the word 'democracy' is synony-
> mous with disturbance, anarchy, spoliation, and mur-
> der, I have attempted to show that the government of
> democracy may be reconciled with respect for property,
> with deference for rights, with safety to freedom, with
> reverence to religion; that if democratic government is
> less favorable than another to some of the finer parts of
> human nature, it has also great and noble elements;
> and that perhaps, after all, it is the will of God to shed a
> lesser grade of happiness on the totality of mankind,
> not to combine a greater share of it on a smaller num-
> ber, or to raise the few to the verge of perfection.

And to his friend, Kergolat, he confessed, "To labor in
this direction is in my eyes a *sainte occupation,* and one
in which one must spare neither one's money nor one's
time, nor one's life."

Tocqueville chose a great subject, and he measured up
to its greatness. He was the first philosophical historian
to write of the American experiment; the first political
scientist to make democracy the primary object of realistic investigation. And it must be accounted a capital
merit in Tocqueville that he had not only a philosophy,

but the right philosophy. He saw that the significance of America in history was to be found in the opportunity it afforded as a laboratory of social, economic, and political democracy, and he fastened his attention on that aspect of America to the exclusion of the merely picturesque or sensational. He had an instinct for the jugular vein in history.

Other observers had lost themselves in the trivial, the irrelevant, the inconsequential; they maundered on about hotel service, the litter on the streets of cities, the hardships of railroad travel, the table manners of their hosts. Tocqueville, too, noted these things, but he did not suppose they were important in themselves or permit them to distract his attention from the object of his investigation—the effect of democracy on manners and morals, politics and religion, business and labor, literature and art, family and social relations. He was concerned, throughout, with fundamental causes and ultimate consequences.

And on almost every page of his book we discern the play of an alert, inquisitive, and critical mind. It is a tribute to the triumph of Tocqueville's method that we are, throughout, more interested in what he has to say about a subject than we are in the subject itself. He had, that is, not only a philosophical but an eminently reflective mind; he had not only a philosophy of history, in the grand manner, but perspicacity and penetration; he was as illuminating in his particular as in his general observations. We are constantly gratified by his shrewd insights and his happy prophecies. Who, after all, has better comprehended the American character than this French stranger who arrived at his understanding almost as by a mathematical formula, so rigorous was his analysis, so logical his conclusions? In his day our literature was still strongly colonial, but Tocqueville foresaw with astonishing perspicuity the effect democracy would have upon it

in the future. He saw, too, that democracy must have its
own History, one in which the individual was subordinate
to the mass, fortuity to great sweeping movements; and
from George Bancroft to Henry Adams and Charles
Beard, American historical litrerature has conformed to
Tocqueville's formula. He penetrated to the gnawing un-
certainty of many Americans about social democracy, the
pretentiousness and insincerity of much of the talk about
the common man by men who invariably made it clear
that they themselves were uncommon men. He understood, as have few foreigners and not many Americans,
the combination—peculiarly prominent in the realm of
politics—of extravagance of language and prudence of
conduct. He noted, as had others, the American passion
for change, and found it the natural consequence of the
restless search for the ideal and the opportunities
afforded all Americans to achieve that ideal. He grasped
the fact, as yet concealed from many of our agitated
Bourbons, that democracy makes for conservatism and
that the surest guaranty of stability is the wide distribution of property. He was the first foreign observer to
appreciate the significance of the dominance of the
American political scene by men trained to the law, and
described in terms still relevant that aristocracy of the
robe which Americans take for granted but which other
democratic peoples look upon with astonishment. He saw
the significance of the interaction of democracy and religion and emphasized throughout his study the place of
the church in American life. He discerned the natural
hostility to the military in a democracy, but foresaw with
startling accuracy the effect of prolonged war on American society and economy and psychology. There was little, indeed, in the American character that his penetrating eye did not see, his luminous mind comprehend.

And Tocqueville's interpretation, for all his aristocratic
and alien background, was almost unfailingly judicious.

He was misled, at times, by the men he consulted, the books he read, but his errors were never malicious. His view of democracy was often pessimistic, but never jaundiced, and it is gratifying that America has confounded its most astute critic where he was pessimistic rather than where he was optimistic. No other interpreter of America, not Grattan nor Bryce nor Münsterberg nor Brogan, has achieved the aloofness, the objectivity, the serene impersonality, that came naturally to Tocqueville. The explanation is, largely, in Tocqueville's own character; it is, in part, that Tocqueville was concerned to instruct his own people rather than to edify the Americans, and that patriotism and morality inexorably required the most scrupulous objectivity.

Finally, it must be counted among the great merits of *Democracy in America* that its style is felicitous and even brilliant. There are no purple patches, there are few epigrams, but there is, throughout, a luminous clarity, a resiliency, a masculine toughness, that contrasts sharply with the rhetoric of Trollope or Martineau, the verbosity of Bryce, the strained brilliance of Siegfried or Maurois. Tocqueville has, above all others who have written about America, the magisterial style.

It is this happy combination of a great theme with a philosophy profound enough to comprehend it, a temperament judicious enough to interpret it, an intelligence acute enough to master it, a style adequate to its demands, that makes *Democracy in America* one of the great and enduring works of political literature. As a young man, Tocqueville confessed, "I do not know any way of life more honorable or more attractive than to write with such honesty about the great truths that one's name becomes known to the civilized world." It is a safe prophecy that as long as democracy itself endures, Tocqueville's name will be known to the civilized world.

CIVIL WAR CARTOGRAPHY

I

"IT MAY be broadly stated," wrote General McClellan of his Virginia campaigns, "that we had no military maps of any value." Colonel Theodore Lyman, noting that this deficiency persisted long after McClellan's departure, spoke bitterly of the "uselessness of the maps furnished to the Staff of the Army of the Potomac previous to the campaign of May 1864." Nor were the Confederates in a more fortunate position. "It is true," wrote Captain Albert Campbell, who was in charge of Lee's "map bureau," "that there were no maps of any account in existence at the time when General Lee assumed the command, that were of use to the Army of Northern Virginia." General Richard Taylor put the matter even more bluntly. "The Confederate commanders," he wrote, "knew no more about the topography of the country than they did about Central Africa. . . . We were profoundly ignorant of the country, were without maps, sketches, or proper

SOURCE: Originally published as the introduction to *The Official Atlas of the Civil War*, ed. Henry Steele Commager (New York and London: Thomas Yoseloff; 1958). Copyright © 1958 by Thomas Yoseloff, Inc. Reprinted by permission.

guides, and nearly as helpless as if we had been suddenly transferred to the banks of the Lualaba."

Here was one of the cardinal facts of the war, and failure to appreciate it has misled many an armchair strategist in his analysis of the realities of tactics, and even of strategy. The awkward, the astonishing fact is that very little of the territory over which Union and Confederate armies fought for four years had been mapped, and that, especially in the first two years of the war, both armies often fought blindly. Stuart has been condemned, and justly, for his excursions around Mc-Clellan's army and into Pennsylvania, but the instinct that led him to these sensational rides was exploratory as well as dramatic. "The day before the battle of Malvern Hill," General Taylor recalled, "President Davis could not find a guide with intelligence enough to show him the way from one of our columns to another." Colonel Lyman submits to our consideration a map of a small section of the Wilderness centering on Chancellorsville, of which he says:

> The junction of the Plank and Brock roads is one and one quarter miles too far to the northwest; Todd's Tavern one mile to the north; Corbin's Bridge, one mile to the northwest; South bend of the Po River, two and three quarter miles to the west; Spottsylvania Court House, two and one half miles to the west, and the house of S. Alsop one and one quarter miles too far to the north. These discrepancies are in a territory only eight miles by nine. ["The Uselessness of the Maps Furnished to the Staff of the Army of the Potomac Previous to the Campaign of May 1864" in *The Wilderness Campaign*, Papers of the Military Hist. Soc. of Mass, 80.]

No wonder the armies blundered!

What was the explanation of this curious, and fateful, situation? After all, Congress had authorized "a geographer and surveyor" as early as 1777, and the Topographi-

cal Engineers had been formally, though not permanently, established in 1813, and re-established in 1838.
Nor had these been wanting in energy. To be sure they
had never been permitted to carry through that comprehensive plan submitted by those remarkable engineers,
Majors Isaac Roberdeau and John Anderson, who proposed to survey not only "topographical details for future
use" but "the knowledge of the condition as well as numbers of the population; a fertile or sterile country, even
the temper, dispositions, and habits of the people, their
mode of life, their food, stock, and civil condition in
relation to their own government." The Topographical
Engineers had, however, been given a large share of
responsibility for river and harbor improvements, roads,
canals, bridges, boundaries, fortifications, coastal de-
fenses, and lighthouses. More to the point they had concentrated their talents on surveys of the Far West, notably such surveys as that for the Pacific Railway in the
mid-forties. And, needless to add, topographical engineers had campaigned with Taylor in the wastes of northern Mexico, marched with Kearny from Leavenworth to
Santa Fé, and fought with Scott from Vera Cruz to the
Halls of Montezuma. In between they had surveyed des-
erts, and made reconnaissance maps, but so little were
they needed for this work that young Lieutenant George
Gordon Meade had been shipped back from Mexico to
Philadelphia as superfluous!

The Topographical Engineers, then, had mapped the
boundaries, the Great Lakes, and the Far West, and
much besides, but not the South from Virginia to Texas.
Nor had any other agency. A few states had carried
through geological and topographical surveys, but the
states of the Confederacy were not among them. The
United States Geological Survey had concentrated on the
West. Alone of government agencies, the Coast and
Geodetic Survey had made contributions that were to be

of value during the war. First, and timidly, under the fantastic Ferdinand Hassler; then systematically, under the bold and ambitious Alexander Dallas Bache, the Coastal Survey had mapped the whole of the Atlantic and Gulf Coast line, bays, inlets, and even rivers. Of the maps available to the Union armies in Virginia, along the Mississippi, and in Texas, those of the Coast and Geodetic Survey were far the most helpful.

What all this meant was that in the beginning the Union and Confederate armies fought quite literally in a wilderness that covered far more than the land between the Rapidan and the North Anna, and that victory often rested not with the heaviest battalions, but with the General who could master the terrain and bring his soldiers into action. It meant that upon the Topographical Engineers, and all who could be pressed into their service, were imposed responsibilities far heavier than they had ever before been asked to bear.

We are staggered by the complete lack of preparation for these responsibilities, and perhaps even more by the lack of any glimmering of their importance that obtained even in high places. Thus the Confederate General Taylor, writing with some bitterness of the failure to keep track of McClellan on the Peninsula, asks us to remember

> that the Confederate commander, General Johnston, had been a topographical engineer in the United States army, while his successor, General Lee—another engineer—had been on duty at the war office in Richmond and in constant intercourse with President Davis, who was educated at West Point, and served seven years, and then think of our ignorance in a military sense of the ground over which we were called to fight. [*Destruction and Reconstruction*, 87.]

Nor was it only the Confederate high command that was unalert and unprepared. Colonel Stephen Long was a

distinguished explorer and engineer, but he was seventy-
seven when the war broke out and he was called back to
Washington to take command of the Topographical Engineers! Not until August, 1861, was the Topographical
Corps increased to a total of forty commissioned officers
and one hundred and fifty enlisted men. No wonder Mc-
Clellan complained that the number was so small he had
to call on the Coastal Survey, and on civilian engineers,
for help, and that the tasks of reconnaissance and surveys fell on his hard-pressed engineers.

At first glance the task confronting the Federals would
seem to have been more arduous than that facing the
Confederates. They were on foreign soil, foreign meaning
unfamiliar as well as hostile. They had neither maps nor
the means of obtaining them; they had to rely on spies,
who were not too clever, and informers, who were notoriously unreliable. The Confederates, on the other hand,
were fighting on home ground, and presumably at home
on that ground. If they didn't have maps it was their own
fault. Except when they took the offensive and stabbed
into Ohio or Pennsylvania, they could carry on topographical surveys and provide themselves with maps without interference.

Actually the balance was much more even than this:
the Federals had many advantages, their opponents
suffered from—or achieved—many disadvantages. Such
maps as had been prepared before the war by the Topographical Engineers, the Geological Survey, and the
Coastal Survey, were all available to Union commanders.
They had facilities, too, for making good their deficiencies: a larger number of trained engineers and expert
civilians; vessels which could explore inlets and rivers;
balloons from which to make military observations; and
an abundance of paper, inks, and photographic and re-
producing apparatus. The Confederates, by contrast, had
no body of maps on which to draw. They had, or devel-

oped, some skillful topographers, but had no reservoir of foreign-trained draughtsmen in the civilian population. And they suffered, throughout most of the war, from a scarcity of the most elementary supplies—paper, ink, chemicals, glass plates, and so forth. They suffered, too, from over-confidence born of their knowledge of the terrain; actually, except for Jackson's Valley campaigns and for some of the fighting in the Wilderness, the Confederates do not seem to have enjoyed the advantages which fighting on home ground should have assured them.

When McClellan took charge of the Army of the Potomac, the expansion of the Topographical Corps was already under way. McClellan promptly appointed the gifted Major A. A. Humphreys chief of the Topographical Engineers; he was later to have a distinguished career as Chief of Staff of the Army of the Potomac and Commander of the II Army Corps. The situation which confronted Humphreys on the eve of the Peninsula campaign is well described by his brother officer, General A. S. Webb:

The Virginia Peninsula, like many portions even of the older States, was practically *terra incognita* for military purposes. Careful surveys of its entire extent had never been made, and when the topographical engineers set to work to construct maps for General McClellan's guidance, in view of his possible movement by that route, their results were necessarily insufficiently full or precise. Major-General A. A. Humphreys, then at the head of the Topographical Corps, consulted every available authority and record bearing upon the features of that region; and this information was used by the Commanding General. Among other maps brought to light were the British plans of the siege of Yorktown, in 1781, and the original survey of the Peninsula from Fort Monroe to Williamsburg, made in 1818 by Major James Kearney. . . . Various outlines were compiled;

but the most elaborate, so far as it went, and the one followed by General McClellan, was that furnished by Lieutenant Colonel T. J. Cram, then serving as engineer and aide-de-camp to General Wool, which embraced Norfolk, Suffolk, and the Peninsula as far as the Halfway House above Yorktown. And yet this map, which, in view of its source, appears to have been regarded as the most reliable, was found to be in error in several important particulars. . . . With these maps before him, it is clear that McClellan did not expect to find the extensive line of defense which . . . Magruder had constructed and occupied. [Alexander S. Webb: *The Peninsula*, 51–2.]

With the energetic support of McClellan, General Humphreys quickly developed and expanded the work of the engineers, and discovered or trained a number of competent military topographers: his assistant on the Mississippi River Survey, Henry L. Abbot, later chief topographical engineer for General Banks; James Duane, later chief engineer of the Department of the South; Truman Seymour, who ended his days as a painter in Florence; Colonel Nathaniel Michler, later chief topographical engineer of the Army of the Potomac, and his assistant, Major John E. Weyss, one of the most prolific of map-makers; and many others. Before the war ended, the Topographical Corps, by then merged with the Corps of Engineers, had been expanded to one hundred and five officers and seven hundred and fifty-two enlisted men, and had attached to it an unknown number of civilians.

In one respect the topographers of the Army of the Potomac had a distinct advantage over their adversaries in the Army of Northern Virginia; that was in aerial observation and reconnaissance. Balloons had been used by the French Revolutionary armies, but not, heretofore, in America. It was a civilian, with the improbable name of Thaddeus Sobieski Coulincourt Lowe, who was chiefly responsible for persuading General Humphreys to adopt balloons for purposes of observation. A few weeks after the attack on Fort Sumter, "Professor" Lowe had sailed— or flown—his balloon from Cincinnati to the borders of South Carolina where he narrowly escaped being mobbed as a spy and had the satisfaction of becoming the first Yankee prisoner. The Confederates might have avoided a good deal of trouble had they interned him; instead they let him go. Back in Washington, Lowe enlisted the interest of Professor Henry of the Smithsonian Institution; Henry, in turn, got him a hearing with President Lincoln. The result was his appointment as chief aeronaut of the Army of the Potomac; before many months were out, the Professor had no less than seven balloons with such happy names as *Enterprise, Intrepid,* and *Eagle,* observing and mapping enemy positions. This embryo American air force did valiant service until, after Gettysburg, it fell victim not to enemy gunnery but to Army red tape, and was disbanded.

The task of mapping the western theater of the war was even more formidable than that of mapping the Virginia front, but it was the boast of the historian of the Army of the Cumberland, Chaplain Thomas Van Horne, that it was better performed. The Topographical Corps of the Army of the Cumberland possessed not only a large staff, but elaborate equipment: a printing press, two lithographic presses, one photographic establishment, arrangements for map-mounting, and a full corps of draughtsmen and assistants. Van Horne tells how all this was used:

Two days before the army started from Chattanooga on the Atlanta campaign, I received notice of the intended march. Up to this moment there was but one copy of the large map of Northern Georgia and this was in the hands of the draughtsmen. I kept it back until the last moment so as to get on it the latest information that

Sergeant Finnegan might be able to extract from the motley crew turned over by the Provost-Marshal General for examination. The map was immediately cut up into sixteen sections and divided among the draughtsmen, who were to work night and day until all the sections had been traced on thin paper in autographic ink. As soon as four adjacent sections were finished they were transferred to one large stone, and two hundred copies were printed. When all the map had thus been lithographed the map-mounters commenced their work. Being independent of sunlight the work was soon done—the map-mounting requiring the greatest time; but before the commanding Generals left Chattanooga each had received a bound copy of the map, and before we struck the enemy, every brigade, division, and corps commander in the three armies had a copy. The copies for the cavalry were printed directly in muslin, as such maps could be washed clean whenever soiled, and could not be injured by hard service. Many officers sent handkerchiefs to the office and had maps printed on them. [Thomas B. Van Horne: *History of the Army of the Cumberland,* II, 457–8.]

"I think," Van Horne concluded, "that the army that General Sherman led to Atlanta was the best equipped with maps of any that fought in the civil war."

Colonel Andrew Talcott, C.S.A., had undertaken a reconnaissance of the country around Richmond as early as the spring of 1861, and, after First Manassas, Captain D. B. Harris spent a month in somewhat desultory mapmaking, but Confederate topography did not really get under way until the appointment of Captain Albert Campbell in June, 1862, as chief of the topographical office in Richmond. Not until after Seven Days had dramatized Confederate ignorance of their own terrain did Campbell get adequate assistance and supplies. Throughout the war the Confederacy was plagued by acute shortages of engraving paper, India ink, tracing cloth, water colors, drawing instruments, and photographic equipment; some of these deficiencies were made good by the

Yankees, others by purchases abroad which successfully ran the blockade. By constantly revising old maps, acquiring Coastal Survey maps, capturing Federal maps, and by continuous reconnaissance, Campbell's office eventually provided Lee with such topographical data as he needed for his campaigns. By 1864, Campbell's office was using photography for multiple map reproduction, and this method, already in use by the Army of the Cumberland and the Army of the Potomac, spread quickly to the Topographical Corps of the Army of Tennessee and the Gulf Department.

The most effective of Confederate topographers was undoubtedly "Professor" Jedediah Hotchkiss of Jackson's command. A Yankee, born in 1847, he had walked from New York to Virginia and, seeing no reason to go farther, had opened an Academy there, and made maps on the side. When, after a brief campaign along the Cheat River, he had reported to Jackson's army as Adjutant of a militia regiment, Jackson sent for him and launched him on his remarkable career: "I want you to make me a map of the Valley from Harpers Ferry to Lexington, showing all the points of offense and defense between those points. . . . Good morning." (Freeman, *Lee's Lieutenants*, I, 321.) It was enough; from then on Jed Hotchkiss was the indefatigable and incomparable surveyor of the Valley, and eventually of all the Virginia battlefields over which the Blue and the Gray fought for three more years. His name appears more frequently than that of any other topographer in the pages of the Official Records, and no less than half of all the Confederate maps that eventually found their way into the *Atlas* were from his hand. As Hotchkiss contributed so largely to the drama of Jackson's triumphs in the Valley, he contributed, in the end, to the drama of the great commander's death. For it was Hotchkiss who found the fatal road around the right flank of Hooker at Chancellorsville.

"His report, with map," wrote Kyd Douglas, "satisfied General Lee that it was practicable, and naturally Jackson was selected to make the movement."

Hotchkiss drew all the maps that bore his name, but most of the maps which are credited to some commanding General in the cluttered pages of the *Official Records* were the work of little-known, or even wholly anonymous, topographers and draughtsmen. What is most impressive is the large proportion of German and French names that connect themselves with so many of the maps. Lithography, engraving, and photography was almost a monopoly of the Germans and French in that generation, and it is not surprising that their special skills should have been levied upon for military purposes. Here, retreating modestly into the smallest print, are Lieutenant Otto Matz, Captain John Rziha, Assistant Engineer Charles Spangenberg, Lieutenant Julius Karnasch, Lieutenant Helmle, Major Franz Kappner, Theodore von Kamecke, Herman Ulffers, F. Theilkuhl, F. S. Gutherz, J. von Glumer, whose origins are obviously German; here are U. de Fonvielle, Captain J. F. Gallimar, Charles Peseux, F. D'Avignon, and William Le Baron Jenny, as obviously French. A Hungarian, John A. Fiala, was Fremont's chief topographical engineer; a Pole, Ladislas A. Wrotnowski, was on General Weitzel's staff in the Army of the James; while August Fosberg, who was topographical engineer in Charleston, and eventually Colonel of the Fifty-first Virginia, was from Sweden.

Before the war was over, topographers and their photographic assistants in the two armies were turning out thousands of maps. There was, however, no systematic provision for their arrangement or preservation. Many of the Federal maps were returned to the War Department; others went back to the Geological Survey or the Coast and Geodetic Survey; still others stayed in private hands, or simply disappeared. Most of the Confederate maps seem to have been destroyed or lost. When Richmond fell, Captain Campbell placed his file of original maps on an archive train bound for Raleigh; the train was wrecked or burned, and the maps lost. The fate of the negatives was even sadder. Captain Campbell himself describes it:

> The *negatives* of the general maps I gave to my private secretary. Some time after he informed me that he had carried them with him in his flight as far as Macon, Georgia, and on his return, for greater security, had placed them in a lady's trunk, a fellow-passenger's. Hearing *en route* that all baggage of returning fugitives was to be examined at Augusta, Georgia, he incontinently *burned them*. [A. H. Campbell: "The Lost War Maps of the Confederates," *Century Magazine*, Vol. 35, p. 481.]

II

While General Grant was hurling his forces at Lee in the Wilderness, Congress rather absent-mindedly authorized the Army to preserve the record of the war. To be sure, nothing happened; not until nine years later, June 23, 1874, was provision made for publication of the official records of the war, and it was another six years before the first volume of what was eventually to be a mammoth one-hundred-and-twenty-eight-volume enterprise was launched. Fortunately provisions of the act of June, 1874, embraced not only formal reports and correspondence but "all official documents that appear to be of any historical value." It was under this broad verbal tent that the *Atlas* eventually found refuge.

In 1887, Lieutenant Colonel Henry Lazelle, a veteran of the Virginia campaigns and one-time commandant of cadets at the Military Academy, was placed in charge of the *Official Records;* two years later Congress provided a board to consist of one officer and two civilians to super-

vise the publication. History tells little about the two
civilians, but the officer, Major George Breckenridge
Davis, was a man of parts. He had seen service in both
the cavalry and the artillery during the Civil War, and on
the frontier thereafter; he taught at various times, Spanish, French, chemistry, geology, mineralogy, history, geography, ethics, and law at the Military Academy. After
teaching law at the Academy, writing a notable volume
on international law, and serving as Judge Advocate, he
got around to a law degree at the Columbian Law School:
this in the moments of leisure during the supervision of
the *Official Records.*

Not until 1889 did the War Department begin work on
the *Atlas;* the enterprise was entrusted, then, not to a
trained topographical engineer, but to a Lieutenant innocent of any knowledge of topography. Yet, as it turned
out, Lieutenant Calvin Duvall Cowles, 23rd United States
Infantry, was an admirable appointment. Born in North
Carolina (he had one uncle in the Confederate Navy and
another in the Confederate Army) he had graduated
from the Academy in 1873, standing an unimpressive
twenty-fifth in a class of forty-one. Thereafter he served
the familiar but dreary round of frontier posts and bar-
racks—at Camp Verde, Arizona; at Fort McPherson, Ne-
braska; at Fort Dodge, Kansas; at the Uncompahgre Can-
tonment in Colorado; in garrison at Fort Mackinac,
Michigan, and David's Island, New York: not, one would
suppose, the ideal preparation for a great scientific and
editorial work. It was on February 13, 1889, that Lieutenant Cowles (his captaincy did not come for another two
years) was assigned to the Rebellion Record Office, and
put "in charge of the map work with instructions to make
a complete index of the maps." He found six hundred and
twenty-six separate maps and five collections aggregating
another hundred and forty-eight, and duly organized and
filed these, happy, as he reported, that he now had six

empty drawers for additional maps when received. But let him tell his own story of the beginning of the great enterprise:

On completion of the rough index I was directed by the officer in charge to ascertain the best method of reducing maps, as it is the intention to reduce all maps to the smallest scale consistent with the clearness. Also to inquire into the general subject of map making. To carry out these instructions I at different times consulted with the following gentlemen or their subordinates, who very kindly gave me such information as they possessed on the subject, viz: the Chief of Engineers, U.S.A., the Superintendent of the U.S. Coast Survey, the Superintendent of the Geological Survey, Messrs. Bartole and McDougal, engravers, and Mr. Peters, photolithographer, all of this city. They explained to me the whole subject of map making, and showed me the different processes in practical operation. . . . I learned that reduction by photography is the best, cheapest, and the only practical method in general use. . . .

Maps engraved on steel or copper are the best. Steel is more durable when the original plate is used in printing, but owing to its great liability to injury from rust is but seldom employed. Fifty thousand copies can be printed from one plate, and about the same number from a copper plate steel faced by the electroplating process. There is a very wide difference of opinion as to the durability of copper plates, when printed from directly, the estimates varying between two and twenty thousand copies. The usual practice is to preserve the Original plates and print from the electrotypes or by transfer to stone. . . . Engraving on stone ranks next in quality, but is little practiced at the present time. . . .

Separate maps of the eleven Southern States, parts of nine border States, and a large number of maps illustrating campaigns, battles &c., will be required in the Atlas in addition to those noted to appear therein.

From an official list prepared at the War Department in 1873, it appears that there were about three hundred and fifty battles and engagements fought during the

war in addition to a large number of actions and skirmishes.

All the battles and engagements and many of the
actions and skirmishes should be illustrated by maps. I
think it is safe to say that about four hundred maps will
be required for the Atlas, in addition to those appearing
in the volumes. Allowing an average of four maps to a
plate, one hundred plates or sets of plates would be
required. . . . [Letter to Colonel H. M. Lazelle, June
21, 1889, in *National Archives,* Cartographic Records
Division.]

In the end, the *Atlas* contained slightly over one thousand
maps and one hundred and eighty-one plates.

Captain Cowles, to give him the rank which he attained in 1891, addressed himself to the preparation of
the *Atlas* with an admirable combination of energy and
conscientiousness. The first, and elementary, task was to
assemble the maps themselves. Some seven hundred and
fifty had already been accumulated; it was necessary to
eliminate duplicates, redraw the crude and the inadequate, correct errors, reduce the over-large and enlarge
the over-small, color the terrain and the opposing army
units, add general maps of regions, military divisions,
and departments, and take care of a hundred other details. A steady stream of letters flowed from Captain
Cowles's office: Would the postmaster at Fredericksburg
check the spelling of places on the Peninsula? Would the
Coast Survey be good enough to forward the map of
Chickamauga with all relevant correspondence? Would
Colonel Owens be good enough to tell what he knows of
the history of the map of Drewey's Bluff? Would the
postmaster at Verdon indicate whether the correct spelling is Lowry, Lowery, or Lowrey? Would General Beaure-
gard identify a series of photographs of Charleston Harbor? Would the United States Geological Survey make
available one of its maps? Would Captain Hotchkiss correct the place names on the map of Winchester? Would

Captain Hotchkiss clear up the position of General Gordon at Hanover Junction? Would Captain Hotchkiss come in for a little talk about some of his maps? In the end it was Hotchkiss who helped more than anyone else, and over one hundred of the maps in the *Atlas* bear his name.

By good fortune the actual engraving and printing of the *Atlas* was entrusted to the firm of Julius Bien, in New York. Bien himself, one of the neglected artists of his generation, was one of the many Forty-Eighters who brought to the new world not only his passion for freedom but technical skills as well. He soon established a fine reputation for craftsmanship in New York City. An interview with Secretary of War Jefferson Davis gave him the contract for making the maps for the great Pacific Railroad surveys of the fifties, and his map of the Trans-Mississippi West was for long to remain authoritative. On the eve of the war he began to reissue Audubon's *Birds of America*. During the war itself he equipped a field map printing outfit, which went with Sherman from Atlanta to the sea. In the generation after the war the firm of Julius Bien had almost a monopoly on providing maps and plates for the government. It did the maps for all the Censuses from 1870 to 1900; the Geological Atlas of Colorado; the Atlas to accompany the Geological Exploration of the Fortieth Parallel; the Atlas for the Geographical Surveys west of the Hundredth Meridian, and many others. We do not know who selected him to make the *Atlas* but it was a happy choice. More and more Cowles came to rely on Julius Bien; his confidence was never misplaced. By 1892 he was writing Mr. Bien somewhat angularly that "your work is very creditably executed as a whole and reflects on your firm." As the preparation of the *Atlas* advanced, ever more responsibility was placed in the practiced hands of Mr. Bien. At the very end came a letter perhaps a little less formal than most: would Mr.

Bien be good enough to hurry as much as possible, as Captain Cowles would like to complete the *Atlas* before he severed his connection with the War Records Office on August 30, 1895.

Mr. Bien would, and Captain Cowles had the pleasure of completing the great undertaking which he had inaugurated.

HOW THE LOST CAUSE WAS LOST

LOOKING back now through the mists of 100 years at the prodigious story of Gettysburg and Vicksburg, we are lost in admiration for the gallantry of those who led the ranks of gray in what we have come to call "the Lost Cause." And we know just when it was lost. It was lost in those fateful days of July, 1863, when Lee's bold thrust into Pennsylvania, which was to have threatened the capital and brought recognition of the Confederacy from Britain and France, was blunted and turned back, and when Vicksburg fell and the Father of Waters went again unvexed to the sea. It was high tide and ebb tide; it was the beginning of the end.

So, at least, most of us suppose. As we contemplate the fall of the Confederacy, we conclude that it was indeed inevitable and that the Confederacy was but a dream:

> *Woe! woe! is us, how strange and sad,*
> *That all our glorious visions fled,*

SOURCE: *The New York Times* (August 4, 1963). © 1963 by The New York Times Company. Reprinted by permission.

Have left us nothing real but our dead,
In the land where we were dreaming.

To most Americans it is inconceivable that the Civil
War should have had any outcome but that registered at
Appomattox. It is inconceivable that the territory which
now constitutes the United States should have been frag-
mented—like that of Latin America—into 20 states. It is
inconceivable that the Confederacy should have made
good its bid for independent nationhood.

But the doctrine of inevitability confronts us with two
insuperable difficulties. If it was clear from the beginning
that the South must lose, how can we explain the fact
that men like Jefferson Davis, Judah P. Benjamin, R. B.
Rhett, Howell Cobb and scores of others, men who were
upright, virtuous, intelligent and humane, were prepared
to lead their people to certain destruction? If defeat was
inevitable, they must have discerned this, too, and their
conduct takes on the character of criminal imbecility.
And second, how can we explain the widespread assumption in Europe—and even in parts of the North—that the
South would make good her bid for independence? How
does it happen that so many otherwise sensible and judicious men were misled?

It is not too much to say that the South held—or
appeared to hold—at least two trump cards in 1861. The
first was what we would now call grand strategy or ultimate war aims. For the fact is that the Confederacy did
not need to win in order to win; it was enough if she held
the field long enough to weary the North with the war.
But the North, in order to win, had to conquer the South,
had to invade and hold an area as great as Western
Europe minus Italy and Scandinavia—an achievement
as yet without parallel in modern history. The Confederacy could afford to lose all the battles and all the campaigns if only she could persuade the North that the price
of victory was too high. The South asked merely to be left

alone, and she proposed to make the war so costly that the North would in the end prefer to leave her alone. After all, the American colonies, and the United Netherlands, had won their independence against even heavier odds than those which faced the Confederacy.

And this suggests the second trump card: foreign intervention. The leaders of the Confederacy had read well the history of the American Revolution, or had heard it from their fathers and their grandfathers—for the Virginians of 1860 were psychologically closer to the generation of Washington than were the Yankees of Massachusetts to the generation of Sam Adams. They knew that the intervention of France and then of other European nations had turned the tide in favor of the Americans, and they assumed that history would repeat itself. They counted with confidence on the intervention of Britain and France—intervention at a practical level on behalf of cotton, intervention at a higher level on behalf of freedom and self-determination.

Quite aside from these two major strategic considerations, the South held other advantages. She commanded interior lines and therefore the ability to shift her smaller forces rapidly from one front to another. She fought on the defensive, and that position (so it was thought) more than made up for her numerical inferiority, since offensive operations, with their implacable demands of transportation, supply, and occupation, required a greater superiority than she felt the Union forces could muster. She had a long and deeply indented coastline, one which presented almost insuperable obstacles to a successful blockade—and, after all, the Union Navy was not above contempt. She had, in her 3,000,000 Negro slaves, a large and, on the whole, loyal labor force which might relieve Southern whites of the many civilian duties and permit them to fight in the ranks. She had, at the beginning, the best generals and a long military tradition. And she boasted—mistakenly as it proved—a broader and deeper unity than the heterogeneous North.

With all these advantages, why did the South lose? Since 1865, students and historians have speculated about this question but no one has answered it. Curiously enough, the leaders of the Lost Cause had little to say about the reasons for defeat. The greatest of them, R. E. Lee, preserved a dignified silence after Appomattox. President Davis wrote two ponderous volumes but they say nothing about the underlying causes of defeat except to blame his political enemies. Vice President Stephens also produced two unreadable volumes on the Confederacy and the war, but failed conspicuously to speculate on the question (in his case, speculation might have proved too embarrassing). Judah P. Benjamin, the most philosophical mind in the Confederate government, might have given us a really penetrating analysis of the problem, but he chose to forget his American past in a more glamorous English present.

Nor do the lesser figures help us much. The literature is voluminous but mostly elegiac and almost all of it is unreflective. Perhaps the Southerner of that generation was, as Henry Adams wrote of his classmate Rooney Lee, by nature unreflective: "Strictly," said Adams, "the Southerner had no mind; he had temperament. He was not a scholar, he had no intellectual training, he could not analyze an idea, and he could not even conceive of admitting two."

Or, more probably, reflection on the responsibility for so great a catastrophe was simply too uncomfortable. And as for the Northerners, by and large they were content with victory, or with easy assumptions about their superiority in arms and in men, or the righteousness of their cause, or the wickedness of the South, or the preference of Providence for the Union.

Why *did* the South lose? Was it because the Confederacy was hopelessly outnumbered? Until 1864, it was able to put almost as many soldiers into battle as the Union— in fact, the South had a numerical superiority at First Bull Run, Pea Ridge, Gaines's Mill, Seven Days, Corinth, Chickamauga, Peach Tree Creek, and Atlanta. Was it for reasons of finance? Lack of money had not prevented the Americans from making good their bid for independence. (And besides, a financial explanation merely begs another question: *Why* did the Confederacy lack money?) Was it due to poor transportation? The South had a much smaller railroad mileage than the North, but she enjoyed interior lines and the advantage of a system of inland waterways. Southern transportation facilities were not, in fact, inadequate in themselves—or at least not irremediably inadequate. The real question is, why did the South fail to use what she had or to develop what she needed?

Was defeat attributable to the failure of the Confederacy to win the border states—Maryland, Kentucky, Missouri? These were, after all, slave states and Southern in culture and social structure. There was every reason to suppose that they would throw in their lot with the South.

> *"Come! For thy shield is bright and strong,*
> *Come! for thy dalliance does thee wrong,*
> *Maryland, my Maryland."*

But she did not come, nor did the other border states— though Kentucky and Missouri were represented in the Confederate Congress! Why not? Was it lack of military skill or political prescience, or simply bad luck that explains why this calculation—like so many others—went wrong?

Or was the underlying fault perhaps, in Jefferson Davis—so brittle, so temperamental, so arrogant? He took the conduct of the war into his own hands; he interfered with the military; he had favorites (like the wretched Braxton Bragg) and enemies (like the brilliant Joseph Johnston). He alienated state Governors and Congressmen and he never won the affections of the Southern people. Yet on balance Davis emerges as a reasonably good President—probably as good as any the Confederacy could have selected at that time. He was tireless, high-minded, courageous, intelligent, indomitable and more often right on major issues than his critics. The real question is why there were so few alternatives to Jefferson Davis.

Or was the South beaten by the blockade? This is perhaps the favorite of all explanations, for ever since Mahan, seapower has been a fashionable key to history. But at the beginning of the war, the North had only an excuse for a navy; not until 1863 was the blockade effective. Why did not the Confederacy bring in whatever she needed before that time? Why did she not utilize her swift privateers to the best advantage? And why, for that matter, were Britain and France willing to respect what was, for a long time, a mere paper blockade? If Cotton was King, why did Europeans refuse to recognize its sovereignty? If Cotton was *not* King, why did Southerners so delude themselves?

When we have considered, and dismissed, these surface reasons for the failure of the Confederacy, we come to more fundamental causes. Three of these, all interrelated, command our attention.

The first was the failure of Southern nationalism. Almost all the ingredients of nationalism were there—indeed, the Confederacy in 1860 had more of the ingredients of nationalism than the Colonies in 1775—but somehow the Confederacy never really became a nation. For all its passionate devotion to Dixie Land, it seemed to lack a sense of nationalism and the will to nationalism. Given the circumstances of its birth, this is not surprising. The Southern states had broken away from the old

Union because the Federal Government—so they alleged
—threatened their rights, and they defiantly founded
their new nation on states' rights and state sovereignty.
The new nation was therefore based on a repudiation of
nationalism.

Even its political institutions reflected this, perhaps
unconsciously. Military leadership in the South was
splendid, but political leadership was weak and vacillat-
ing. The Confederacy had its Lee and its Jackson to
match—perhaps to outmatch—Grant and Sherman, but
where was its Lincoln? Where for that matter were its
Seward, its Stanton, its Stevens, its Sumner, its Trumbull; its diplomats like Charles Francis Adams; its war
governors like Andrew of Massachusetts or Morton of
Indiana? There were local factions but no political parties, and therefore no safety valve for political discontent.
There were strong state supreme courts, but, notwithstanding the provision of the Confederate constitution,
Congress never created a Confederate Supreme Court.

State sovereignty is not necessarily fatal to nationalism
or to union in time of peace and order, when no grave
problems confront a government and no stern crises challenge the people. Had the North permitted the "wayward
sisters to depart in peace," the Confederacy might have
survived long enough to develop the essential institutions, political habits and administrative practices. But to
build a nation on state sovereignty in time of war is to
build upon a foundation of quicksand.

The second fundamental cause of failure was, in fact,
this very issue of states' rights, which steadily eroded the
strength of the Confederacy. State Representatives at
Richmond devoted their energies to thwarting Jefferson
Davis. Vice President Stephens retired to his Georgia
home to wage relentless war on the President. State supreme courts nullified Confederate laws, and there was,
as we have seen, no Confederate Supreme Court to which

to appeal. States put their own interests ahead of the interests of the embryo nation. Even in the first year of the war, the states jealously held on to their arms and supplies. Had they surrendered them to the Confederacy at the beginning of the war, it could have put 600,000 men into the field instead of 400,000, and that might have made all the difference.

State governors like Brown of Georgia and Vance of North Carolina exempted thousands of their citizens from conscription and their judges protected deserters and refugees from capture and restoration to the ranks of the Confederate armies. The governor of Mississippi exempted over 4,500 militia officers and others in his state from the operation of the conscription laws, and the governor of Alabama almost the same number.

All through the war, state governors withheld desperately needed supplies. Thus Brown of Georgia not only kept his Georgia troops well supplied with uniforms and blankets but had a surplus in his warehouses sufficient to have outfitted the whole of Lee's army—and kept it there! At a time when "Lee's Miserables" were going barefoot and freezing in the terrible trenches of Petersburg, Governor Vance of North Carolina had 5,000 complete uniforms and an equal quantity of shoes and blankets in his warehouses—and kept them there!

States' rights, instead of being the rock on which the nation was built, was the reef on which the nation foundered. There is a moral here, even for our own time.

The third fundamental cause of Southern defeat was slavery itself—that "peculiar institution," as the South euphemistically called it. It was slavery that the war was ultimately about; it was slavery that ultimately doomed the South to defeat. For it was slavery that decisively prevented the one move which might have saved the South, even after Vicksburg and Gettysburg—European intervention. As late as 1863, British aristocrats—a

Cecil, a Halifax, a Gregory, a Linsay, a Vansittart—organized the Southern Independence Association which dedicated itself to intervention. It was in the summer of 1863 that the British navy yards were building the famous Laird rams that almost got away—almost, but not quite!

Had Britain intervened to break the blockade—and France would have followed her lead, and Mexico, of course—there is every likelihood that the Confederacy would have won independence. With Britain ready to provide the Confederacy with money, arms, munitions, food and drugs, and ready to buy her cotton and other produce, the Confederacy could have fought on indefinitely, just as the Americans did once they had supplies and money from France after 1777. And had the Union government responded to such intervention by a declaration of war—as it almost certainly would have done—it would probably have signed its own death warrant.

What prevented intervention from abroad? Not the failure of the South on the battlefield, for that failure was not decisive until after the midsummer of 1863. And it was not sympathy for the government of the Union, for there was very little of that in the ruling circles of Britain or France. No, more than anything else, it was slavery. The upper classes might be sympathetic to the Confederacy, but the powerful middle and working classes were passionately on the side of the North. It was not merely that the North represented democracy—although that was a consideration; it was, far more, that the South represented slavery. Public opinion, that newly emerging and still amorphous thing, simply would not tolerate going in on the side of slavery.

But, it will be asked, why did not the South see what we now see? Why did not Southerners see the necessity of a strong national government in time of war and create one? Why did they not see the pernicious conse-

The Search for a Usable Past

quences of states' rights in time of crisis and restrict them? Why did they not see the blight of slavery and move against it, move to win public opinion abroad by some dramatic gesture of gradual emancipation?

Here we come to something very fundamental—to the psychology, the philosophy associated, perhaps inevitably associated, with slavery.

Slavery was the foundation of the South, and slavery carried with it the enslavement of the mind of a people. For thirty years the South had felt herself misunderstood, condemned and beleaguered. For thirty years she had rallied her resources to defend the "peculiar institution," and she had finally convinced herself that slavery was not a necessary evil but a positive good, not a curse but a blessing. She realized, however, that she was almost alone in this opinion and, feeling herself increasingly isolated, she withdrew into her own intellectual and moral fortress.

Whoever criticized slavery in the South was an enemy of society, a traitor to the Southern way of life. Preachers who questioned slavery from their pulpits were deprived of their churches; teachers who criticized slavery were driven out of their colleges and universities; editors who dared raise their voices against slavery saw their presses destroyed. If the United States mails carried abolition or antislavery literature, the mails were rifled, the pernicious literature burned. Libraries were purged of offensive books—even Hinton Helper's *The Impending Crisis of the South* was publicly burned. The whole South, in short, closed ranks to defend and exalt the "peculiar institution."

Now when you prevent the free discussion of the greatest of public issues, you prevent the discussion of almost all issues. When you drive out critics, you leave behind the noncritics. When you silence dissent, you assure only approval. When you intimidate criticism, you discourage the habit of critical inquiry. When you stop agitation, you guarantee complacency. We have learned in our own time the price that a society pays when it intimidates the independent mind, when it silences criticism.

The habit of independent inquiry and criticism all but disappeared in the South of the eighteen-fifties and sixties—and has not yet really returned. There was no real discussion of slavery, and because there was no discussion there was no probing of alternatives. There was no real debate over secession—at least, not on the principles at stake. As Southern political thought had gone slowly bankrupt after Calhoun, so Southern political discussion went bankrupt—in the Confederate Congress and in the newspapers of the Confederacy. There were a few bold spirits who questioned secession; there were some who doubted the ability of the South to win a war against the North; there were some who saw that slavery would become the Achilles' heel of the Confederacy. But there was no discussion of real issues, as in the North, and no statesman to lead the people out of the labyrinth in which they found themselves and on to a high plateau from which they could see their life and their society in perspective.

There is, perhaps, a certain poetic justice in all this. The Confederacy, which was founded on state sovereignty, was destroyed by state sovereignty. The Confederacy, which was founded on slavery, was destroyed by the state of mind which slavery imposed upon its other victims—the white people of the South. The failure of the Confederacy was ultimately a monument not to a failure of resolution or courage or will, but to a failure of intelligence and morality.

THE HOPE OF REFORM,
1890–1917

I

BY 1912 Eastern liberalism was swerving to the left. That year Walter Weyl championed the New Democracy— what with the New Nationalism and the New Freedom and even the *New Republic*, everything was new then— and his opening chapter furnished a mordant analysis of the "disenchantment of America." The revelations of the Pujo Committee provided abundant support to the theory of disenchantment, and those who boggled at government reports could read the same story, with no perceptible improvement in style, in Dreiser's *The Financier*. The undismayed Roosevelt, always radical during election years, led his shouting followers out of the Grand Old Party to some Armageddon where they prepared to battle for the Lord, and for T. R. At Baltimore Woodrow Wilson, with the aid of the veteran Bryan, nosed out the noncommittal Champ Clark for the Democratic nomination, and that November the New Freedom officially sup-

SOURCE: *Literary History of the United States*, ed. Robert E. Spiller et al., Vol. II. Copyright 1948, The Macmillan Company. Reprinted by permission.

planted the New Nationalism and the promise of American life seemed not hopelessly beyond fulfillment. The Eastern intellectuals—older men like Wilson and Brandeis and Villard, and younger men like Croly and Weyl and Lippmann—prepared to catch up with the homespun Western radicals after a lapse of only twenty years.

There was, to be sure, little that was new about the stirrings and strivings of the second decade of the new century, except the stage on which they were presented and the accent in which they were expressed. Even here the change was but relative. Jacob Riis, after all, had told how the other half lived, and Henry George had campaigned for the mayoralty of New York, and De Leon had taught socialism at Columbia University back in the eighties and nineties. Nor was there much the Pujo Committee could uncover that had not been known to Henry Demarest Lloyd, or much the *New Republic* could say that had not been anticipated by Flower's *Arena,* while men like Altgeld and Weaver and "Sockless" Jerry Simpson had known the realities of disenchantment long before Croly learned the meaning of the word. Indeed it is difficult to discover anything in the New Nationalism or the New Freedom that was not explicit or implicit in the Populism and the socialism of the nineties, except respectability. Otherwise, the distinction was quantitative rather than qualitative: whereas Bryan had persuaded but six and one-half million voters, Wilson, Roosevelt, and Debs, together, attracted more than eleven million. These figures dramatized the fact that public opinion had at last become aware of the problems that had confronted America ever since the decade of the nineties.

For in the second decade of the twentieth century the nation faced a crisis in the conflict of forces within itself that had first declared themselves in the nineties, and creative energies were released, with their doubts as well as their confidence, into literature and criticism. The outlines of that conflict had by then emerged clearly and even boldly. On the one side lay an America predominantly agrarian, concerned with domestic problems, conforming—intellectually at least—to the political, economic, and moral principles inherited from the eighteenth century: an America still in the making, physically and politically, an America on the whole self-confident, self-contained, and conscious of its unique character and of a unique destiny. On the other side lay the modern America, predominantly urban and industrial, inextricably involved in world economy and politics, troubled with the social and economic problems that had long been thought peculiarly the burden of the Old World, desperately trying to accommodate its traditional institutions and habits of thought to conditions new and in part alien.

II

The New Freedom (1913–17) was the climax of the age of reform—the following years were anti-climax. That age (1890–1917) was experimental rather than dogmatic, given to exploration rather than to the establishment of sovereign claims. It was a time of protest and change, of the rejection of what was old and the championship of what was new, of speculation and experiment. There was boundless enthusiasm for good causes and compulsive tinkering with the political machinery. Armies of reformers advanced upon the battlements of vested interests, bands of humanitarians waged guerrilla warfare upon every form of social injustice, visionaries imagined felicitous Utopias and some even indulged in them, less felicitously. There was a youthful ardor to weed out abuses, democratize government, redistribute property, humanize industry, improve the lot of the workingman and the farmer, rescue the victims of social in-

justice, elevate the moral tone of society. It was the day
of the music makers and dreamers of dreams, of world
seekers—though rarely of world forsakers. The great figures in politics were reformers, the great movements
were reform movements. Bryan, La Follette, Roosevelt,
Wilson, and Debs bestrode the national political scene;
Altgeld, Tom Johnson, "Golden Rule" Jones, Hazen Pingree, Charles Aycock, Ignatius Donnelly, "Bloody Bridles"
Waite, Tom Watson, Joseph U'Ren, gave color to state
and local politics.

The era was ushered in by the Populist Revolt in the
nineties, bowed out by the New Freedom and the crusade
to make a democratic world. Agrarian reformers captured the Democratic party, and urban progressives the
Republican; socialism became respectable and was taken
up by the churches, and settlement houses blossomed in
every slum. New England liberals emerged to take up the
battle for the Negro and the Indian and, after Manila
Bay, a crusade against imperialism enlisted the intellectual elite of the whole country. There were countless
other crusades: for temperance, for conservation, for
peace, for woman suffrage, for children's rights, for civil
service reform. The conscience of the nation was troubled, and each exposure of sin or neglect brought contri-
tion and penance. In those years Americans learned *How
the Other Half Lives,* heard *The Bitter Cry of the Children,* were shocked by *The Shame of the Cities,* outraged
by the *Treason of the Senate,* revolted by the fate of *The
Daughters of the Poor,* initiated into the iniquities of
Frenzied Finance, alarmed by *The Greatest Trust in the
World,* came at last to understand the dichotomy of
Wealth Against Commonwealth. As a result, laws to clear
slums, protect women and children, curb monopolies,
supervise insurance companies, free the public lands,
save the forests, frustrate corruption, and safeguard the
ballot box crowded the statute books.

All this was eloquent of optimism. Despair leads to apathy or revolution, it is the incorrigibly hopeful who spend their energies in reform. Though the bright promise of American life seemed to be fading, there was no inclination to despair of the Republic, to abandon democracy, or even to challenge a capitalist economy. There was, on the contrary, an all but universal confidence in the beneficent workings of democracy and of the profit system—if only they could be operated honestly and by virtuous men. Carnegie's lyrical description of American material prosperity was, after all, entitled *Triumphant Democracy.* There was nothing fundamentally wrong with American institutions; it was merely that abuses had crept into them, that they had been exploited by shortsighted men to selfish purposes. What was needed was not the abandonment of democracy, but more democracy, not the abolition of private property, but the wider and more equitable distribution of property. "The evil," said Woodrow Wilson in his first inaugural address, "has come with the good, and much fine gold has been corroded." The task was to get rid of the evil and hold fast to what was good.

This is what explains the crusade for Social Justice, for the Square Deal, for the New Freedom, for all those catchwords and phrases which confessed a reassuring— and perhaps a naïve—optimism. Was democracy failing? The answer was to double the electorate by giving votes to women. Was there corruption at the ballot box? The Australian ballot, or formidable corrupt-practices acts, would eliminate that. Were legislatures deaf to the voice of the people? The initiative and the referendum would once more give expression to that voice. Was the Senate a stronghold of privilege? Elect senators by direct vote, and that body would become a stronghold of democracy. Was Congress caught in its own cumbersome machinery? A revival of the Jacksonian doctrine of presidential leader-

ship would make the cumbersome machinery of government work. Did bosses manipulate political parties?
Direct primaries would circumvent them. Were wealth
and privilege entrenched in the judiciary, as Jefferson
had warned? The recall of judicial decisions, or even of
judges, would assure a democratic interpretation of the
Constitution.

In the economic arena, too, there was confidence in the
soundness of institutions and the virtue of the majority
of men. Roosevelt could talk of "malefactors of great
wealth," but he distinguished sharply between "good" and
"bad" trusts, and the moral distinction was carried over
into the judicial realm as "reasonable" or "unreasonable"
restraint of trade. The Grangers had denounced the railroads as the Great Monopoly, and the Populists had demanded that they be publicly owned; but these demands
were easily watered down to regulation and supervision,
and Roosevelt—who better than any other figure typified
the optimism and opportunism of the reform movement
—compromised even here. There was much ado about
the maldistribution of wealth, but no attack upon wealth
itself, and if the reformers were not quieted by Carnegie's
admission that it was a disgrace to die rich they were
willing enough to settle for income and inheritance taxes.
Communism was not unknown, but it completely lacked
the native roots of the earlier Utopian movements; and it
was the Debs wing of the Socialist Party, not the radical
De Leon wing, that won.

All this suggests that the reform movement was thoroughgoing in criticism, but opportunistic in its tactics. It
formulated no logical system, subscribed to no universal
principles. It accepted in practice Justice Holmes' dictum, "Legislation may begin where an evil begins," and
had put a touching faith in the efficacy of legislation. It
was romantic in its philosophical implications, but realistic
in its recognition of the economic basis of politics. It was,

above all, secular—even the Christian Socialists seemed more socialist than Christian, more concerned, that is, with the material than with the spiritual welfare of men. It lacked, or rejected, the basic philosophy that had animated the reformers of the 1840's—the passionate religious conviction of the identity of man with God, of the infinite worth of every human soul. It was more concerned, indeed, with equality of income than with equality of soul, and demanded justice in the name of the Declaration of Independence and the Populist platform rather than of the New Testament.

There was disintegration, but no reintegration. Pragmatism, for all its merits, offered not stability but an open universe and the chance to make ideals truth; and most of the reformers were pragmatists even when they used the vocabulary of mechanistic determinism. Fiske, to be sure, illuminated history with Cosmic Philosophy, but Fiske's day was past, and Henry Adams had already traced the explosion of unity into multiplicity. Veblen was profound but scarcely constructive, and Lester Ward, who was constructive, was largely neglected. Holmes, greatest of American jurists, had no confidence in abstract notions of Law or Justice and no faith in reform, but merely an unassailable conviction that he was not God, and that in a democracy people had a right to make fools of themselves. Even criticism in the grand manner had lost its earlier assurance; it was significant that when Bryce came to portray America he was descriptive and tentative where Tocqueville had been analytical and magisterial, and that even Bryce seemed profound by comparison with native American interpreters.

By 1912 the reform movement began to seem curiously opportunistic and fragmentary. The agrarian reformers were not, on the whole, concerned with the welfare of the workers. Labor, especially after the demise of the Knights and the advent of the Federation, seemed completely self-centered and even boasted its opportunism; its leaders rejected Marxist philosophers and asserted: "We have no ultimate ends. We are going on from day to day." Many of the muckrakers were reformers only fortuitously, and few of them were inspired by ideals or sustained by convictions. It was not surprising that Ida Tarbell, who had laid bare the malpractices of Standard Oil, should later write a laudatory biography of Elbridge Gary; that John Spargo, who had first heard the bitter cry of the children, should end as an implacable opponent of the New Deal; that Burton Hendrick, who exposed the iniquities of life insurance, should celebrate the virtues of Andrew Carnegie. It was characteristic enough that Moorfield Storey should champion the cause of the Negro but bitterly oppose the elevation of Brandeis to the Supreme Court and the admission of Jews to Harvard University; that Tom Watson should fight for the tenant farmer and the mill hand, but inflame his followers against Negroes, Jews, and Catholics; that William Allen White should expose the corruption of politics and of wealth, but oppose Bryan, Wilson, and F. D. Roosevelt. Bryan was radical enough when it came to banks and railroads, but reactionary in matters of religion and education; Thedore Roosevelt enunciated reform principles, but exhibited distaste at their practical application; even Wilson, who spoke eloquently of the New Freedom, acquiesced in the suppression of freedom of speech and of the press during the war.

Because the reform movement lacked a pervasive and sustaining philosophy there is about it a depressing inconclusiveness. Many of the reformers lacked staying power; few of them were concerned with the whole scene. They dissipated their strength, they wandered off on strange bypaths, they compromised. Their followers were even more unreliable. For most of them a touch of prosperity was all but fatal. With an increase in the price of wheat the agrarian revolt collapsed. Gold in the Klondike ended the free-silver crusade. Labor was persuaded by the argument of the full dinner pail. Southern deserters came trooping back to the ranks of the Bourbon Democracy when the bogy of race equality was dangled before their horrified eyes. The succession of Roosevelt by Taft in 1908, the readiness to jettison La Follette for Roosevelt in 1911, the disintegration of the Progressive Party after 1913, all cast a curious light on the sincerity or the intelligence of the reform movement as it entered the new century.

III

Even before the opening of the new century the geographical center of reform had shifted from the Middle Border to the urban East. If, as Denis Brogan has observed, farmers confessed to few ills that dollar wheat wouldn't cure, the Eastern reformers recognized few that would not yield to Honesty and Philanthropy. These end-of-the-century reformers—men like Norton and Atkinson and Storey in Boston, like Gilder and Low and Roosevelt in New York—constituted a distinguished group. Their radicalism, however, was tempered by good manners and by a total inability to understand violence. They were the heirs of Godkin and Curtis rather than of Horace Greeley or Wendell Phillips. They had gone to the best schools— one sometimes feels that a degree from Harvard was a prerequisite to admission to their club—associated with the best people, read the *Nation* and the *Independent,* and knew poverty only at second hand. Their intentions were laudable, but their vision was limited and their interests narrow. They thought of reform almost exclusively in terms of politics, and they were inclined to think that honesty in politics was the sum of political science. Good government, they thought, would follow inevitably from the civil service system and gentlemen in politics. They had the same abiding faith in the efficacy of noble moral sentiments that Wells ascribes to the English liberals of the same period in *The New Machiavelli*. When they thought of the civil service they thought of England. When they thought of gentlemen they thought of one another, and though animated by no vulgar ambition for office, they were not unwilling, from time to time, to sacrifice themselves to the public good.

They had no interest in the agrarian crusade, little sympathy for organized labor, and they thought panaceas like the Single Tax or Bellamy's Nationalism as eccentric as Mormonism. Free silver they held to be simple dishonesty, and outbreaks like the Haymarket riot and the Pullman strike filled them with horror. They were equally fearful of socialism, communism, and anarchism, and inclined to place any economic heresy indiscriminately in one of these categories. For men like Bryan and Weaver they had only contempt. Altgeld and Debs they damned as un-American.

Yet they had both sympathy for the poor and the underprivileged and a strong feeling of social responsibility. They were ready enough to remedy injustice or alleviate misery, when made aware of them by a Jacob Riis or a Jane Addams. Like the Western agrarians they opposed trusts and protective tariffs, approved government regulation of railways, urged the conservation of natural resources, and worked to wipe out slums, protect women and children, ameliorate race relations, humanize industry, and "socialize" Christianity. It was the humanitarian strain that was most pronounced in them. Because most of them were economically immature, had been raised in a Christian tradition of charity, and were heirs to the social tradition of *noblesse oblige,* they turned instinctively to good works rather than to the state. They engaged in earnest efforts to organize charity, help newsboys, maintain lodging houses, save delinquent girls, rescue homeless waifs, enforce Sunday closing hours, eliminate the sweatshop, mitigate the rigors of the penal code.

The best representative of this Eastern group is its most prominent member—the ebullient Theodore Roosevelt. He was, like most of the good-government enthusiasts, primarily a moral crusader. His earliest venture into politics had been on behalf of tenement house reform— reform nullified by the courts. Under the tutelage of Jacob Riis he had seen Mulberry Bend and Poverty Lane, the sweatshops, the vice and crime of the lower East Side. He had fought the machine, and been rewarded with an appointment as civil service commissioner. His enthusiasm for reform was temporarily dampened by the radicalism of Bryan and then deflected into navalism and nationalism. Later, as governor of the Empire State, he renewed his attack upon the bosses and consolidated his reputation as a liberal.

In Roosevelt, even before he came to the Presidency, we see harmoniously blended the qualities characteristic of the Eastern reformers: optimism and opportunism; distrust of economic, and confidence in political, panaceas; sentimentality and superficiality. Alert, zealous, and upright, he no sooner saw an evil or an infirmity than he exposed and excoriated it. He was against corruption, bosses, those who betrayed the public trust or looted the public domain; he opposed trusts and monopolies, impure foods and drugs, the exploitation of women and children; he was for honesty in politics and the Square Deal and conservation and red-blooded Americanism. Elihu Root once chided him for thinking that he had written the Ten Commandments. Sensitive as he was to wrongdoing, he could never see that particular injustices were the natural product of an inequitable economy or believe that any evil was so deep-seated that it could not be cured by tinkering with the political machinery.

Because Roosevelt compromised on every important issue and evaded every dangerous issue, the transition to Taft seemed natural enough. Yet it was the Taft administration that brought home to the nation the failure of the reform movement. For while Roosevelt sounded like a progressive even when he acted like a conservative, it was Taft's misfortune to sound like a conservative even when he acted like a progressive. By the end of the first decade of the century it was clear that the Roosevelt-Taft brand of progressivism was inadequate to the needs of the day. With all the frenzy of trust busting, the trusts were stronger in 1910 than they had been in 1890 or 1900. With all the fever of railroad regulation, the railroads still managed to evade effective regulation of rates. With all the denunciation of malefactors of great wealth, the distribution of wealth was more inequitable at the end than at the beginning of the period. The protective tariff was untouched; centralized control of banking, unaffected; even conservation—the most sincere of all Roosevelt's reforms—proved woefully inadequate; the forests and soil of the nation disappeared with terrifying rapidity.

With the election of Wilson in 1913 the Progressive Movement reached such maturity as it ever attained. Both the country and Wilson had caught up with the radicalism of the nineties and were prepared to do, now, what should have been done twenty years earlier, as well as to make clear what had to be done twenty years later. Wilson, for all his academic antecedents, his passion for Mill and Bagehot, his curious reluctance to include Jefferson in his calendar of great Americans, his hostility to socialism and Populism, proved a far more realistic, thoroughgoing, and idealistic reformer than Theodore Roosevelt—and a far more effective one.

Like Roosevelt, Wilson was a moralist in politics, though his morality was more personal than that of his great rival, more a matter of principles than of good or bad men, more of the New Testament than of the Old. He was a Southern gentleman, brought up on the tenets of Manchester liberalism, Godkin respectability, and Virginian *noblesse oblige*. He had achieved a national reputation by playing the role of St. George with the dragon of corruption in New Jersey; and, except among those dazzled by the brilliance of T. R., the support of liberals and radicals throughout the country came to him almost by default. His mind was logical and consistent, and when he found himself cast in a democratic role he embraced the whole reform program much as he might have embraced the conclusion of a mathematical theorem. To a profound, almost a religious, conviction of the rightness of such causes as he espoused, he added an astonishing capacity for learning, genius in the manipulation of public opinion, and an iron determination to have his way. No wonder that he succeeded where Roosevelt had failed, and no wonder that his success, and the methods whereby he achieved it, outraged his critics and alienated his friends.

It is legitimate to personify the New Freedom in Woodrow Wilson, but a capital error to suppose that it was all Wilson's achievement. Without Wilson the New Freedom might have been inconclusive; without the support of public opinion it would have been impossible. Wilson had behind him not only the Bryan wing of the Democratic Party, but a substantial part of the Progressive Party. The nation, as a whole, was impatient for reform and ardent for leadership. As Wilson said, with characteristic eloquence:

> The Nation has been deeply stirred, stirred by a solemn passion, stirred by the knowledge of wrong, of ideals lost, of government too often debauched and

made an instrument of evil. The feelings with which we
face this new age of right and opportunity sweep across
our heartstrings like some air out of God's own presence, where justice and mercy are reconciled and the
judge and the brother are one.

The country was ready, too, for a positive program which
would translate these noble sentiments into constructive
legislation.

That legislation came, the most comprehensive and
effective program since the days of Polk, and under Wilson's driving leadership the progressive forces came
closer to realizing their objectives than at any earlier time
in our history. The Underwood Tariff, the Federal Reserve System, the Clayton Anti-Trust Act, and Federal
Trade Commission Act, the Adamson eight-hour law, the
income tax, farm relief, child-labor laws, the good-neigh-
bor policy, all brought to a logical and impressive climax
the agitation of a generation of reformers.

Yet even in the years of triumph it was clear that
something had gone out of the reform movement. It had
lost something of that elemental strength, that emotional
fervor, that economic realism, which had characterized it
in the days of Henry George and Peter Altgeld and Tom
Johnson. Most of the leaders who had inspired it and
molded its character had passed from the scene, or di-
verted their energies into different channels. Bryan, to be
sure, retained his simple idealism; but he seemed to have
lost touch with his old associates, and concerned himself
increasingly with temperance and peace. Roosevelt, em-
bittered by the spectacle of Wilson playing the role he
felt rightly his, abandoned himself to vindictiveness and
chauvinism. La Follette lingered on, harsh and irascible,
flouted except in his own state. With the transfer of power
from state to federal government, local reform movements
diminished in importance. The shift was fateful. When
the reactionaries moved in and took over, there were no

local or regional groups powerful enough to counteract them or to maintain laboratories of liberalism in the states.

I V

The First World War marked the end of the great reform movement which had set in about 1890. That the war, and the peace which followed, brought disillusionment is clear; what is not clear is why they should have done so. Historians have neglected the anatomy of reaction after 1918, though the manifestations of that reaction are more obvious than its pathology. Just as the Civil War had canalized all the reform movements of the forties and fifties into the crusade against slavery and disunion, so the First World War canalized the reform movements of the previous decades into an all-embracing crusade for world democracy. After 1917 the interests and energies of the nation were deflected into new channels; prosperity, war, and the post-war problems of international order made most of the issues which had agitated the previous generation seem remote and unreal. Then, too, the inevitable idealization of the crusade for democracy brought an almost equally inevitable reaction into cynicism, while the identification of reform with Wilson himself involved it in the general repudiation of Wilson and Wilsonism. His collapse at Wichita undermined domestic liberalism as well as internationalism. Finally, the wartime emphasis on national unity made it easy to distort even constructive criticism into obstructionism and disloyalty, and seemed to justify not only the deportation hysteria and the Red scares but also state and federal laws destructive of free thought and speech.

The details of the reaction are too familiar to justify repetition. President Harding in 1920 dedicated his administration to the return to "normalcy"; Coolidge in 1924 to the proposition that "the business of America is business"; Hoover in 1928 to the Spencerian concept of "rugged individualism." There was widespread hostility to foreigners and to foreign ideas: indeed, ideas themselves were suspect as somehow contrary to genuine Americanism. Aliens suspected of radical notions were rounded up and deported by the thousand; legislatures were purged; teachers were required to take loyalty oaths, and textbooks revised to conform to the concepts of Americanism entertained by the American Legion and the Daughters of the American Revolution. The Ku Klux Klan, which boasted a membership running into the millions, anticipated Nazi doctrines of Aryan supremacy, and its hooded Klansmen intimidated Catholics, Negroes, Jews, and radicals. Religious fundamentalists sponsored laws against the teaching of evolution in the public schools or the dissemination of information about birth control, and censorship laws emasculated moving pictures, plays, and books. In two notorious cases—those of Sacco and Vanzetti in Massachusetts and of Mooney and Billings in California—the victims were punished more for their radicalism than for any crimes proved against them. The Supreme Court, by its genial reinterpretation of the antitrust laws and its nullification of child labor and minimum wage laws, revealed its sympathy with the reactionary tendencies of the time.

There is no more representative figure in this whole period than William Allen White, of Emporia, Kansas. He tells us, in his charming *Autobiography,* how, in the 1920 convention, he led the Kansas delegation onto the Harding bandwagon.

> I was too heartsick [he wrote] to rise and fight. . . . The whole liberal movement which had risen so proudly under Bryan, Theodore Roosevelt and La Follette, was tired. The spirits of the liberals who called themselves Progressives were bewildered. The fainthearted turned cynics. The faithful were sad and weary.

Not all of them, to be sure; there were some who fought
on. Eugene Debs kept socialism afloat, and even from his
cell in the Federal Penitentiary at Atlanta commanded
almost a million votes. New parties arose in the Northwest, only to be paralyzed by the hostility of bankers and
shippers. That sturdy oak, La Follette, refused to bend to
the new winds howling out of the caves of Mammon and,
in 1924, organized a party that won five million votes—
and disappeared. The *Nation* and the *New Republic* kept
up their shrill clamor for social justice; but only the
faithful read them, and there were few converts. The
liberal movement persisted—without it there could have
been no New Deal—but it was a thin and shallow stream
running beside the mighty torrent of reaction.

The whole intellectual atmosphere changed, too—
more sharply perhaps than in any previous decade in our
history. It was not that the artists and writers acquiesced
in the new dispensation, but that their rejection of it was
so desperate. The novelists and scholars and artists of the
Bryan-Roosevelt era had been in revolt, but their revolt
was not an expression of their alienation from or contempt for their society, but of indignation and pity. Their
protests were designed not to display their own superiority, but to improve the common lot. No one could doubt
their sincerity or integrity. When they spoke the language
of the farm or the street it was because that language was
rightly theirs, not because they wanted to deride it. They
were not afraid of passion or indignation, and they directed these toward the oppressors, not toward the victims of oppression. Though they were often troubled by
the contemplation of the helplessness of man, it never
occurred to them that the only significant thing about
man was his insignificance.

The intellectuals of the twenties revealed the same
talent for exposure, the same revolt against the farm and
the village, the same distaste for Mammon and for Mrs.

Grundy, that had animated their predecessors. But they were more concerned with dissociating themselves from these things than with improving or changing them. They did not suffer, like Garland, with the farmers and villagers but, like Lewis, from them. They were not really rebels, but iconoclasts, which is a very different thing. They were too sure of their own superiority to be greatly troubled by the lot of the average man and woman, and their hatred of injustice was not nearly so lively as their hatred of vulgarity and spiritual decline. Others, like Willa Cather and Ellen Glasgow, turned to the past and celebrated the ideals, the achievements, and the failures of earlier Americans rather than attempting to reform their own times. They served art better than most of their predecessors, but lost force as propagandists for a new order. Where the writers of the nineties found it intolerable that a virtuous people should suffer, the literary rebels of the twenties found it intolerable that virtue should be so dull, and financial success so devoid of spirituality.

For all their rage and frustration, the writers of the twenties, with few exceptions, showed little concern for reform. They were not conspicuous in the fight for the League of Nations or the cleansing of politics or the improvement of the lot of the workingman and the farmer. There were no farm novels like Garland's *A Spoil of Office,* no labor novels like Sinclair's *The Jungle,* no political novels like Churchill's *Mr. Crewe's Career.* One might almost say that, even with the celebration of Freud, there were no sex novels like Crane's *Maggie* or Phillips's *Susan Lennox,* for the interest in sex, as in almost everything else, had become psychoanalytical rather than sociological. It was somehow appropriate that the 1890's should be ushered in with *How the Other Half Lives,* and the 1920's with *Main Street* and *This Side of Paradise.*

LESTER WARD AND THE
WELFARE STATE

I

THE student of the American constitutional system is confronted at the very outset by a paradox. The term "General Welfare" is written twice into the Constitution: once in the Preamble, as part of the broad statement of the purpose of the Constitution itself; once in what may (or may not) be a more restricted sense in section eight, which confers power on the Congress. But the injunction on government to serve the general welfare was not new: the phrase appears twice in the Articles of Confederation as well.

Yet notwithstanding the broad statement of purpose and the more specific grant of power to raise money "to provide for the common defense and general welfare," Congress allowed the authority—if it was indeed an authority—to "provide for the general welfare" to go by

SOURCE: Originally published as the introduction to *Lester Ward and the Welfare State*, copyright © 1966, by Henry Steele Commager, reprinted by permission of the publishers, The Bobbs-Merrill Company, Inc.

default, while courts and commentators alike disputed the meaning of the phrase. When, from time to time, Congress did find it desirable to expand its legislative powers, it did so either under the commerce clause or the war power, authorities whose effectiveness varied (as the Passenger, the Prize, and the Legal Tender cases revealed) with the character of courts and judges.

It is a further paradox that not until the 1880's did Congress begin in any serious fashion to explore these grants of power specified in the Constitution. There had been tariffs, to be sure, and internal improvements, and railroad legislation, and an occasional assertion of power in the territories, but though these exercises of power inspired acute constitutional controversies, they were far from exhausting constitutional potentialities. Not until a century after the original constitutional grant did Congress exercise its power over immigration, or enact a general commerce law, or make even tentative gestures towards the regulation of business and industry. Meantime, the Court had formulated the principle of affectation with a public interest, but when states attempted to test somewhat gingerly the contours and the limits of this principle, courts hastened to discourage them, while the principle itself was held not to apply to Congressional authority.

By this time a constitutional and political crisis was upon the country, a crisis that was to test whether government in America had the power to do those things which governments elsewhere took for granted, and whether such powers as government did have were national or local.

II

Three interrelated aspects of the crisis enlist our attention: the economic, the political, and the philosophical.

The economic crisis was brought on by the rapid and unregulated growth of industry, transportation, and capital, by the chaotic upsurge of cities, by mass immigration —over five million in the eighties—and by concentration in industry, transportation, and capital without a comparable concentration among farmers, workers, or consumers.

The political crisis was the failure, or incompetence, of government to deal with economic problems. The explanation of that failure is complex. It was in part the tradition of dual federalism and the discovery of a twilight zone in which neither state nor federal government operated. It was in part that those who controlled national politics were not interested in effective regulation of the industrial order. It was in part that the courts seemed to be engaged in a kind of conspiracy to paralyze governmental power, denying the states authority to regulate corporate business by a broad construction of the due process clause of the Fourteenth Amendment, and denying the national government authority by a narrow construction of the commerce and the tax clauses.

The philosophical crisis was in some ways the most intransigent. The roots of *laissez faire* went deep into American history and experience. To the generation that won independence from the Old World nothing was more dramatic or more edifying than the contrast between the role of government in the Old World and the New. In the Old World government maintained standing armies and indulged in incessant wars, supported an established church and rigorously enforced religious conformity, levied crushing burdens on the poor for the benefit of the rich, administered one standard of justice for the powerful and the privileged and another for the weak and the unprivileged. There government was indeed the enemy to liberty, to toleration, to equality. But in the New World government was in fact almost nonexistent for fortunate

America: no king, no court, no aristocracy; no armies, no church, no inquisition; no levies on the poor, no crushing taxes. The lesson seemed plain: that government is best that governs least.

Besides, Americans were able to fend for themselves without government, or so it appeared. Men could take care of themselves, and did, through voluntary associations. Thus they provided for their own religious needs by building churches and supporting them; they provided for their educational needs by setting up schools and academies and colleges; they provided for defense through the militia or—along perilous frontiers—by organizing their own military units; they created companies to build roads and bridges and canals. "Wherever," as Tocqueville later observed, "at the head of some new undertaking, you see the government in France, or a man of rank in England, in the United States you will be sure to find an association."

Federalism, too, or what came to be called dual federalism, contributed to and facilitated the habits of *laissez faire*. For federalism distributed powers among governments, and inevitably this distribution precipitated controversies which delayed or discouraged the application of power and created an area in which no government appeared to have power. Whether this was logically necessary is disputable, but it is undeniable that institutions like slavery or corporations which desired to avoid any regulation did take refuge in the interstices of the federal system.

A fourth ingredient in the development of *laissez faire* in America was the special position and power of the business community. For a variety of reasons business had, almost from the beginning, greater prestige and power in America than in the Old World. In Old World countries—Britain or France, for example—business was a comparatively new phenomenon and had to adjust

itself to a political and social world already dominated by
the crown, the church, the aristocracy, the army, the
guilds, and other ancient institutions. It accepted such
terms as these were prepared to grant and accommodated itself to ancient laws and practices. Not until the
nineteenth century did it command significant social
prestige; in France, for example, the aristocracy was not
permitted by law to engage in business; in England successful merchants hastened to provide themselves with
landed estates and to marry into the landed gentry. But
in America commerce, trade, and business had few com-
petitors for power or for prestige. There was no court, no
aristocracy, no church, no army or navy, no guild system.
There were few barriers, legal or otherwise, to the indulgence of private enterprise, and there were many incen-
tives. In America the merchant, the entrepreneur, the
banker, did not so much fit into the rules as make the
rules. They did not have to adapt their activities to some
traditional doctrines of public interest; what they did
was, clearly, in the public interest. A later generation was
to look back on the railroad builders, the captains of
industry, and the titans of finance as "robber barons," but
most of their contemporaries regarded them as public
benefactors.

By the 1870's and 1880's business had even developed
its own philosophy, one which levied arrogantly on economics, law, biology, and even religion to justify the
special privileges it enjoyed. We have come to call this
philosophical potpourri "Social Darwinism." It was made
up of five not wholly harmonious ingredients. First, the
principle drawn from Jeffersonian agrarianism and Manchester liberalism that that government was best which
governed least, and that government should keep its
hands off business. "All experience," wrote the most vigorous of the Social Darwinists, Professor William Graham Sumner, of Yale University, "is against state regula-

tion and in favor of liberty. The freer the civil institutions are, the more weak and mischievous state regulation is." Second, the principle of the peculiar sanctity of property —including, of course, corporate charters and franchises —in our constitutional and economic system. Third, the quasi-religious principle that the acquisition of wealth was a mark of divine favor and that the rich therefore had a moral responsibility both to get richer and to direct the affairs of society. Judge Elbert Gary, who had refused to talk to the representatives of steelworkers who worked twelve hours a day, seven days a week, in his mills, put it simply. "Moral principles," he said, "are the base of all business success."

Fourth was the principle of white, and Nordic, supremacy, which seemed to justify the exploitation of the Negro by Southern whites and of newly arrived immigrants from Italy, Poland, Rumania, and other non-Nordic countries by industry, and which, on a larger scale, was invoked to throw a halo around imperialism and the "white man's burden." The findings of social workers and the teaching of sociologists commonly supported this principle of Nordic supremacy, for somehow their findings went to show that "new" immigrants and Negroes contributed far more than their proportionate share to crime and vice and disease.

Spencer's basic principle was that society is an organism, like all other organisms, and subject to the same evolutionary laws as all others. Any attempt, therefore, to remove human society from the laws that operate uniformly and implacably upon nature was foredoomed. "Political schemers," as Spencer called them, who look on society as a "manufacture" rather than as a natural growth and attempt to "supersede the great laws of existence," may do incalculable harm.

Where government was concerned, Spencer was not merely a Manchester Liberal, he was almost an anarchist. Because government, he believed, is based on the necessity of dealing with evil in man, it is itself a reflection of that evil. If men could but learn to cooperate with nature, they would not need government at all; like the Marxists, he looked forward with confidence to the eventual withering away of government. Meantime there were a few, a very few, things which government might rightly do: defend the nation, keep the peace, and enforce justice. But that virtually exhausted the legitimate area of governmental activities; all others—even the postal service, even public health, even education—were misguided. They were misguided on practical grounds, for the individual was more efficient than the state. They were misguided on natural grounds, for they encouraged the survival of the unfit, while nature preferred and progress required the survival of the fit.

It demands an effort of the imagination now to appreciate the dominion which Spencer exercised over American thought in the quarter century or so after the Civil War and, in some quarters, down to the eve of the First World War. Henry Holt testified that "no other philosopher ever had such a vogue as Herbert Spencer"—he was speaking of his own country, to be sure—and John Fiske asserted that Spencer's genius surpassed that of Aristotle as the telegraph surpassed the carrier pigeon. Andrew Carnegie considered Spencer more important than Charles Darwin, and Frederick Barnard was prepared to insist that his was "the most powerful intellect of all time." As late as 1916 Truxton Beale brought out a new edition of *The Man versus the State,* and great national figures like William Howard Taft, Henry Cabot Lodge, Elihu Root, and Nicholas Murray Butler were honored to contribute introductions to single chapters.

Even more impressive, and certainly more revealing, were the tributes that came from the business community and its spokesmen, like William Graham Sumner of

Yale University, and Edward Youmans, editor of the widely-read *Popular Science Monthly*. When in 1881 Henry Demarest Lloyd launched his first attack on the Standard Oil Company, one great industrialist wrote indignantly that "the donkeys who can't see the operation of natural laws in fixing the rates of transportation now, rely mainly on the Standard Oil Company as an example. [But] the Standard Oil Company is simply a product of natural laws which it is not safe to touch." Clearly John D. Rockefeller agreed with this interpretation. "The American-beauty rose," he said, "can be produced in the splendor and fragrance which bring cheer to its beholder only by sacrificing the early buds which grow up about it. This is not an evil tendency in business. It is merely the working out of a law of nature and of God."

III

It is interesting to reflect that Spencer enjoyed no comparable vogue in Britain or on the European continent. The explanation is simple enough. European economic and social thought was more mature and sophisticated than American, with traditions that traced back to Johann Wolff and Vico and Montesquieu. Also, Europeans had long been habituated to assuming that government had the authority and the responsibility to hold a just balance between conflicting interests and orders and to carry through whatever reforms were called for. Social Darwinism made little sense in the highly urbanized and industrialized Britain of Gladstone or the Germany of Bismarck; where it did seem to make sense and where it flourished was in the colonial empires of these two powers. But the American tradition was not one of strong, but of weak, government, not of government which held or imposed a balance of power in society, but one of multitudinous interests, groups, and factions which themselves balanced out. And in America, which was still wide open and still in the making, which still offered immense scope to individual initiative, much of what Spencer and his disciples had to say seemed but a reformulation of familiar experience.

Yet every year America was getting more and more like Europe economically, socially, even intellectually. America, too, was becoming urbanized and industrialized, and facing problems very much like those which western Europe faced. It was almost inevitable that sooner or later Americans would find the simple solutions of Spencer irrelevant to the realities of life.

Though they borrowed Social Darwinism from abroad, where it was not popular, they did not look abroad for the counterphilosophy, which was popular. To an astonishing extent their counterphilosophy was indigenous. Though Europe first created the welfare state—in Germany, Scandinavia, and Britain—it is no exaggeration to say that Americans were the first to develop the philosophy of the welfare state. That was something of a reversal of customary roles, but a reversal natural enough in the light of the needs and circumstances of the two Atlantic societies.

For at no time did the Spencerians have things their own way in the United States. So commanding is the fame of Spencer that we tend to underestimate, or to forget, the strength and pervasiveness of the revolt against his teachings and those of Manchester. From the mid-seventies on, that protest welled up from every part of the nation, and in many voices, which in the end found their own harmony. Most eloquent, perhaps, was the social-gospel group, the clergymen and their allies outside the church, men like Washington Gladden of Columbus, Ohio, Lyman Abbott of New York, Octavius Brooks Frothingham, who was a proper godson to Theodore Parker and who developed a religion of humanity, and Walter Rauschenbusch, who organized the "Brother-hood of the Kingdom" and whose *Christianity and the Social Crisis* was one of the significant documents of the Progressive movement. Equally important were the economists, pioneers like Henry George, whose *Progress and Poverty* touched a responsive chord in a dozen countries, the pioneering Richard Ely of Wisconsin, with his colleague John R. Commons, the hardbitten Thorstein Veblen, the philosophical Simon Patten from Philadelphia, and E. Benjamin Andrews and Edward Bemis, who were forced out of their academic posts because of their radicalism.

The jurisprudents were fewer but even more distinguished—young Louis Brandeis, who was already becoming the people's counsel, the German-born Ernst Freund, and Judge Walter Clark in North Carolina, and at Harvard two erudite deans, James B. Thayer and Roscoe Pound. They had this in common, these men of the law, that they distrusted the theories and fictions of natural law and the pretensions of judges, and thought that law, like other institutions, should be required to serve the needs of society. Then there were the social workers, with Jane Addams at their head and her associates at Hull House—Florence Kelley and Dr. Alice Hamilton and Julia Lathrop and Sophia Breckenridge—and settlement-house workers throughout the country; their influence was nationwide. There were reformers like Jacob Riis, author of *How the Other Half Lives*, and economists like Richard Ely and E. A. Ross, at Wisconsin, and the defrocked Congregationalist minister George Herron. There were the politicians, most of them more at home in the Populist or Socialist than in the "major" parties, which were engaged in a kind of conspiracy of silence, men like Governor Altgeld of Illinois, Pingree of Michigan, and the incomparable La Follette of Wisconsin, and in Ohio "Golden Rule" Jones of Toledo, Tom Johnson of Cleveland,

and scores of others who refused to accept the dominance
of the great corporations as somehow ordained by nature
and by God, and who tried to rally the farmers and workingmen and intellectuals to a common cause. For the
intellectuals were involved too: William James and John
Dewey, the Georgia-born poet Sidney Lanier, whose *Symphony* was one of the earliest assaults on the sins of
industrialism, the transcendentalist New Englander William Vaughn Moody, whose *Gloucester Moors* raised fundamental questions about the social order, and most of
the leading novelists—Mark Twain, William Dean Howells, Frank Norris, Stephen Crane, and Hamlin Garland
among them.

Of them all—the economists, the jurists, and the political reformers, the Christian socialists and the philosophers and the men of letters—none contributed more to
undermining Social Darwinism and to laying the foundations for the welfare state than that government clerk
whose business was with immigration statistics, with the
census, with the flora and fauna of the West, with fossils
—Lester Ward.

I V

Lester Ward has some claim to be regarded as the
philosopher, the protagonist, even the architect, of the
modern welfare state. Neglected in his own day (though
never quite as neglected as he liked to suppose) and
almost forgotten since, he was, as were so many of the
leaders of the intellectual revolution at the turn of the
century (Thorstein Veblen, for example, Charles Beard,
Frederick Jackson Turner, Louis Brandeis, Roscoe
Pound, Frank Lloyd Wright, and Jane Addams), a product
of the Middle Border. His father was an engineer of sorts
(untrained, like Ward himself), a mechanic who special-
ized in building locks and dams. He had fought in the

War of 1812—how quickly we get back to the generation
of the Founding Fathers—and many years later he was
able to collect a quarter section of land in Iowa for his
military services.

Born in 1842, Lester Ward grew up in what was still
frontier country along the banks of the Desplaines and
the Rock and the Fox rivers in Illinois and Wisconsin,
getting what schooling he could, which was not much,
and learning from nature what he could, which was a
great deal. In the mid-fifties the family moved to that
quarter section in Iowa, but Ward was not attracted to
farming, and after his father's death he and his brother
Cyrenus—another unsung genius—went east to Pennsylvania to work in a wheel hub shop. It was a thankless job,
but somehow Ward managed to pick up a bit of Latin and
Greek, French, and mathematics as well; and when the
wheel hub venture failed, he took to schoolteaching; he
began and closed his career that way. He was fully conscious of the ragged and desultory character of his education:

> Perhaps the most vivid impression that my early experi-
> ence left on my mind was that of the difference be-
> tween the educated and the uneducated person. I had
> had much to do with the uneducated, and I could not
> believe that the chasm between these and the educated
> people was due to any great extent to their inherent
> nature. . . . The influence of education and environ-
> mental conditions took an ever stronger hold on me.
> [*Glimpses of the Cosmos*, Vol. III, p. 147.]

He took a few courses at the Susquehanna Collegiate
Institute; he continued his own studies of Greek and
Latin and added German; he kept a diary in French,
partly for practice, partly for privacy—for he was indulging in a romantic and passionate love affair and the
diary told all. When the Civil War came, he enlisted in
the Pennsylvania Volunteers and marched off to Virginia,

where he managed to get himself wounded three times. And if he did not read quite as much into that experience as did Justice Holmes, for whom it was central, he did, like Holmes, draw from it a sense of the national power.

Out of the army, Ward found a job with the Bureau of Statistics, and after that with other government departments—the Bureau of Standards, the Census Bureau, the Bureau of Immigration; and meantime he was busy educating himself, faithfully attending night classes at the Columbian University (now George Washington University) and somehow managing to pick up degrees in both medicine and law. The degrees were not much, but he was able to win admission to practice before the bar of the Supreme Court—that was something for a self-educated young man from the Illinois frontier.

Somehow, too, he found time to launch a little magazine named, prophetically enough, *The Iconoclast* and dedicated to embalming the ideas of Tom Paine and echoing those of Bob Ingersoll. He edited it and wrote most of it but soon tired of it and turned to more serious interests. By now Ward was settling down. He had his degrees; he married, only to lose his wife, whom he loved, and his next marriage was not very successful. His interests were turning increasingly to science, especially to geology, paleontology, and paleobotany, and he found a job in the United States Geological Survey under the dynamic and inspiring John Wesley Powell, to whom he was to dedicate his first book. But he found himself increasingly distracted from science to larger social problems. He was a child of Darwin, to be sure, a committed evolutionist, a scientist who worked by preference in the field, off on one expedition after another, jogging along dirt roads in Alabama or exploring the Bad Lands of the Dakotas, just at the time Theodore Roosevelt was discovering them, or floating down the Missouri in a flatboat. Clearly he was a product of the age of science and

of evolution; but he was a product, too, of the new spirit
of unrest and revolt against Victorian complacency and
the triumph of the new plutocracy, a product of the age
which produced the Greenbackers and the Grangers, the
Populists and the Socialists, and it was with these that he
could cast his lot. He lived in Washington where he
might watch politics at first hand, but Washington meant
to him not politics but government, not spoils but power,
and if he took little interest in the politics of the Gilded
Age, he learned well the lessons of power. But Washington did provide Ward with a great company of scientists
—no university of that time could boast a scientific faculty to equal that which worked in the Smithsonian and
in the various departments of the government. As early
as the seventies, when Ward himself was barely in his
thirties, he began to make those contributions to science
and to social science that were destined to mark him
eventually as one of the leading explorers of his generation in both realms.

Nothing is more astonishing than how early Ward
found what were to be his lifelong interests, unless it is
the assiduousness with which he cultivated them. As
early as 1869 he had drawn up an elaborate prospectus of
the book that was to appear fourteen years later as *Dynamic Sociology*—and this while he was still working for
his degrees. He gives us a blow by blow—or chapter by
chapter—account of the composition of that book in one
of the autobiographical notes in *Glimpses of the Cosmos;*
and he gives us, too, without the slightest embarrassment, the three reviews which he himself wrote of his
book in different journals. If we take 1869 as the starting
point of Ward's inquiries into science and sociology, we
can say that the scholarly monument which he built
engaged his undivided attention for forty-five years.

There was, indeed, a formidable intensity about the
young man—and the old man, too—and with it a hard,

almost implacable quality. There were few grace notes in
Ward, few concessions to style and, for all his concern
with the psyche, little interest in the life of the imagination. We can see this quality in the boy who took up the
study of Greek and Latin, French and German, and mastered them; we see it in the relentless pursuit of academic
degrees; we see it in the unswerving commitment to the
one great principle of sociology which he formulated
early in his studies and upon which he played variations
for the rest of his life—the principle of the psychic control of evolution.

Ward never outgrew his early suspicion of the respectable elements of society. That suspicion grew deeper with
the passing years. He was, almost by instinct, a dissenter,
even something of a dreamer. It is hard to see a dreamer
in that hardbitten, humorless, prematurely old government clerk, busy with his immigration statistics and his
fossils. Yet there was romance there, and excitement. He
knew America intimately, knew her as did only a handful
of his contemporaries, explorers and scientists, men like
Major Powell and Clarence King, Ferdinand Hayden and
Raphael Pumpelly, all at one time or another connected
with the Geological Survey. As a boy he had grown up on
the frontier of the Middle Border, and later he was to
crisscross the plains and the mountains of the Far West,
the Yellowstone, the Colorado, Utah and Arizona, sleeping out and writing his books by the light of log fires,
studying the flora and fauna of the West, building up
fossil collections for the Geological Survey. He knew the
plain people, too, those who rode coaches instead of Pullman Palace cars, or who rode no cars at all, farmers and
cattlemen, workingmen, privates in the army, the civil
servants of Washington, the immigrants, the poor, the
denizens of the slums, whom he thought potentially the
equals of the rich and the privileged.

Somehow in the midst of all his professional activities

he mastered a dozen fields of knowledge, until he became in the end perhaps the most variously learned man in the country. And—except in a few areas—that learning was not superficial but professional. What he knew, he knew thoroughly; what he did, he did not only well but expertly. A master of half a dozen fields of science, he was a master, too, of social science—in a sense he may be said to have created it. When at the end of his life he attached himself to Brown University, he gave a course which he called—perhaps it was his one gesture of humor—"An Outline of All Knowledge."

The protest movement was, to be sure, well under way when Ward enlisted in it, but it was disparate, amorphous, and even fortuitous in the sense that it took its tone from the evils which it attacked rather than from the virtues which it extolled. That is one reason why, compared with the great sweeping reform movement of the pre-Civil War years, this one appears so miscellaneous. It was—and the historical name is right here—an era of social protest rather than an era of social achievement, and a disproportionate amount of its energy was devoted to criticism. What it lacked was a philosophy that would bind together its disparate activities and enthusiasms.

It was this that Ward undertook to provide, a philosophy that could be relevant, comprehensive, fundamental, and positive. First came that book which, he hoped, would sum up the problem and settle it, too—*Dynamic Sociology*. "All things considered," wrote the Chicago sociologist Albion Small years later, "I would rather have written *Dynamic Sociology* than any other book ever published in America." A decade later, in 1893, came *Psychic Factors of Civilization*, in some ways Ward's most important book, succinct, original, and persuasive. This little masterpiece was followed in turn by *Outlines of Sociology* (1898), *Pure Sociology* (1903), and *Applied Sociol-*

ogy (1906). There was, in addition, that curious hodge-podge which Ward with unconscious vanity called *Glimpses of the Cosmos,* originally designed to fill twelve stout volumes but restricted in the end to six, a collection of almost everything that Ward had written of a fragmentary character, whether scientific, sociological, or merely occasional.

Few men of his day ranged so widely or saw so deeply as Lester Ward. In the realm of social economy he anticipated Thorstein Veblen, who owed much to him. In the realm of education he anticipated John Dewey and supplied him with a scientific basis for much of his educational philosophy. In the realm of politics he provided the intellectual foundations on which such man as La Follette and Wilson and Franklin Roosevelt were later to build.

This is what particularly concerns us, for these notes do not attempt to represent the whole range of his intellectual or professional interests nor the whole of his philosophy. They are confined to the presentation of what was, in retrospect, the central thrust of Ward's social thought and what has proved to be, in our current situation, the most lasting and most significant of his contributions—his formulation of the philosophy of the welfare state.

V

Ward's sociology was all of a piece. Like so many great social thinkers, Comte, for example, and Herbert Spencer and perhaps even Veblen, he was a man of one great idea. He was consumed by this idea, and he devoted much of his life to advancing it—that part left over, in any event, from the demands of his professional work. And what was that one great idea? It was this: that man is not the subject but the master of nature, and that all

progress is achieved by the conscious exercise of that
mastery over the impersonal and chaotic forces of nature. It is the mastery over nature that distinguishes man
from all other creatures. All of nature and all forms of
life are subject to the iron laws of evolution, but man—
and man alone—through the psychic forces of mind and
spirit can control and direct those laws.

Almost all of Ward's voluminous writings in the field
of sociology were variations on this theme. Certainly this
was true of his first book, *Dynamic Sociology*—a book
which he had hoped would sum up the whole of his
message. That hope proved mistaken; Ward found that
he had to restate his case over and over in different ways.
And that is what much of his later work was: the penetrating *Psychic Factors in Civilization*, the abstruse *Pure
Sociology*, the intensely practical *Applied Sociology*. Like
so many philosophers and social thinkers, Ward had a
habit of cannibalizing himself: he nourished himself on
his own ideas, digested them well, and brought them out
again in new forms and patterns. But along with the
exposition of his own philosophy went another task, time-
consuming but unavoidable. That was to clear away the
debris which, he thought, littered the sociological landscape.

In the preface to *Dynamic Sociology* he wrote:

A growing sense of the essential sterility of all that has
thus far been done in the domain of social science has
furnished the chief incentive to the preparation of this
work. Just as Comte could complain that the philosophy
of Hobbes, Locke and Voltaire, was negative, so it may
now be maintained that the school of Mill, Spencer, and
Fiske is almost negative. . . . The latter has only advanced to the passively dynamic stage which recognizes
only the changes wrought by nature, unaided by art;
but before the science of society can be truly founded,
another advance must be made, and the actively dynamic stage reached in which social phenomena shall

be contemplated as capable of intelligent control by
society itself in its own interests.

Ward had no doubt, from the beginning, that he had
made that advance, and in the notice which he himself
wrote of *Dynamic Sociology* he staked out his claim:

> Seizing upon the new conception of universal develop-
> ment or evolution [he wrote], Mr. Ward fits everything
> into its appropriate niche in his progressive scheme of
> having man in his highest social stage at its head in
> showing how this system of things has been evolved,
> the higher from the lower forms. Our author is in entire
> harmony with most of the modern philosophers who set
> out with the facts of the known universe as the basis of
> their ideas, but at this point he finds himself compelled
> to diverge from the main path of the most advanced
> modern thought, and to introduce new elements which
> he regards as being of paramount importance. Without
> ascribing to man any divine attributes not originally
> attained through spontaneous evolution like all the rest,
> he does maintain that the development of the psychic
> faculty, and especially the appearance of the rational
> intellect of man, introduced a set of factors into the
> general problem of evolution. . . . [*Glimpses of the
> Cosmos*, Vol. III, pp. 232–3.]

"Is it true," Ward asked, "that man shall ultimately
obtain dominion of the whole world except himself?"
Those who subscribed to the doctrine of *Social Statics* as
formulated by Spencer were forced to confess that it was.
But sociology, Ward insisted, was a positive and dynamic
science, and properly applied, it would enable man to
control the evolutionary process. The psychic factors, he
maintained, count more than the natural, for they condition and control the natural. "The advent with man of the
thinking, knowing, foreseeing, calculating, designing, in-
venting and constructing faculty, which is wanting in
lower creatures, repealed . . . the law of nature, and
enacted in its stead the psychologic law, or law of mind,"
he wrote. The capital error of the Spencerian system was

its failure to appreciate the role of mind in creative evolution, and this error Ward set about to repair. "Thus far," he wrote, "social progress has in a certain awkward manner taken care of itself, but in the near future it will have to be cared for. To do this, and maintain the dynamic condition against all the hostile forces which thicken with every new advance, is the real problem of sociology considered as an applied science."

More clearly than any of his contemporaries Ward saw that though environment transforms animals, man transforms environment, and he insisted that the transformation be not haphazard but planned—and so planned as to produce not only material abundance but intellectual and spiritual well-being. He set himself, therefore, to rescue evolution from the creeping paralysis with which Spencer had infected it, release its energies for the use of society, and make it the servant rather than the master of man. Throughout all his writings there runs, as Frank Giddings wrote, one dominating and organizing thought. "Human society as we who live now know it, is not the passive product of unconscious forces. It lies within the domain of cosmic law, but so does the mind of man; and this mind of man has knowingly, artfully, adapted and readapted its social environment, and with reflective intelligence has begun to shape it into an instrument wherewith to fulfill man's will."

If the mind of man was to function in this benign fashion, it was necessary to rid it of those superstitions that still held domain. Of these, *laissez faire* was the most stupefying, and it was on the doctrine of *laissez faire* that Ward trained his heaviest guns. *Laissez faire*, Ward argued, was incoherent, fragmentary, and futile, scarcely consistent with the law of nature and wholly inconsistent with the law of man. It repudiated the past and condemned the future, denied scope to the creative faculty of man and barred the road to progress. Civilization as we know it, he argued, is the triumph of man over the blind forces of nature and the deliberate application of human genius to the task of emancipating man from the tyranny of those forces. "We are told," he wrote, "to let things alone, and allow nature to take its course. But has intelligent man ever done this? Is not civilization, with all it has accomplished, the result of man's not letting things alone, and of his not letting nature take its course?" Nature is prodigal and ruthless, indifferent to man's fate and to time; it is only when man breaks in upon nature's course that he can free himself from the fate to which all other forms of life are condemned:

> This iron law of nature, as it may appropriately be called, was everywhere found to lie athwart the path of human progress, and the whole upward struggle of rational man . . . has been with this tyrant of nature —the law of competition. And in so far as he has progressed at all beyond the purely animal stage he has done so through triumphing little by little over this law and gaining somewhat the mastery of the struggle. In the physical world he has accomplished this through invention, from which have resulted the arts and material civilization. Every implement or utensil, every mechanical device . . . is a triumph of mind over the physical forces of nature in ceaseless and aimless competition. All human institutions—religion, government, law, marriage, custom—together with innumerable other modes of regulating social, industrial and commercial life are, broadly viewed, only so many ways of meeting and checkmating the principle of competition as it manifests itself in society. [*Psychic Factors of Civilization*, pp. 261–2.]

The notion of the "survival of the fittest" Ward repudiated as either meaningless or pernicious. Assuredly, said Ward, mere fitness to survive is no criterion that civilization can accept, and here he echoed Huxley's statement that "social progress means a checking of the cosmic process at every step. The more advanced a society becomes, the more it eliminates the struggle for existence." It was only when man intervened that nature's products became fit for man, and it is only when society or government intervenes, Ward asserted, that man's products become fit for society. Competition is, in fact, not the law of life, as so many of Ward's contemporaries believed, but the law of death: the whole of medicine and surgery, according to that argument, would be a violent interference with biological competition. Man, thanks to the possession of mind, repudiates nature and applies art—or that which is *artificial*. "The constant tendency," Ward pointed out,

> is to render everything more artificial, which means more and more perfect. Human institutions are not exempt from this all-pervading spirit of improvement. They, too, are artificial, conceived in the ingenious brain and wrought with mental skill born of inventive genius. The passion for their improvement is of a piece with the impulse to improve the plow or the steam engine. Government is one of these artificial products of man's devising, and his right to change it is the same as his right to create it. [*Psychic Factors*, pp. 287–8.]

He protested equally the inconsistency and the insincerity of the doctrine of *laissez faire* as applied in America. It was applied to public associations but not to private, and Ward had been too long a civil servant to accept the curious theory that a peculiar iniquity attached to governmental activities from which the comparable activities of corporations were miraculously free. He knew that *laissez faire* was a rationalization rather than a first principle. Business did not embrace competition in response to philosophical precepts; those precepts, rather, flowed from the felt needs of business. *Laissez faire* was the validation rather than the inspiration of the economic conduct of the age of corporate business. And Ward saw, too, what even William Graham Sumner, for all his hostility to the protective tariff, had failed to see, that business had already made a travesty of the doctrine of *laissez faire*, invoking it only to prevent regulation which might interfere with profits but rejecting it out of hand whenever questions of tariffs, patents, copyrights, or corporate charters were at stake.

All this meant inevitably an enlargement of the role of government. Unlike most of his contemporaries, unlike many of our own contemporaries, Ward did not fear this but looked upon it with approbation.

Government was, as he saw, the most fundamental and the greatest of man's inventions, the one without which all the others were doomed to futility. Man and the state were not incongruous, as Spencer had insisted, but interdependent: imagine man without the state! Ward, to be sure, did not think of "man" but of "mankind"; a collective title for his books might have been "Society and the State." His political philosophy—we can use the term for Ward as for Montesquieu or Rousseau or John Stuart Mill—can be stated succinctly, though he himself argued it elaborately and pervasively. First, all invention is an intervention in nature, and all invention is social. Second, government is the greatest of all inventions for intervening in and controlling nature. Third, almost everything government undertakes—in a democracy, in any event—it does better than private enterprise can possibly do. Fourth, the major defect of government, so far, has been caution and ineffectiveness; and as long as government is controlled by private and selfish interests, it will continue to be cautious and ineffectual. And, finally, the function of government should be not negative but positive, not merely the prevention of crime or subversion or conquest but the organization of the energies of society for beneficent purposes. Government must, of course, guard against crime and injustice and chaos—these duties are elementary. But the larger end of government is

the manufacture of intelligence and happiness and the
advancement of the general welfare.

"Modern society," wrote Ward, "is suffering from the
very opposite of paternalism—from under-government.
. . . The true function of government is not to fetter,
but to liberate the forces of society, not to diminish but to
increase ther effectiveness." It was a bold thing for a
scholar to announce in the 1890's, when even the Interstate Commerce Act seemed vaguely socialistic and when
Henry Wood, whose *Political Economy of Natural Law*
purveyed Spencer in capsule form, was insisting that
"freedom of the individual contract is the chief corner-
stone in the structure of any system of liberal government. . . . Any legislation or even prevailing custom,
which tends to its impairment, is tyrannous."

William Graham Sumner had said the same thing. "All
experience is against state regulation," he asserted
roundly. But Ward was not inclined to apologize for the
state. Government had already extended its jurisdiction
over broad areas of life—justice, national defense, agri-
culture and the public domain, science and education—
and no one could say that it had done badly. "In all those
affairs which the state can manage more advantageously
than the individual," he concluded, "it has in fact managed well, and such as have passed from private to public
control are better administered by the state than they
were by the individual."

The question of government intervention, as Ward
saw, was one not of theory but of fact, and the wisdom of
particular legislation was to be determined by experience
rather than by *a priori* reasoning. That realization made
him impatient with discussions of abstractions like "cen-
tralization," "paternalism," "bureaucracy," "socialism,"
and similar terms that lost all their meaning when they
were treated as absolutes rather than as techniques. He
had the same test for legislation that William James had

for truth: good legislation was what worked. Nor was his
political pragmatism less idealistic than James's philosophical. What worked was what contributed most in the
long run to the spiritual and intellectual as well as to the
material welfare of mankind.

The trouble with legislation, as Ward saw it during the
last quarter of the nineteenth century, was threefold: it
was limited in scope and in imagination; it reflected the
will of special pressure groups rather than the needs of
society as a whole; it was haphazard and unscientific.
What was needed, therefore, was a positive program, one
not hamstrung by those predatory interests that were so
ready to use government for their own advantage and so
reluctant to permit society to use it for social advantage.
Ward himself was not tempted to shift from his study to
the political hustings. He was more concerned for the
establishment of right principles than for the agitation of
current issues. "It is not indifference, now, that resigns
me to events," he wrote, "but a sense of the infinitesimal
effect of anything I could do, especially of the utter pow-
erlessness of the hortatory method." He had small faith
in the mere tinkering with the political or the economic
machinery of society. What was needed was new machinery altogether, machinery to "manufacture intelligence"
and to apply it scientifically to the needs of society.

One way to begin here was to formulate a science of
politics and to provide scientific training for legislators
and social scientists.

Before science taught man the nature of physical laws,
all attempts at invention except of the simplest kind
were just such wretched miscarriages as attempts at
progressive legislation are today, and for the same reason, viz., that the inventors possessed no science of the
field of natural forces over which they sought to exert
an influence. Before progressive legislation can become
a success, every legislature must become, as it were, a
polytechnic school, a laboratory of philosophical re-

search, into the laws of society and of human nature.
No legislator is qualified to vote on or propose measures
designed to affect the destinies of millions of social
units until he masters all that is known of the science
of society. Every true legislator must be a sociologist.

The legislation of the future, Ward wrote elsewhere, "will
consist of a series of exhaustive experiments on the part
of true scientific sociologists, and sociological inventors,
working on the problems of social physics from the practical point of view." As a contribution to this end Ward
proposed the establishment of a national academy of the
social sciences which should train public administrators
and study the great social problems of the age.

For intelligence, too, was a manufacture. "The origina-
tion and distribution of knowledge can no longer be left
to chance and to nature. They are to be systematized and
erected into true arts." This, as Ward saw it, was the
major task of society—to provide education for all, to
discover talent and develop it and enlist it in the attack
on social problems. Faith in education was nothing new
in America, but no earlier American educator—neither
Jefferson nor Horace Mann nor Henry Barnard—had
based his educational program so firmly on scientific
foundations or faced so clearly its logical implications
and consequences. He believed both in the potential
equality of intelligence and in the manufacture of knowledge. There is, he asserted, no aristocracy of talent; intellectual ability is the product of opportunity and privilege,
not of native capacity. "The denizens of the slums," he
asserted, "are not inferior in talent to the graduates of
Harvard College," and criminals are "the geniuses of the
slums. Society has forced them into this field, and they
are making the best use they can of their native abilities."
Nowhere is Ward's quarrel with Spencer sharper than
here. "It is a frequent delusion," Spencer had said in reply
to an inquiry about the future of America, "that educa-

tion is a universal remedy for political evils." But for
Ward education was "the great panacea." And it was, like
civilization itself, a violent and calculated interference
with nature. It was, of all the activities of civilized man,
the most thoroughgoing departure from *laissez faire*.

VI

Ward's significance as prophet has been overshadowed
by his role as critic. The first sociologist to challenge the
doctrine of *laissez faire* on scientific grounds and to articulate social to natural evolution, he was the first, too, to
embrace the full implications of pragmatism and to give
sociology a scientific foundation. From the beginning he
ranged himself on the side of the plain people, fighting
their battles with weapons more formidable by far than
those which Sumner and his followers could muster, and
he inspired a generation of scholars and social workers to
believe that it was possible to rebuild society on sounder
foundations, with more honest materials, and on a more
symmetrical plan; new generations that did not know
him fought with his weapons and built with his tools. He
lived just long enough to hear Woodrow Wilson inaugurate the New Freedom in words that might have been
taken directly from his own writings:

> There can be no equality of opportunity if men and
> women and children be not shielded in their lives, their
> very vitality, from the consequences of great industrial
> and social processes which they can not alter, control,
> or singly cope with. . . . Society must see to it that it
> does not crush or weaken or damage its own constituent
> parts. The first duty of law is to keep sound the society
> it serves.

If this was not the end of *laissez faire*, it was the
beginning of the end; if it was not the triumph of the
welfare state, it was the end of the beginning of that

process. For the New Freedom was to be succeeded by the bolder and more far-reaching New Deal, and that by the New Frontier, and that in turn by the Great Society—a term and a concept first formulated by Ward's fellow worker Graham Wallas in 1914. It is no hyperbole to call Ward the prophet and the protagonist of all those movements looking to the reconstruction of the American economy and society through governmental intervention —the most striking development of American politics in the past half century—or to name him the philosophical architect of the welfare state.

JANE ADDAMS AT HULL HOUSE

EVEN as a little girl in the pastoral community of Cedar-ville, in northern Illinois, Jane Addams was—as she herself tells us—"busy with the old question eternally suggested by the inequalities of the human lot." There were not many inequalities in Cedarville, but even there were poverty and frustration: the war widows, the forlorn old couple who had lost all five of their sons, the farmers who were victims of the postwar depression, and the newcomers who could never really get started. And when she visited the neighboring town—was it Freeport?—she was shocked by the "horrid little houses" and, characteristically, wondered what could be done to make them less horrid. She could sympathize with the misfits and the victims of society for she was herself a misfit—so she felt anyway—"an ugly, pigeon-toed little girl whose crooked back obliged her to walk with her head held very much upon one side," who was constantly afraid that she might embarrass the handsome father she adored.

At nearby Rockford Seminary, too—it was not yet a

SOURCE: Originally published as the foreword to the edition of *Twenty Years at Hull House* by Jane Addams published by The New American Library, Inc. Copyright © 1961 by Henry Steele Commager. Reprinted by permission.

college—the air was heavy with a sense of responsibility—moral, cultural, and even social. Here the girls,
most of them deeply religious, encountered a strong
missionary tradition, and here too a compelling sense of
the obligation of women to prove themselves in what was
still a man's world. It was all very Victorian: the passion
for Culture, the passion for Good Works. Miss Addams's
Greek oration on Bellerophon and his fight with the Mino-
taur "contended that social evils could be overcome by
him who soared above them into idealism"—not precisely
the doctrine that she later espoused.

There was a brief effort to study medicine—still a bit
daring in the eighties—then a breakdown, and after that
a long visit to Europe. She was sent abroad to drink up
the culture of the Old World, like any Daisy Miller
(Henry James was a fellow passenger), but she would
have none of it. She wrote later, and bitterly, of "the
sweet dessert in the morning, and the assumption that
the sheltered, educated girl has nothing to do with the
bitter poverty and the social maladjustment which is all
about her, and which, after all, cannot be concealed, for
it breaks through poetry and literature in a burning tide
which overwhelms her; it peers at her in the form of the
heavy-laden market women and underpaid street labor-
ers, gibing her with a sense of her own uselessness."

This assumption was valid enough for most of the girls
who made the Grand Tour in the comfortable eighties,
but not for Jane Addams nor for her friend Ellen Starr,
who was her companion. Miss Addams's travels on the
Continent and in Britain merely strengthened and deepened her already lively concern for the welfare of those
whom Jacob Riis was to call "the other half." What she
visited was not cathedrals and galleries, but factories and
slums. It was on one of these visits in London's East End
that she found herself looking at the spectacle of hunger
and want through the eyes of literature, instead of the

thing itself, and concluded even then that "lumbering our minds with literature only served to cloud the really vital situation." She had already visited Toynbee Hall, which applied Christian Socialism to the needs of the London poor, and she saw that if she would be true to herself she would have to cast her own lot in with the poor and the neglected, with those whom Theodore Parker called "the dangerous and perishing classes." She too would open a settlement house—not another Toynbee Hall, for it could not be religious or even give the appearance of a gesture of *noblesse oblige*. With Ellen Starr she returned to Chicago, and on that long *via dolorosa*, Halsted Street, found a decayed mansion that had been built by a merchant, Charles Hull, and now belonged to the ever-generous Helen Culver. On September 18, 1889—a day that Chicago should commemorate—Hull House opened its doors to those who cared to enter. Jane Addams liked to remember that her father had never locked his doors; the doors of Hull House were always open to the world.

As Miss Addams saw it, there was nothing dramatic about the opening of Hull House; yet it was an historic event. For here was the beginning of what was to be one of the great social movements in modern America—the Settlement House movement; here, in a way, was the beginning of social work. As yet there was no organized social work in the United States—the beneficent program of Mary Richmond was still in the future—and as yet there was not even any formal study of sociology. It was no accident that the new University of Chicago, which was founded just a few years after Hull House, came to be the center of sociological study in America, and that so many of its professors were intimately associated with Hull House—Albion Small and John Dewey and the wonderful Miss Breckenridge and the two famous Abbott sisters, Edith and Grace, and thereafter two generations of academic reformers.

The time was ripe and the place logical. By 1890, just a hundred years after the founding of the Republic, the "Promise of American Life" was becoming an illusion. The extremes of wealth and poverty were as great as those in the Old World. Millions of immigrants crowded into the slums of American cities, constituting a proletariat not only impoverished but alien: these newcomers were the first immigrants who had not been absorbed. The Negro had achieved his freedom, but as yet not acceptance or recognition. Unemployment plagued the land, organized labor was in retreat, farmers were becoming peasants. As Woodrow Wilson was to say in his First Inaugural Address, we were in a hurry to be great and did not stop "to count the cost of lives snuffed out, of energies overtaxed and broken, the fearful physical and spiritual cost of the men and women and children upon whom the dead weight and burden of it all has fallen pitilessly the years through." It was an America familiar to us in the novels of Theodore Dreiser and Upton Sinclair, an America that accepted uncritically the grim doctrines of Social Darwinism that promised success to the strong and the ruthless, and remorselessly condemned the weak and the helpless to defeat. The welfare state was as yet unknown and almost unimagined; even social legislation was a thing of the future. Men worked twelve or fourteen hours a day, and thought themselves lucky to have work. Women toiled long hours at night as well as day; even little children of five or six were unprotected by enforceable legislation. Slums grew apace, and with them disease and crime and vice. Business and government combined to smash strikes, break unions, silence critics, and jail agitators who disturbed their peace.

As for Chicago, all the evils and vices of American life seemed to be exaggerated there. It was, wrote Lincoln Steffens at this time, "first in violence, deepest in dirt; loud, lawless, unlovely, ill-smelling, new; an overgrown gawk of a village, the teeming tough among cities. Criminally it was wide open; commercially it was brazen; and socially it was thoughtless and raw." Happily, it had other qualities, too—the qualities that built the University of Chicago, established the Art Museum and maintained the great symphony orchestra, laid out a network of parks and boulevards, and responded to the challenge that young Jane Addams flung before it.

If there was one part of Chicago that dramatized all its problems more than any other, it was the five miles of Halsted Street from the Chicago River to the stockyards—the great street teeming with Irish and Germans and Russians and Italians and Poles, lined with dingy saloons, pawnshops, and—on the side streets—houses of prostitution. It was to Halsted Street that Jane Addams came, and Ellen Starr, and they were soon joined by Julia Lathrop and Florence Kelley and the wonderful Dr. Alice Hamilton, and a score of other intrepid women, and men, to inaugurate what was to be a great experiment in social service.

A great experiment. She thought of it as a simple matter of neighborliness. "It is natural to feed the hungry and care for the sick," wrote Jane Addams. "It is certainly natural to give pleasure to the young, comfort the aged, and to minister to the deep-seated craving for social intercourse that all men feel." That is what they proposed to do and that is what they did.

The "first resident" was an old lady who had lived at Brook Farm and had known Emerson and Bronson Alcott and that pioneer of social reform, Theodore Parker. Soon men and women and children of all ages thronged through the hospitable doors of the old mansion now reborn to new life; before long two thousand people crossed its portals every day. Hull House caught the imagination of Chicago—as it was to catch the imagination of the whole nation. There were gifts of buildings and of

land from the ever-benevolent Miss Culver and eventually
of money from many others. Hull House grew and spread
until in time it came to be a kind of community center for
the whole of Chicago: a boys' club, an art museum, a
theater, a music school, a gymnasium, and a dozen other
buildings, all in use from morning until late into the
night. Children came to play; the young to act or to draw
or to dance; girls in trouble who had been turned out of
their homes; men out of work, or on the run; the sick and
the tired and the frightened and the lonely, and along
with them scholars from universities, like John R. Commons and E. A. Ross, down from nearby Madison, or
John Dewey, or young Robert Morss Lovett. And along
with them came the leaders of Chicago society, for Hull
House had become fashionable.

Calm and serene and authoritative, Jane Addams presided over it all. She took care of babies, even acting as
midwife—had she not planned to be a doctor? She super-
vised all the varied activities of the sprawling community, kept the accounts, dealt with the scores of visitors,
found work for the eager assistants and even trained
them; she lectured, she wrote articles and books; she
carried on a tremendous correspondence with social
workers throughout the country, she served on committees and pleaded with legislatures and won over governors. Nothing was too difficult for her, and nothing too
simple. She tells us of the tasks that fell to her in the
early weeks—and that continued to make demands upon
her:

> For six weeks after an operation we kept in one of our
> three bedrooms a forlorn little baby who, because he
> was born with a cleft palate, was most unwelcome even
> to his mother, and we were horrified when he died of
> neglect a week after he was returned to his home; a
> little Italian bride of fifteen sought shelter with us one
> November evening to escape her husband, who had
> beaten her every night for a week when he returned

from work because she had lost her wedding ring; two
of us officiated quite alone at the birth of an illegitimate
child because the doctor was late in arriving, and none
of the honest Irish matrons would "touch the likes of
her"; we ministered at the deathbed of a young man
who, during a long illness of tuberculosis, had received
so many bottles of whisky through the mistaken kind-
ness of his friends that the cumulative effect produced
wild periods of exultation, in one of which he died.

Over the years Jane Addams built a bridge between the
immigrants and the old-stock Americans, between the
working classes and the immigrants, between the amateur reformers and the professional politicians, even between private philanthropy and government. She made
Hull House a clearing house for every kind of social service, an experimental laboratory in social reform, in art
and music and drama and education as well; she made it
a school of citizenship and a university of social work.

It was all done so simply and so naturally, so much as
part of the day by day housekeeping, that contemporaries
did not always realize that it was a product of head as well
as of heart. Miss Addams knew what she was about; she
has told us that

> The Settlement then, is an experimental effort to aid in
> the solution of the social and industrial problems which
> are engendered by the modern conditions of life in a
> great city. It insists that these problems are not con-
> fined to any one portion of a city. It is an attempt to
> relieve, at the same time, the overaccumulation at one
> end of society and the destitution at the other. . . .
> The one thing to be dreaded in the Settlement is that it
> lose its flexibility, its power of quick adaptation, its
> readiness to change its methods as its environment may
> demand. It must be open to conviction and must have a
> deep and abiding sense of tolerance. It must be hospita-
> ble and ready for experiment. It should demand from
> its residents a scientific patience in the accumulation of
> facts and the steady holding of their sympathies as one
> of the best instruments for that accumulation. It must

be grounded in a philosophy whose foundation is on the solidarity of the human race, a philosophy which will not waver when the race happens to be represented by a drunken woman or an idiot boy. Its residents must be emptied of all conceit of opinion and all self-assertion, and ready to arouse and interpret the public opinion of their neighborhood.

Jane Addams had many talents, but none more remarkable than her ability to work from the immediate to the general, from practical problems to philosophy, and even from the local to the national and the international. She always began with the task at hand, no matter how elementary or undignified; she took on the job of inspector of garbage removal for her Ward to show how it should be done—and did it so well that the boss had to abolish the job itself in order to protect those collectors who held their jobs as sinecures; she went to the Illinois legislature with case histories of working women to push through labor legislation—legislation struck down by the courts. What she saw of children on the city streets ended up as a program of school playgrounds; what she learned of children in trouble with the law ended as the first juvenile courts in the nation.

She had another genius, too. "You utter instinctively the truths we others vainly seek," William James wrote her. Yet it was not really instinct, but experience and wisdom—experience so full and wisdom so deep that they functioned like a second nature. Long before Lincoln Steffens she learned that corruption in politics was not the exclusive privilege of the wicked but stemmed from the respectable as well, and she learned, too, that it was possible to win politicians and spoilsmen to your side. *Democracy and Social Ethics* anticipated E. A. Ross's penetrating discovery that personal virtue was not enough—that social virtue was necessary to triumph over social sin. Her essay on the Pullman strike, "A Modern

King Lear," saw the problem of capital and labor not so
much in moral as in psychological terms, and she anticipated scholars like Frank Tannenbaum in seeing the
deep social conservatism of the labor movement. And in
her appreciation of art as experience, her realization that
"life consists of processes . . ." and that "democracy is
that which affords a rule of living as well as a test of
faith," she both anticipated and influenced John Dewey.

Yet to what end all of these melioristic activities? "In
the face of desperate hunger and need," Jane Addams
wrote in 1894, the depth of the worst of our depressions,
"these activities could not but seem futile and superficial." More and more she came to feel like Alice with the
Red Queen: no matter how fast she ran, she was still in
the same place; the poverty, the slums, the crime and
vice, the misgovernment, the illiteracy, the exploitation,
the inhumanity of man to man—all these were still there.
How futile to bind up wounds that should never have
been inflicted; to put together parts of lives that should
never have been shattered; to rescue girls from city
streets when fair wages would have kept them safely at
home in the first place; to give children a chance to play
in the late hours of the evening when the whole day
should belong to them; to provide emergency nursing for
diseases that should never have infected their victims.
How futile was the cure, how imperative was prevention!

One of the many merits of *Twenty Years* is that it
dramatizes to us that lesson which every generation has
to learn anew if it is to achieve understanding of either
past or present: that those who stand at the levers of
control, whether they are Southern slaveholders in the
1850's, or industrial barons in the 1890's, or labor bosses
in the 1950's, tend to use power ruthlessly, and that there
seems to be a close correlation between the social respectability of power and the ruthlessness. Certainly no

farmer or labor organization in our history ever displayed the contempt for law, the brutality toward women and children, the prejudice against aliens, the ferocity toward those who stood in their way, that corporate wealth displayed in the Chicago, and in the Illinois, that Miss Addams describes in these tragic pages.

Very early Miss Addams and her Hull House associates found that they had to move into the political arena. They helped push through labor legislation, set up juvenile courts, provided school playgrounds, worked for adequate enforcement of housing and sanitation laws, improved the school system, agitated for broader participation in politics—including woman suffrage—called for legal protection for immigrants, served as an embryonic Civil Liberties Union to preserve due process. They turned first to the municipal government, then at the very apex of corruption; then to Springfield, which was not much better. Eventually they looked to Congress and the President for national action. By the end of the first twenty years so lovingly chronicled in these pages Jane Addams was ready for a national crusade for social justice—a crusade to be waged in politics. Another five or six years and the World War launched her on an international crusade: the last years of her life were dedicated to the cause of peace, and the little girl from Cedarville who had always walked a few steps behind her father ended up by organizing the women of Austria and Italy, Japan and India, for world peace. She became the first woman to win the Nobel Peace Prize. That is the story of the Second Twenty Years.

Yet, of course, Hull House remained the center of her interest, and indeed of her world, and when she came to record the later years and the larger crusades she called the story, quite appropriately, *The Second Twenty Years at Hull House.* There it was, growing, flourishing, spreading its influence throughout the city, the state, the nation,

the entire world. It was, in all these years, a Settlement
House, a cultural center, a social service training school,
a university, and almost a church. An institution, it has
been said, is the lengthened shadow of one man. Hull
House is more than the shadow of Jane Addams; it is the
very substance.

Miss Addams's earlier activities on behalf of labor laws
and slum clearance and the rights of the poor and the
despised had earned her the suspicion and hostility of
some businessmen and of some conservative politicians;
her later activities on behalf of what we would call
the welfare state, and the cause of peace, won for her the
hatred and contumely of the professional patriots. The
American Legion denounced her as un-American, and
the Daughters of the American Revolution stigmatized
her as "a factor in a movement to destroy civilization and
Christianity." She was used to these pin pricks; she had
fought stouter opponents most of her life. Nor did she
ever allow her serenity to be ruffled by attack, or her
judgment to be warped by bitterness.

In time, of course, she weathered all attacks; in time,
the querulous dissents were drowned out by a ground
swell of acclamation and affection. She had long been the
first citizen of Chicago; by the second decade of the new
century she was widely regarded as the first citizen of the
nation, and she came in time to occupy something of the
place in the affection and admiration of the world that
Eleanor Roosevelt holds today.

Jane Addams had many talents; not the least of them,
and not the least astonishing, was her literary talent. She
wrote for the best of reasons, because she had something
that very much needed to be said. She wrote with the best
of styles—direct, lucid, and simple. She knew by instinct
what the great encyclopaedist Jean D'Alembert taught:
"Have lofty sentiments and your manner of writing will
be noble." Miss Addams did not consciously entertain

lofty sentiments, but her whole character was noble, and so too her style. She never thought of herself; even her autobiography is the story of Hull House. Was there ever a more impersonal autobiography? Henry Adams pretended to impersonality by using the third person, but it is Adams, Adams, all the way, and in the end the cosmos is invoked to explain the Adams family. Miss Addams does not ask us to consider her, but only the society she served; yet how luminously her character shines through: firm, just, gentle, efficient, tenacious, upright, and endlessly compassionate.

She was, the British labor leader John Burns said, "the only saint America had produced." It was as Saint Jane that she was known to millions around the earth and who now will challenge her right to that name?

JOHN FISKE:
AN INTERPRETATION

IN 1900 Americans were able to read John Fiske's last book, *The Life Everlasting*, and, in translation, Ernst Haeckel's *Riddle of the Universe*; thus, appropriately, the finale of eighteenth- and the prologue of twentieth-century philosophy merged in curious discord. For to Fiske, with his confident assurance of immortality as a scientific and philosophical truth, the universe was no riddle; it meant intensely and meant good, and to find its meaning was his meat and drink. He had found that meaning, indeed, forty years earlier when, browsing in Little, Brown's bookstore, he had come across the *Social Statics* and the *Principles of Psychology*, together with a prospectus of the cosmic plan already elaborated by the Englishman Herbert Spencer, and he had never felt compelled to seek another. He had promptly subscribed, not only because he was interested, but, he confessed, as "his duty to mankind," and thereafter he was assiduous in performance of duty. Two years later, under the trees of Petersham, he was reading choice passages from the *First*

SOURCE: *Proceedings of the Massachusetts Historical Society* (October 1936–May 1941), Vol. LXVI.

Principles to his fiancée, and these auspices attended his courtship, his marriage, and his early ventures into law and journalism. To the end of his life, indeed, Fiske devoted the major part of his energies to understanding and restating the doctrines of Herbert Spencer.

And what were those doctrines? They were, briefly, those of social evolution, the application of the Darwinian thesis to human society. They taught that man had evolved, socially as well as biologically, from the simple to the complex, that all human institutions had experienced this process, and that the process was governed by what Fiske himself called cosmic laws. They revealed that man had progressed, in accordance with these laws, from savagery to civilization, from chaos to order, from anarchy to law, and they promised further progress in accordance with the irresistible workings of cosmic forces.

To Fiske, as to Spencer and his disciples in England, this was indeed a gospel of good cheer. For it appeared to solve a problem that was gravely troubling the most thoughtful men of that generation. That was the problem of the validity of the moral and religious teachings that had been taken for granted in the eighteenth and early nineteenth centuries, but that were now seriously challenged by the findings of science. The philosophy of the Enlightenment, with its faith in reason and in law and its acceptance of absolutes, had been found wanting. The defects did not appear fatal, and they had been partially healed by Transcendentalism, with its assertion of the validity of truths that transcended reason and made proof superfluous. In many respects there was harmony rather than conflict between the Enlightenment and Transcendentalism; as every student of Jefferson and Emerson knows, they complemented each other. Both assumed a universe governed by law and knowable to reason; both taught that God—or providence—was good,

nature benevolent, and man and society alike perfectible.
To both, man was the center of the universe, and to both,
the laws that controlled nature and society were absolute,
and assured, in the end, the infinite happiness of mankind.

But Transcendentalism itself threatened the integrity
of the Enlightenment because it relied so largely upon
subjective and *a priori* rather than sensational facts. By
the mid-nineteenth century Transcendentalism—and its
manifestations in Romanticism—had lost respectability
almost everywhere but in America; in America it was
respectable but ineffectual. The early nineteenth century
offered nothing in place of reason and idealism; neither
Hegelianism nor Positivism nor the Scotch common-
sense philosophy could restore to Americans their waning
faith in man, in reason, and in progress, nor stem the
rising tide of materialism.

At this juncture the evolutionary philosophy of Herbert
Spencer saved the day, and it was the privilege of Fiske to
carry the glad tidings to his fellow countrymen. The new
teachings answered perfectly the needs of the time. They
gave new assurance of a universe governed by law and of
the progressive destiny of man. And now, at last, it was
all based, not on fallible reason nor on mere intuition,
but on the irreproachable findings of science. Evolution
outmoded Transcendentalism, but it did not overthrow
Transcendentalism, for if its methods were profoundly different, its conclusions were the same. Reason and intuition had wrestled vainly with the problem of evil in a
universe logically or ideally good; evolution made the
problem irrelevant. The Enlightenment had built a Heavenly City, and Transcendentalism a Utopia; but evolution held out to man the dazzling prospect of a future
more glorious than anything which either had imagined,
and its promise carried conviction.

It was the historical function of John Fiske to explain

and popularize to Americans these findings of Darwin and Spencer, to square them with religious orthodoxy, adapt them to American society, and apply them to American institutions. He lulled a generation of Americans into the conviction that there was no conflict between science and religion, helped them to sublimate their acquisitive economic practices into a philosophical system, furnished them a new basis for their belief in progress, and inculcated in them faith in the destiny of their own country and the ultimate destiny of man.

To Fiske, more largely than to any other American, was due the immense prestige which Herbert Spencer enjoyed in the United States. Youmans was, to be sure, the pioneer; but Youmans did not live to see the fulfillment of his efforts. Fiske was the ideal spokesman. He was zealous, enthusiastic, eloquent, and indefatigable; he was persuaded that Spencer was the greatest philosopher of all time and that evolution concluded all philosophy, and he won his generation to this persuasion. The influence of Spencer is, indeed, the most striking phenomenon in the intellectual history of the United States in the last quarter of the nineteenth century. The formal philosophers and academicians were not greatly impressed by him; but to the average man he was the Luther of the philosophical Reformation. And this was not only because the assiduity of Youmans and the zeal of Fiske made him plausible, but because his teachings, popularized and even vulgarized, furnished a rationalization for rugged individualism and exploitative economy. He appealed to philosophical liberals like Edwin L. Godkin and Henry Holt; he appealed no less persuasively to beneficiaries of that liberalism like Andrew Carnegie. It is not remarkable that Spencer was more widely read in the United States than in England, or that when misfortune threatened the completion of his great project, it was Americans who came to his aid. His audience here was ready and eager, and Fiske had merely to explain, not to convert.

Yet Fiske's own concern was less for the social and economic implications of the doctrine of evolution than for the religious, and he early dedicated himself to the task of reconciling evolution with orthodox Christianity. It is difficult now to appreciate the shock with which devout Christians of the 1860's received the theory of evolution. When Darwinism first burst upon the faithful, it seemed to threaten the very foundations of their faith. It rejected special creation and design, and challenged every system of philosophy or religion which reserved to man a privileged place in the universe. These threats, to be sure, had been anticipated, but neither the Deism of the eighteenth nor the liberal Unitarianism of the early nineteenth century had penetrated deep into American orthodoxy. Darwinism was far and away the most formidable danger which orthodoxy had till now encountered. Yet within a comparatively short time an accommodation was reached, and the issue, which might permanently have arrayed science against religion, was resolved or avoided.

For this happy solution Fiske was in large part responsible. For the rôle of conciliator he was admirably equipped. He had been born to orthodoxy, he was early familiar with the gentle heresies of the Transcendentalists, he was thoroughly at home in science as in religion. He was, in short, precisely the man to reassure the pious that evolution, far from threatening the foundations of faith, strengthened them. This was the thesis not only of the great *Cosmic Philosophy* but of a dozen other volumes of essays, lectures, and sermons. For it was inescapably clear to Fiske that evolution implied the existence of a creative mind and of a plan, that it required belief in an omniscient God and a beneficent nature. But there was more here than even Spencer had supposed. Not only religion as an institution, but faith itself was part of the great evolutionary process. This was the substance of Fiske's cosmic theism, suggested with originality, argued with plausibility, elaborated with learning, dimly anticipating some of William James's later intuitions.

The ethical note is, indeed, far stronger in Fiske than in his master, and it permeates all his writings, historical as well as philosophical. Fiske was at bottom a moralist, just as the great Transcendentalists, Emerson, Parker, Alcott, had been moralists. Science was for him no mere objective study, nor was the universe that science revealed impersonal and amoral. "The distinction between right and wrong," he asserted, "is rooted in the deepest foundations of the universe." And again: "I think it can be shown . . . that the cosmic process is ethical in the profoundest sense, that in the far-off morning of the world, when the stars sang together and the sons of God shouted for joy, the beauty of self-sacrifice and disinterested love formed the chief burden of the mighty theme."

Fiske remained, then, the most notable and certainly the most articulate representative of Victorian optimism. He was sure that he could read the cosmic processes and that they promised well for man. He thought the world good but knew that the best was yet to be. He expressed in prose, usually sober but sometimes lyric, the buoyant faith of Matthew Arnold and Robert Browning, the faith in an eternity which affirmed the conception of an hour. Yet even as he wrote and preached so confidently, science was abandoning the positions which he thought impregnable, and philosophy, too. A new physics was to unveil a mechanistic and impersonal universe in which man was insignificant, to substitute energy for purpose, and to match evolution with entropy; a new philosophy confessed that progress was a fiction and moral laws illusions with which men momentarily consoled themselves.

But all this Fiske stubbornly ignored, and his letters as

well as his more formal writings are innocent of any recognition of its import. Other Americans, notably Henry Adams, were much concerned with the meaning of the new physics and with the effort to apply it to society. Of all Americans of the post-war generation, Fiske and Adams present perhaps the sharpest contrast. Both New Englanders, reared in the Puritan tradition, molded by Harvard College and its associations, self-trained to history and to science, at home in English thought and society, their differences in outlook were far more significant than their similarities in station. Fiske preached a genial optimism, Adams a dark pessimism; Fiske was confident of progress, Adams no less sure of degradation; Fiske insisted stubbornly on preserving the ethical elements in science, Adams was indifferent alike to ethics and to religion. To Fiske the universe was an organism evolving inevitably toward perfection, and the destiny of man was to share in this evolution; to Adams the universe was a clock that was running down, and the destiny of man a steady deterioration ending in death.

In another respect, however, Fiske bears a superficial resemblance to the melancholy Adams. Not only were both historians, but both attempted to formulate laws of history. In that generation, as Adams tells us, every historian thought that he was on the verge of discovering some great law that would do for history what Newton had done for the natural sciences. Adams himself formulated a law, and so, too, did his brother Brooks and the scientist, John William Draper. Even in more limited fields there were efforts to find some framework that would explain or organize historical development—the frontier, geography, democracy, race, economics. Adams presented his law after he had written his histories, and one looks in vain through the brilliant pages of the *History of the United States* or the *Life of Albert Gallatin* for any application of the second law of thermodynamics. Fiske formulated his law first, but he applied it to history only incidentally. That law was, very simply, the law of evolution. It was Spencer applied to historical as well as to sociological processes.

The logical laboratory for the testing of such a law was, of course, the American. For America was, clearly, the climax of the evolution of European society. Here in this new world the interaction between inheritance and environment could be most clearly observed; here social and political institutions had developed most naturally; here the whole process was so recent and so fully recorded that it afforded invaluable data to the evolutionary-minded historian. As early as 1879 Fiske mapped out a course of lectures on the genesis of American political ideas "treated according to the law of evolution," and he had the assurance of Spencer himself that if he would stick to history, he could "go beyond anything ever yet done." He did stick to history, but he did not go very far—not, indeed, beyond his generalizations.

The trouble was, of course, that the scheme was too large for practical purposes, too large and too generalized. Fiske was brave enough in the announcement of his formula but timid in its application. Spencer had pointed the way toward emphasis upon the particular, and his synthetic philosophy was the result of an accumulation of a multitude of facts. Fiske confined himself to a few, more obvious, facts and failed to achieve a synthesis. Notwithstanding his interest in the evolution of institutions, the history that he actually wrote was orthodox political and military narrative, narrow in scope and parochial in point of view. He was concerned with the modification of old-world inheritance by new-world environment, but he limited his study of inheritance to Anglo-Saxon law and politics, and of environment to the Atlantic coast. He was concerned with institutions, but he left out economics, and his social history, though charming, was merely descriptive. His philosophy of history, in short, was promising, but the promise was never fulfilled.

It is not for their philosophy, however, that Fiske's histories are remembered and sometimes read, but for other qualities of a very different character. Fiske had a talent for the organization and exposition of historical materials that amounted to genius. No American historian was ever more successful in unraveling the tangled skein of history and reweaving it into a pattern bright and clear. There was no room for confusion in Fiske's historical scheme, for evolution does not permit of confusion. Scarcely less important were a breadth of learning and urbanity of treatment, an old-fashioned scholarship that was at home in ancient, medieval, or modern history, familiar with ethnology and anthropology and mythology, ready with an apt allusion from homely experience or an appropriate quotation from literature. Together with this there was everywhere the play of a lively intelligence—a quality reflective rather than philosophical—a readiness to interpret character or moralize about events that fitted well the Victorian mood. And all these qualities were enhanced by a style always smooth and clear, usually felicitous, and occasionally brilliant.

These qualities grace most of Fiske's sweeping panorama of our colonial history. Everywhere—in the *Old Virginia and Her Neighbours*, the *Beginnings of New England,* the *Dutch and Quaker Colonies*, and the posthumous *New France and New England*—one is beguiled by a warm feeling for the physical environment, a generous recollection of illuminating details, brilliant portrayal of character, a sense of life and of movement, a lively humor, a spaciousness and sophistication of treatment. Everywhere the learning is unobtrusive, the imagination controlled, the argument firm and independent. Modern scholarship discounts some of the interpretation—the insistence upon the dominant Cavalier element in the

Old Dominion, for example—but modern scholarship has yet to paint a more picturesque canvas of colonial history than that which came from Fiske's expert brush.

Yet, notwithstanding these literary virtues, Fiske is no longer widely known or widely read. Scholars still consult *The Discovery of America;* students who gag at McMaster or at Hildreth read *The Critical Period;* but Fiske has no audience comparable to that which his contemporaries, Parkman and Adams, command. The fact is that in his own day Fiske's fame derived very largely from his lectures. It was for lectures that he prepared his histories, and it was, appropriately, as a lecturer that he was most familiar to his own generation.

This is the story most elaborately set forth in Fiske's voluminous letters, and it is a story not without its sober overtones. As a lecturer on historical topics Fiske served a useful purpose; to him, more largely than to any other, is due the credit for reviving an interest in American history and for giving that interest a scholarly rather than a merely rationalist quality. His audience, to be sure, was ready and sensitive. The Centennial Exposition had reawakened interest in the American past, and the Civil War had inspired a pride in nationalism that was easily canalized into an interest in national history. Fiske's first historical lectures were given to English audiences, and his fame reverberated back to his own country; if the English were interested in the American past, certainly it was respectable for Americans to confess the same interest. In 1879 Fiske gave a course on American history at the Old South Church in Boston; "the applause was great," he wrote, "and I had a sort of sense that I was fascinating the people and it was delicious beyond expression." He was, indeed, fascinating, and the demands upon him were incessant. Soon he was bounding about the country, hurrying from town to town, from state to state, his hirsute behemoth figure familiar to audiences from Cape

Cod to Puget Sound. Lecturing brought him fame and fortune, and soon it was fame and fortune that he was interested in. He abandoned the Harvard College Library and his ambitions for a teaching position, abandoned, too, his ambitious scholarly projects, and threw himself wholeheartedly into his lectures. After a time Major Pond got hold of him: Pond who had promoted Beecher and Mark Twain and many others. Fiske loved the excitement of it all, compared himself cheerfully to the circus, the opera, the Greek play, and boasted of a "Fiske season." He conquered New England, he harried the Middle West, he carried the Pacific coast by storm. In 1881 he "made a pile of money" in Wisconsin, for "they're lively folks out there, want to hear all the new notions"; three years later he was sure of ten thousand dollars for the season; in 1888 he acknowledged 143 lectures. He was a veritable Chautauqua, a peripatetic chair of history and philosophy, and he cheerfully accommodated his menu to the taste of his audiences. He lectured to universities and learned societies and to the President's cabinet; he lectured to ladies' clubs and sipped tea; he lectured to girls innocent of history but eager for culture, and counted five courses at fashionable schools in one winter. Thus he laid waste his powers.

In all this Fiske illustrated a development characteristic of the postwar generation: a watering down of the spiritual content of philosophy, an acquiescence in materialism, an admiration for the public manifestations of success. An earlier generation, too, had taken to the lecture platform, but one looks in vain through the letters of Emerson or Parker or Alcott for any such concern with social prestige and financial returns as permeates the correspondence of Fiske. These giants of an earlier day were men with a message. They, too, counted their audiences, but they counted them with a view to the influence that they might exert, the converts they might make.

There is much in Fiske's letters about his audiences, but little about history or philosophy.

This materialism, emanating from the lecture platform, affected many aspects of Fiske's character. It explains, in part, his desertion of philosophy for history, and it explains the kind of history that he wrote. He confessed that he preferred ancient or medieval to American history, but he willingly adapted himself to his market. He took on job after job and regretted that he had so little time for study or thought. Even Harvard College, finally, was admirable because its fellowship brought material rewards, his observation on college friendships was not entirely facetious: "the moment a little favor is desired, you have only to suggest it, and it's 'Come on, my dear fellow, we'll do what we can for you.' That's why I say, let all my boys go to Harvard College; it pays."

In other respects, too, Fiske illuminates certain traits characteristic of his time. Perhaps the most interesting of these was that return to colonialism which Mr. Van Wyck Brooks has recently noted as an essential element in the New England mind of the postwar years. Fiske himself was a Yankee born and bred, the product of an environment more parochial than most parts of the United States. It was New England that he loved, and he resisted every inducement to live in any other section. To walk beneath the elms of Cambridge was his delight, and to tramp the fields of Petersham was very heaven. Yet even in this Connecticut Yankee there were distinct traits of the new colonialism. Compare Emerson in England with Fiske, a quarter-century later: Emerson studying English traits but preserving his American traits with austere dignity; Fiske reveling in English society, eager for English patronage. Imagine Emerson writing, as did Fiske: "This X club that I dined with last Thursday is the most powerful and influential scientific coterie in England. . . . You see they are an influential set of chaps, and there are ever so many fellows in England who would have thought it a great thing to be invited to dine with them. They are exclusive enough, and not lavish with their compliments to folks. Besides all this, they have a good deal of indirect influence with the best Reviews, and so on." Fiske's physical roots were in New England, but his intellectual in Old. There, he felt, was his spiritual home, and tea in London with the right people surpassed anything that Boston had to offer.

It was not only that England was the source of the new philosophy, the home of Darwin and Spencer. In other respects, too, Fiske looked to England—in literature, education, and the arts. The persistent colonial, he was sure that only in Europe did they know about painting and sculpture and the arts, and, if we are to go by his letters he had never heard of Richardson or Sullivan, Saint-Gaudens or La Farge; for him Homer and Ryder and Eakins painted in vain. He had grown up in the midst of the pleasantest architecture in America, but he was irritated that we did not "honestly confess our stupidity . . . by copying Oxford or Cambridge buildings literally." It was English literature that he read, English poetry that he quoted, English character that he liked.

So far as his letters indicate, indeed, Fiske was more familiar with and more interested in English than in American public affairs. The indifference which he managed to display toward the great issues agitating American society during his lifetime suggests a curious dissociation from the fundamental interests of that society. He was a young man at college when the batteries at Charleston barked at Fort Sumter, and he congratulated himself that defective eyesight made him ineligible for military service. Nor did he later show any active interest in the issues of the war or in its outcome; his study of the

Mississippi Valley in the Civil War was purely military.
So, too, with the issues and events that dominated American
life through the last third of the century. Fiske's
letters do not recognize any of the great political questions:
reconstruction, impeachment, the contested election,
civil service reform, tariffs, trust and railroad regulation,
the money question, expansion, and imperialism.
They are equally innocent of reactions to social and economic
issues. During the years of Fiske's maturity the
country was swept by two major panics, by agrarian revolt,
by profound disturbances in the relations of capital
and labor. Farmers gathered in Grange halls and denounced
monopolies; Greenbackers called for inflation;
western legislatures struck at the railroads, and the Supreme
Court sustained them; anarchists rioted in Haymarket
Square, and innocent men were held responsible
for the riot; Pinkerton detectives fought a pitched battle
with workingmen on the banks of the Monongahela; the
Pullman strike tied up transportation throughout the nation,
and Cleveland sent troops to Chicago in defiance of
Altgeld. Populism swept the West, farmers clamored for
free silver, Bryan rejected the cross of gold, and a bumptious
nation went to war with Spain and was perplexed at
the consequences. Not a word of all this disturbs the
placid surface of Fiske's correspondence. Through it all
he went serenely on, preparing his courses, counting his
auditors, and rejoicing in success.

This divorce from current affairs was in one particular
especially remarkable. That was with respect to practical
progressivism. Fiske devoted a good part of his lifetime to
preaching philosophical progressivism; but in contemporary
efforts to secularize that philosophy he had no interest.
He had grown up in the atmosphere of the greatest,
the most profound, the most sweeping of all reform
movements in our history, and he reached the height of
his powers at the time when the progressive movement of

the nineties was enlisting the energies of men and women all over the country. Henry George, Bellamy, Debs, Altgeld, Bryan, Riis, Storey, Gladden, and a hundred other crusaders were wrestling with the task of ameliorating the crowding evils that afflicted American society. But if Fiske had knowledge of or interest in all this, he failed to reveal it. Perhaps the explanation is to be found in the consolation which the Spencerian doctrine did, after all, afford the philosopher: that though the cosmic processes worked slowly, they worked surely, and all would come right in the end. Certainly it was to the conservatives, the defenders of the status quo and of *laissez faire*, that Spencer irresistibly appealed, and these, in their struggle against radicalism, Fiske all unwittingly supported.

Even in Fiske's professional work there appears something of this same insularity. He was a purveyor of philosophy but scarcely a philosopher—as his contemporaries Royce and James were philosophers—and his professional contacts were meager. Neither his letters nor his writings reveal any interest in the philosophy that antedated Spencer—in Plato or Aristotle or Aquinas or Spinoza or Kant; nor did he trouble himself with contemporary movements other than the Spencerian. He appeared at the Concord School of Philosophy but ignored the weary Transcendentalists who sponsored it. He lectured regularly in St. Louis but was not interested in the Hegelianism which had here put down uncertain roots. He associated with William James but not with James's new pragmatic philosophy.

In history, too, Fiske's professional isolation is striking. The most widely known historian of his day, his responsibility for the revival of interest in American history was a compelling one, but he did not interpret it as requiring any association with fellow workers in the field or recognition of their harvest. Just at the time when Fiske himself turned to history, the study of history in the United States was becoming organized and professionalized. Scholars trooped hopefully over to the German universities and, returning with their Ph.D.'s, conducted seminars dedicated to the study of manuscripts and the production of monographs. History emancipated itself from its antiquarian and its filiopietistic bonds, divorced itself from literature, and married science. Scholars like Schouler, Winsor, Rhodes, McMaster, Adams, and a host of others reexamined and rewrote the history of the American past, and the professional journals groaned with the products of their disciples. It is not apparent that any of this new ferment affected Fiske. One would not know, from his writings, that any contemporary historian had written anything of the slightest interest to him. Much of *The Critical Period* was based upon the first volume of McMaster's *History*, but one searches in vain for any reference to that scholar. In 1895 Fiske gave a lecture on the Frontier in American History, but his letters do not mention the fact that Turner had announced the frontier theory two years earlier.

Indeed, in history as in philosophy, it is difficult to escape the impression that Fiske was a magnificent amateur and, toward the end of his career, something of a dilettante. This is not to suggest that his scholarship was not thorough nor his purpose serious, but that his significance lies largely in his successful popularization of the findings of others. His own contribution—and it was important—was limited to his doctrine of the social significance of the prolongation of infancy. In philosophy he was, as his friend Howells observed, "the mockingbird of Spencer," and with the passing of Spencer, Fiske's philosophical writings have taken on a faintly antiquarian character. In history he made some original contributions, but nothing that he wrote has the permanence of the best of Parkman or of Henry Adams, and for the most

part he was content to polish the nuggets quarried by
others. He consistently accommodated himself to his patrons, in philosophy and in history alike; even his books,
with their neat arrangements and their dramatizations,
are evidence of that. His talents for organization and
exposition were of so high an order that they overwhelmed those talents for original scholarship which he
had possessed. His mind was uncreative, his genius sec-
ondhand. And in this, too, he reflected his age, which
exploited the past for the necessities of the present, ra-
tionalized its will into a religion, and laid up little of use
to the future.

But no interpretation of Fiske that confined itself to
his intellectual significance and ignored his personality
would be complete. The explanation of his immense popularity is not to be found exclusively in the gospel that
he preached, but rather in qualities of character and
personality that endeared him to his contemporaries and
recommend him to posterity. For he was, indeed, a wonderful creature, so large and energetic, bubbling over with
life, breathless with enthusiasm, buoyant and cheer-
ful and generous, an intellectual dynamo with a mind
that raced like electricity and an inexhaustible store of
learning, prodigal of his talents and of his affections; a
great, companionable person out of Pickwick, happy in
the inns of London or on the highroads of England, reveling in long talks and long bouts with beer and tobacco
and ready to leap to the defense of these with his indomitable pen, confessing cheerfully his enjoyment of food
and drink. Nothing wearied him, not the endless succession of books to be catalogued or to be read or to be
written, or of lectures to be delivered; he would edit an
encyclopedia or furnish copy for the newspaper or preach
a sermon or sing songs on demand; even travel was not
tedious, and he never grumbled at the discomforts of the
railroad or of small-town hotels, but found it all refresh-

ing. He was incurably romantic: about his wife whom he adored and his children who tumbled around him; about beauty in every form—the snug hills of Petersham or the lochs of Scotland or the blue waters of Puget Sound, the beeches of England, and the fragrant roses that he cultivated. And he was happiest when he could sing the lyrics of Schubert or play the sonatas of Beethoven. He delighted in the richness of life; and in his felicity he embraced with gusto his work, his family, his friends, his books, knew no hesitations or frustration, never doubted that his world was good or that his feet were set firmly upon the right path. This is the Fiske who emerges, living, from his letters; and he is, for all his limitations, one of the most lovable figures of his generation.

SHOULD THE HISTORIAN SIT IN JUDGMENT?

I

IN 1847 that Boston gentleman and man of letters William Hickling Prescott concluded twenty years of labor on the history of the expansion of Spain under Ferdinand and Isabella, the conquest of Mexico and of Peru. It was a noble edifice that he had raised, the most impressive literary monument yet reared in the New World. So said Daniel Webster: a comet had blazed out on the world in full splendor. So said Lord Holland, over in London: it was the most important historical work since Gibbon. So said the great Alexander von Humboldt, who had embraced the entire cosmos. The Royal Academy of History at Madrid, the Royal Society of Berlin, the Institute in Paris welcomed the Bostonian to honorary membership. And from John Quincy Adams came the grudging tribute that the reader could not tell whether the author was Protestant or Catholic, monarchist or republican.

To Prescott that was the highest praise of all. Confronted with three of the most blood-stained chapters of history—Spain of the Inquisition and the expulsion of

SOURCE: Originally published as "Should the Historian Make Moral Judgments?" in *American Heritage* (February 1966). Copyright © 1966 by Henry Steele Commager.

the Moors, the conquest of Mexico, and the conquest of Peru—Prescott tried to avoid moral judgment. How easy to condemn Ximenes for his reliance on the Inquisition; how easy to denounce Cortés for the treachery and greed and brutality which accompanied the swift conquest of Mexico; how easy to execrate the wretched Pizarro for cruelties almost unparalleled in the history of conquest. Prescott was not unaware of the embarrassments of impartiality. "To the American and the English reader," he wrote in the Preface to his *Mexico*, "acknowledging so different a moral standard from that of the sixteenth century, I may possibly be thought too indulgent to the errors of the conquerors." And he confessed that he had indeed "given them the benefit of such mitigating reflections as might be suggested by the circumstances and the period in which they lived." Two considerations, not entirely consistent, stayed the intuitive judgment of the moralist in Prescott. First, the familiar argument that the standards of the sixteenth century were not those of the nineteenth, and that we should not arbitrarily impose our standards upon the past. "It is far from my intention," wrote Prescott, "to vindicate the cruel deeds of the old Conquerors. Let them lie heavy on their heads. They were an iron race who periled life and fortune in the cause; and as they made little account of danger and suffering for themselves, they had little sympathy to spare for their unfortunate enemies. But to judge them fairly we must not do it by the lights of our own age. We must carry ourselves back to theirs, and take the point of view afforded by the civilization of their time" (*Mexico*, I, p. 425).

The second plea in extenuation was broader—and more dubious; it was also more Victorian. It was that the cruelty and bloodshed which accompanied the destruction of the two great civilizations of the New World were, in a sense, the price of progress. The Aztecs and the Incas were, after all, so he asserted, backward and even barba-

rous peoples. It is therefore pure sentimentalism for us to
"regret the fall of an empire which did so little to promote
the happiness of its subjects or the real interests of humanity." The Aztecs, particularly, "were a fierce and bru-
tal race, little calculated, in their best aspect, to excite our
sympathy and regard. Their civilization . . . was a generous graft on a vicious stock, and could have brought no
fruit to perfection." We cannot choose the instruments or
the vessels of the spread of civilization and of Christianity; these are often blunt and warped. But over the generations and the centuries we can see that this is the way
progress works to eliminate the weak and the backward
and to make room for the strong and the progressive.
May we not, therefore, conclude, that "it was beneficently
ordered by Providence that the land [of the Mexicans]
should be delivered over to another race who would rescue it from the brutish superstitions that daily extended
wider and wider?" (*Mexico*, II, p. 350; I, p. 75)

The Reverend Theodore Parker—known in his day as
"the Great American Preacher"—was both a scholar and
a moral philosopher. As a scholar he was prepared to be
indulgent toward Mr. Prescott's histories, for superficial
as they were, they had their points. But as a moralist
Mr. Parker had no patience with Prescott's apologies and
evasions and extenuations. In two long essays in the
Massachusetts Quarterly Review—which he edited—
Mr. Parker raked Mr. Prescott fore and aft for what he
regarded as moral cowardice. At every point in his narrative the historian of the conquests of Mexico and Peru
had excused, palliated, and condoned, until in the end we
were forced to conclude that his moral sensibilities were
as calloused as his judgment was warped. Who was Mr.
Prescott that he should suspend judgment over the hide-
ous cruelties and iniquities of the conquistadores?

> Mr. Prescott shows little horror at these [Spanish] cru-
> elties, little sense of their injustice; nay, he seems to

seek to mitigate the natural indignation which a man feels at such tyranny of the strong over the weak. We confess our astonishment that an historian who thinks the desire of converting the heathen was the paramount motive in the breast of Cortez has no more censure to bestow on such wanton cruelties, so frequently perpetrated as they were. [*Works,* X, p. lvi.]

It is one thing to explain, but another thing to condone, the crimes of the past. "Crime is one thing," thundered Parker,

but the theory which excuses, defends, justifies crime is quite a different thing, is itself not to be justified, defended or excused. We are sorry to add the name of Mr. Prescott to the long list of writers who have a theory which attempts to justify the crime against mankind, the tyranny of might over right. We are sorry to say of this work . . . that it is not written in the philosophy of this age, and still worse, not in the Christianity, the wide humanity, which is of mankind." [*Works,* X, p. 150.]

What all this meant was that Mr. Prescott had failed to fulfill the high duty of the historian. The Rev. Mr. Parker made clear the nature of that duty. "In telling what has been, the historian is also to tell what ought to be, for he is to pass judgment on events, and to try counsels by their causes first, and by their consequences not less. When all these things are told, history ceases to be a mere panorama of events having no unity but time and place; it becomes a philosophy teaching by experience and has a profound meaning and awakens a deep interest, while it tells the lessons of the past for the warning of the present and edification of the future" (*Works,* X, p. 86). Parker's final verdict followed unequivocally: "Thus, lacking philosophy, and having more of the spirit of chivalry than of humanity, it is impossible that Mr. Prescott should write in the interest of mankind, or judge men and their deeds by . . . the immutable law of the universe."

Now let us look across the sea. It is forty years later, but Queen Victoria is still upon the throne, and literature is still regarded as a moral enterprise. In 1887 the Reverend Mandell Creighton, canon of Worcester Cathedral and professor of ecclesiastical history at Cambridge University, published the fourth and fifth volumes of his magisterial *History of the Popes*. He promptly sent the volumes off to his old friend and distinguished fellow historian Lord Acton. Acton was a Catholic, perhaps the most famous Catholic historian in all Europe. A scholar of prodigious learning, he took the whole of history into his embrace, including, needless to say, the history of the medieval church; his specialty was the history of liberty. Lord Acton had immense respect for Creighton's scholarship but less for his judgment. What disturbed him was that Professor Creighton had recorded the melancholy history of the papacy during the late Middle Ages without disapproval or censure. "The Popes of the thirteenth and fourteenth century," wrote the great Acton, "instituted a system of persecution. . . . It is the most conspicuous fact in the history of the medieval Papacy." Creighton had not made the fact of persecution central to his tale, nor had he sufficiently condemned the intolerance and cruelty of such popes as Innocent IV, Innocent VI, and Sixtus IV, who bore so heavy a burden of guilt.

Clearly there was a real principle at stake here, a principle of historical interpretation and even of historical philosophy. "You say that people in authority are not to be snubbed or sneered at from our pinnacle of conscious rectitude," wrote Lord Acton. "I cannot accept your canon that we are to judge Pope and King unlike other men." And then came the statement of principle: "The inflexible integrity of the moral code is to me the secret of the authority, the dignity, the utility of history. If we may debase the currency for the sake of genius or success or reputation, we may debase it for the sake of a man's

influence, or his religion, or his party. . . . Then history
ceases to be a science, an arbiter of controversy, a guide
to the wanderer. . . . It serves where it ought to reign,
and it serves the worst cause better than the purest."
Professor Creighton put Acton off with soft words, but to
another historical friend he complained that Acton demanded that "history should be primarily a branch of the
moral sciences." But "my view of history," he added, "is
not to approach things with any preconceived ideas,
but with the natural *pietas* and sympathy which I try
to feel towards all men who do and try to do great
things. . . . I try to put myself in their place; to see their
limitations; and leave the course of events to pronounce
the verdict upon a system and men alike. No doubt Acton
is more logical, but his view would reduce history to a
dreary record of crimes, to which I am unequal."

In this fascinating exchange between two of the great
figures of English historical scholarship the issue was
joined, an old and familiar issue which is still with us. To
judge or not to judge? Should the historian sit in judgment over the great drama of the past and the men and
women who performed on that vast and crowded stage,
exposing evil and celebrating virtue and damning and
praising famous men? Or should he observe the historical
processes with scientific detachment and record them as
automatically as a tape recorder, rigorously excluding
personal, national, or religious considerations? Is he competent to perform either of these functions—the function
of the judge or the function of the impartial reporter?

The problem is difficult and perhaps insoluble. It raises
hard questions about the purpose of history, the duties
and responsibilities of the scholar, the nature of historical
judgment, and the distinctions, if any, between what
might be called moral and secular judgment. It raises
questions, too, about the competence of any historian to
judge the past, and the sanctions, if any, behind such

judgments as are rendered. And it requires us to weigh
the dangers implicit in moral neutrality against those
inherent in moral arrogance and intellectual parochialism.

Earlier generations of historians were not seriously
troubled by this problem of judgment. The Greek historians Herodotus and Thucydides were surprisingly free
from the urge to judge, but their successors in the ancient
world took for granted that their function was to edify, to
instruct, and to judge. Livy invited his readers to ponder
the moral lessons taught by the history of Rome—as he
presented it—and to observe how Rome rose to greatness
through her virtues and how the decay of these virtues
brought ruin. Tacitus thought the highest function of
history was to "rescue merit from oblivion" and "to hold
out the reprobation of posterity as a warning and a rebuke to all base conduct." Plutarch, who wrote some sixty
Moral Essays, compiled his famous *Parallel Lives* not to
adorn a tale but to point a moral, and he succeeded
beyond his furthest imagination.

Medieval historians knew perfectly well what were the
moral standards to which history was obliged to conform,
and they knew, too, the penalties of nonconformity; for
what was history but the working out of God's will with
man? Even the great eighteenth-century historians, Gibbon and Hume and Robertson, Rollin and Voltaire and
Raynal, accepted Bolingbroke's aphorism that history was
philosophy teaching by examples, and they assumed that
its lessons were moral and that it was the duty of the
historian to point them. Only with the rise of "historicism" in the nineteenth century—there were antecedents, to be sure, in such historians as Machiavelli and
Vico—did the question of the propriety and the validity of
moral judgment come to the fore. Ranke, and his successors and disciples in almost every country, abjured moral
judgment, or said that they did, and set themselves the

task of simply recording what had actually happened with a minimum of comment and with neither approval nor disapproval. Theirs was the ideal that Henry Adams later found so futile: "To satisfy himself whether, by the severest process of stating, with the least possible comment, such facts as seemed sure, in such order as seemed rigorously consequent, he could fix for a familiar moment a necessary sequence of human movement" (*Education of Henry Adams*, p. 382).

There was bound to be a reaction away from this austere principle, especially as so few of its protagonists actually lived up to it. The Victorian era, which in Germany saw the triumph of historicism, was also the era of morality, of moral preaching in law and in economics, in politics and in history, as in art and in literature. It is difficult to know whether such historians as Froude in England, Michelet in France, Treitschke in Germany, or Motley in America considered themselves primarily ethical leaders or historical scholars; in fact they did not distinguish sharply between the two roles. "The eternal truths and rights of things," said James Anthony Froude in his inaugural address as rector of St. Andrews University, "exist independent of our thoughts or wishes, fixed as mathematics, inherent in the nature of man and the world."

That was Thomas Carlyle's view, too—Froude, rightly enough, wrote his biography. Listen to Carlyle—it is in his essay on Goethe—commenting on philosophy in general and historical philosophy in particular:

> To the faithful heart let no era be a desperate one! It is ever the nature of Darkness to be followed by a new nobler Light; nay, to produce such. The woes and contradictions of an Atheistic time; of a world sunk in wickedness and baseness and unbelief, wherein also physical wretchedness, the disorganisation and broken-heartedness of whole classes struggling in ignorance and pain will not fail: all this, the view of all this, falls

like a Sphinx-question on every earnest heart to deliver
itself from, and the world from. Of Wisdom cometh
Strength: only when there is "no vision" do people
perish. . . . Woe to the land where, in these seasons,
no prophet arises; but only censors, satirists and embit-
tered desperadoes, to make the evil worse; at best but to
accelerate a consummation, which in accelerating they
have aggravated! Old Europe had its Tacitus and Juvenal; but these availed not. New Europe too has had its
Mirabeaus, and Byrons, and Napoleons, and innumerable red-flaming meteors, shaking pestilence from their
hair; and earthquakes and deluges, and Chaos come
again; but the clear Star, day's harbinger, had not yet
been recognised. [*Critical and Miscellaneous Essays,*
Vol. IV, pp. 164–5.]

John Lothrop Motley imported moral judgment even
more directly into his history; here is his final verdict on
Philip II of Spain:

There have been few men known to history who have
been able to accomplish by their own exertions so vast
an amount of evil as the king who had just died. If
Philip possessed a single virtue it has eluded the conscientious research of the writer of these pages. If there
are vices—as possibly there are—from which he was
exempt, it is because it is not permitted to human
nature to attain perfection even in evil. The only plausible explanation—for palliation there is none—of his
infamous career is that the man really believed himself
not a king but a God. He was placed so high above his
fellow creatures as, in good faith perhaps, to believe
himself incapable of doing wrong; so that, whether
indulging his passions or enforcing throughout the
world his religious and political dogmas, he was ever
conscious of embodying divine inspirations and elemental laws. When providing for the assassination of a
monarch, or commanding the massacre of a townful of
Protestants; when trampling on every oath by which a
human being can bind himself; when laying desolate
with fire and sword during more than a generation the
provinces which he had inherited as his private property or in carefully maintaining the flames of civil war

in foreign kingdoms which he hoped to acquire; while maintaining over all Christendom a gigantic system of bribery, corruption and espionage . . . he ever felt that these base or bloody deeds were not crimes, but the simple will of the godhead of which he was a portion. [*United Netherlands*, Vol. V, pp. 74–5.]

And in case his readers might think that he had stepped out of his province in thus condemning the Spanish monarch, Motley added a word on the responsibility of the historian:

> When an humble malefactor is brought before an ordinary court of justice, it is not often, in any age or country, that he escapes the pillory or the gallows because, from his own point of view, his actions, instead of being criminal, have been commendable, and because the multitude and continuity of his offenses prove him to have been sincere. And because anointed monarchs are amenable to no human tribunal, save to that terrible assize which the People, bursting its chain from time to time in the course of the ages, sets up for the trial of its oppressors, and which is called Revolution, it is the more important for the great interests of humanity that before the judgment-seat of History a crown should be no protection to its wearer. There is no plea to the jurisdiction of history, if history be true to itself.
>
> As for the royal criminal called Philip II., his life is his arraignment, and these volumes will have been written in vain if a specification is now required. [*United Netherlands*, Vol. V, p. 79.]

In a Carlyle or a Motley moral judgment was a form of self-indulgence. But there was more to it than this, there was high duty! The clearest and most persuasive statement of the moral function of the historian came from Lord Acton himself. Eight years after his exchange with Canon Creighton, Acton was appointed Regius Professor of History at Cambridge University. In his inaugural address he once again exhorted his listeners—and all students of history—"never to debase the moral currency or

to lower the standards of rectitude, but to try others by
the final maxim that governs your own lives, and to suffer
no man and no cause to escape the undying penalty
which history has the power to inflict on wrong. The plea
in extenuation of guilt and mitigation of punishment is
perpetual. At every step we are met by arguments which
go to excuse, to palliate, to confound right and wrong
and reduce the just man to the level of the reprobate. . . .
Opinions alter, manners change, creeds rise and fall,
but the moral law is written on the tablets of eternity."
"We have the power," he concluded, "to learn from un-
disguised and genuine records to look with remorse upon
the past, and to the future with assured hope of better
things; bearing this in mind, that if we lower our standards in History, we cannot uphold it in Church or State."

We cannot glibly ascribe Acton's philosophy to his Ca-
tholicism; he was not a very orthodox Catholic, and his
quarrel with Creighton—and with his old master, Johann
Döllinger—was that they had not sufficiently rebuked the
medieval popes. Such diverse contemporary historians as
Veronica Wedgwood, Isaiah Berlin, and Arnold Toynbee—none of them Catholic—all acquiesce in the necessity of moral judgment in history. Thus Miss Wedgewood,
who has done so much to illuminate the great political
and religious issues that stirred England in the seventeenth century, warns us against "the confusion into
which historians fall when they make allowances for
'the standards of the age.' Their intention is to understand and be just to the past, but the result in the long
run may be unfair to the present, because this outlook
steadily and stealthily fosters the conviction that nothing
is good or bad in itself, but only in relation to its sur-
roundings. . . . The aspiration to understand and to
forgive is noble and valid in personal relationships between the living but," she concludes, "the application of
the principle of . . . forgiveness to historical personages

is a sentimental fallacy" (*Truth and Opinion*, pp. 48–9).

Arnold Toynbee, who has concerned himself more consistently with the universal and the eternal than any other modern historian, has remained throughout his distinguished career a Christian moralist, ready to judge the past and the present: his assertion that the expulsion of the Arabs from Palestine by the Israelis was no less a crime than the Nazi murder of some six million Jews precipitated an international controversy.

All of this constitutes what might be called a moral argument in favor of moral judgment. The moral laws are universal and timeless; murder is always murder and betrayal is always betrayal, cruelty and intolerance are always the same; the historian cannot stand above the moral laws, or stand aside from them, but must acknowledge them and participate in them and apply them. If he does not, he will fail the cause of morality—and of history as well—and forfeit the confidence and respect of his peers.

There is, however, another and perhaps more persuasive argument for moral judgment in history, one that rests not so much on moral as on psychological grounds. It is that the historian cannot, in any event, help himself, and that he might as well acknowledge what is inherent and implicit in his condition. He is, after all, a creature of his time, his society, his faith. Even if he resolutely refrains from overt moral judgment, he will surely be guilty of covert judgment: his choice of subject, his selection of facts, his very vocabulary, will betray him. How much better, then, how much fairer and more honest, to acknowledge his position in advance; how much better to call his book—it is Charles A. Beard who makes the point—*An Economic Interpretation of the Constitution* rather than to fall back on a title like *The Making of the Constitution,* one that "does not advise the reader at the

outset concerning the upshot to be expected." History is
not a science and the historian is not a scientist. "The
supreme command," therefore, "is that he must cast off
his servitude to the assumptions of natural science and
return to his own subject matter—to history as actuality."

This is the argument, too, of the distinguished Oxford
philosopher Sir Isaiah Berlin, who sees in the passion for
scientific impartiality yet another expression of the misguided and pernicious belief that history is a science.
"The case against the notion of historical objectivity," he
writes, "is like the case against international law, or international morality; that it does not exist." And he adds the
warning that

> Except on the assumption that history must deal with
> human beings purely as material objects in space,
> must, in short, be behaviourist,—its method can scarely
> be assimilated to the standards of an exact natural
> science. The invocation to historians to suppress even
> that minimal degree of moral or psychological eval-
> uation which is necessarily involved in viewing human
> beings as creatures with purposes and motives . . .
> seems to me to rest upon a confusion of the aims and
> methods of the humane studies with those of natural
> science. It is one of the greatest and most destructive
> fallacies of the last hundred years. [*Historical Inevita-
> bility*, pp. 52–3.]

II

But the stout champions of moral judgment do not
have things all their own way. Not at all. Here comes a
whole phalanx of historians with a formidable arsenal of
counterarguments.

First, while it is true that history tries to observe something like historical "due process," it cannot in the nature
of the case do so. The past is not there to defend itself.
We cannot recall the witnesses, put them on the stand,
question and cross-examine them. It is difficult enough to

render a moral verdict on anything so recent as, let us say, Hoover's dispersion of the "bonus army" or the conduct of the Vichy government or the resort to the atomic weapon at Hiroshima; how much more difficult, then, to sit in judgment on the character of Alcibiades, the justification for the murder of Caesar, the conduct of the Norman invaders of England, or of the Spanish Conquistadors.

Second, while technical judgment is essential in the law, in the civil service, in the university, in athletics, if society is to function, such judgment does not pretend to be moral but purely professional. A university professor who permitted his moral views of a student to dictate his grades, a referee whose decisions were based on moral considerations, even a judge who allowed his private moral convictions to influence his decisions on questions of contracts, wills, liability, or bankruptcy proceedings, would be regarded as not only incompetent but expendable. There are reasonably clear standards for such practical judgments as society requires—laws, rules, tests—but as parents, psychiatrists, and priests so well know, moral judgments present questions of labyrinthine complexity even when all the relevant evidence appears to be in. Where history is concerned, the conduct of men or of nations in past centuries, all the relevant evidence, is never available, and there are no universal standards. What the historian does, when he judges, is merely to identify his own "can't-help-but-believes" with eternal verities. Herodotus made this point twenty-five centuries ago. When Darius was upon the throne, he summoned

> into his presence the Hellenes at his court and asked them for what price they would consent to make a meal of their fathers when they died. The Hellenes replied that all the money in the World would not induce them to do such a thing, whereupon Darius summoned the Callatian Indians, who do eat their parents, and asked

them (in the presence of the Hellenes, who were kept informed, through an interpreter, of the tenor of the conversation) for what price they would be willing to burn their fathers when they died. The Indians shrieked aloud and begged him not to pursue an unmentionable subject—a story which illustrates the habitual attitude of Mankind towards this question, and which, in my opinion, justifies Pindar's poetic aphorism that "Custom is king of all."

Justice Holmes made the point with even greater succinctness. "I prefer champagne to ditch-water," he said, "but I see no reason to suppose the cosmos does."

If history "tells us" anything, it tells us that standards, values, and principles have varied greatly from age to age and from society to society; indeed, that they have varied greatly from one generation to another within the same society. Popes chosen for their learning and their virtue were certain that morality required that they put down heresies with fire and sword, cruelty and torture; sixteenth-century Spaniards had little compunction about killing Indians, because the Indians had no souls; learned and upright Puritans readily sent witches to their death; and nineteenth-century Christians in the American South regarded slavery as a blessing. And we are as shocked at Hellenic notions of love as the Hellenes of whom Herodotus tells us were at the notion of eating their dead fathers. Consider, for example, Plato's defense of a practice which most of our contemporaries regard not only as immoral but as pernicious, and which our military and civil authorities combat with sleepless zeal:

> I cannot say what greater benefit can fall to the lot of a young man than a virtuous lover and to the lover than a beloved youth. . . . If then there were any means whereby a state or army could be formed of lovers and favorites, they would administer affairs better than all others, provided they abstain from all disgraceful deeds and compete with one another in honest rivalry, and

such men, together with others like them, though few in number, so to speak would conquer the world. [*Symposium*, ¶ 178–9.]

Consider a problem that has confronted—and perplexed—American historians for a hundred years: slavery. Surely if anything is wrong, slavery is wrong. No social institution more deeply offends our moral sensibilities than this; no other collective experience induces in us a comparable sense of shame. Slavery, we are all agreed, corrupts alike the slave and the master; slavery corrupts the body politic, the poison still infects us.

This is the vocabulary of morality, and it is this vocabulary that we invoke, almost instinctively, whenever we discuss what was long euphemistically called the "peculiar institution."

Yet when we come to pronounce judgment on slavery, we are met at the very threshold with the most intransigent consideration: generation after generation of good, humane, Christian men and women not only accepted it but considered it a blessing. What are we to say when confronted by the fact—a formidable body of evidence permits us to use that word—that so many of our own forebears, only two or three generations back, embraced slavery, rejoiced in it, fought to defend it, and gave up their lives confident that they were dying in a good cause.

Clearly we cannot fall back on the simple explanation that all of these men and women—those who owned slaves and those who sustained the slave system—were bad. These beneficiaries of and defenders of slavery were neither better nor worse than their cousins north of the Mason and Dixon Line who had managed to get rid of the "peculiar institution" one or two generations earlier; they were neither better nor worse than we are. Whatever may be said on practical grounds for the moral righteousness and self-righteousness of abolitionists who fought slavery, it can be said that no comparable pressures weigh upon us as historians. It is absurd in us to pass moral judgment on slaveholders, absurd to indict a whole people or to banish a whole people to some historical purgatory where they can expiate their sins. Lincoln saw this, Lincoln who saw so much. The people of the North and South, he said in his Second Inaugural Address, "read the same Bible and pray to the same God, and each invokes His aid against the other. It may seem strange that any men should dare to ask a just God's assistance in wringing their bread from the sweat of other men's faces. But let us judge not, that we be not judged."

We can agree now, most of us, that slavery was an unmitigated evil, but we cannot therefrom conclude that those who inherited it, were caught in it and by it, supported it and fought for it, were evil men. What we can say is that but for the grace of God, or the accident of history, we might ourselves have been caught up in slavery and bound by it and habituated to accepting it, just as our forebears were. What we can say is that if earlier generations—North and South alike—bore the burden and the guilt of slavery, we have born the burden and the guilt of racial discrimination, and that morally there is not much to chose between the two.

Clearly, different generations have different moral standards; it is a form of intellectual arrogance for us to impose ours upon the past. We do not accept *ex post facto* laws, bills of attainder, or guilt by association in our legal system; we should not apply these concepts or rules retroactively to the past. Far better to refrain from the folly and the vanity of moral righteousness about the past; far better to accept Lincoln's admonition to judge not, that we be not judged. The historian's task is not to judge but to understand. How did it happen that men dedicated to carrying out the precepts of the Sermon on the Mount could send those who disagreed with them to the stake? How did it happen that men dedicated to the expansion of European civilization could carry fire and sword to the hapless inhabitants of the American continents? How did it happen that men and women who dearly loved their own children and whose days were bound each to each by natural piety could bitterly oppose laws designed to protect little children from the awful burden of work in factory and mine? How did it happen that Christian men and women could look upon slavery as a blessing? How did it happen that a people who boasted a high civilization, who had produced Leibniz and Kant, Beethoven and Mozart, Goethe and Heine, Rilke and Thomas Mann, could stand by while six million Jews were done to death?

Tout comprendre, tout pardonner. But it is not true that to understand all is to forgive all. It is the historian's business to "understand," it is not the historian's business either to condemn or to forgive. He is not God.

And here is a third argument against moral judgment in history—that the historian is not God. He is not called upon to judge the quick or the dead; indeed he is not called upon to judge. If he sets up as a judge, he changes the whole pattern of his intellectual and professional role from one dedicated to objective inquiry to one devoted to prosecution or defense. As the distinguished historian of the Russian Revolution, E. H. Carr, observes, the attempt to erect standards of historical judgment "is itself unhistorical, and contradicts the very essence of history. It provides a dogmatic answer to questions which the historian is bound by his vocation incessantly to ask. The historian who accepts answers in advance to these questions goes to work with his eyes blindfolded, and, renounces his vocation." And how interesting that Allan Nevins, who asserted in the first edition of his classic *Gateway to History* the necessity of the application of rigorous moral standards which "ought to be held absolute and applied to all modern ages," and who quoted with approval Acton's admonition to his fellow historians

"never to debase the moral currency" or "suffer any man
to escape the penalty which history inflicts upon wrong,"
later abandoned this position and substituted the simple
assertion that "what is important is not to denounce Abdul Hamid for his crimes but to understand what gave
birth to Abdul Hamid and his policies" (*Gateway to History*, 1962 edn., p. 259).

The historian is not God; he is a man, and like other
men. He confesses to most of the failings, responds to
most of the pressures, succumbs to most of the temptations that afflict his fellow men. Consciously or unconsciously he is almost always taking sides. Can we really
trust Carlyle on Cromwell, Motley on Philip II, Charles A.
Beard on the causes of the Civil War, or Vernon Parrington on John Marshall? Can we trust either Macaulay or
Winston Churchill to write impartially about the Duke of
Marlborough? Can we trust Lord Acton or Benedetto
Croce on a subject so close to their hearts as the history of
liberty? Clearly we cannot. The historian, like the judge,
the priest, or the statesman, is a creature of his race,
nationality, religion, class, of his inheritance and his education, and he can never emancipate himself from these
formative influences and achieve Olympian impartiality.
Where he undertakes to judge, he does not even have the
prop of professional training and traditions to sustain
him, as he does when he records and reconstructs. His
judgments are, therefore, as Herbert Butterfield has observed, but "pseudomoral judgments, masquerading as
moral ones, mixed and muddy affairs, part prejudice,
part political animosity, with a dash of ethical flavoring
wildly tossed into the concoction." And because not even
a Ranke, not even a Mommsen, not even a Toynbee can
survey the whole of history, his forays into the past are
bound to be haphazard and fortuitous as well. For purposes
of reconstructing the past, that is not a fatal handicap; others will fill in the gaps. But for purposes of for-

mulating a moral code and applying it systematically and impartially, it is a fatal handicap.

We may, then, accept the findings of the historian in matters of fact—always subject to subsequent revision, to be sure—but why should we accept his conclusions in matters of morality? "I beseech you in the bowels of Christ," wrote Oliver Cromwell in his Letter to the Church of Scotland, "think it possible you may be mistaken." Alas, the historians have so often been mistaken. Over the centuries they have stood ready to pronounce judgments which differ little from the tainted and tarnished judgments of statesmen, soldiers, and priests. Catholic historians have sustained the persecution of Protestant heretics, and Protestant historians looked with equanimity upon the persecution of Catholics. National historians have almost invariably defended and justified the conduct of their own nation and as regularly rendered judgment against the enemies of their nation; more, they have themselves provided the arguments for chauvinistic nationalism, imperialism, and militarism. No wonder that the chief professional preoccupation of the historian in our day is revision!

There is no special dispensation for the historian. He is not exempt from the prejudices, the ambitions, the vanities, the fears, that afflict his fellow men. When he dons his professional robes, he is an impressive and sometimes a majestic figure; when he is persuaded to put on the robes of the moral judge, he is as naked as the unhappy emperor of Hans Andersen's story.

We come then to a fourth consideration, practical rather than philosophical: the futility of moral judgment in history. Surely, say those who insist that the historian be a judge, it is proper that the historian reprobate the Inquisition and exalt tolerance, that he deplore slavery and celebrate freedom, that he execrate Hitler and Nazi genocide and rejoice in the triumph of the forces of liber-

ation. But why should the historian go out of his way to
condemn or to praise these things? The assumption behind this expectation is that the reader has no mind of his
own, no moral standards, no capacity to exercise judgment; that he is incapable of distinguishing between slavery and freedom, persecution and tolerance, but depends
upon the historian to do this for him. Are those who are
mature enough to read serious histories really so obtuse
that they cannot draw conclusions from the facts that are
submitted to them? Is there really any danger that students will yearn for slavery or rejoice in the Inquisition or
admire Philip II or Adolf Hitler if the historian does not
rush in and set them right? Alas, if the reader does not
know that Hitler was a moral monster and that the murder of six million Jews was a moral outrage, nothing the
historian can say will set him right; if he does not know
in his bones that slavery corrupts both slave and master,
nothing the historian can say will enlighten him. Is there
not, indeed, some danger that if the historian continually
usurps the role of judge, the reader may react against his
judgments; that if the historian insists on treating his
readers as morally incompetent, they may turn away
from history altogether to some more mature form of
literature?

There is a further consideration, which might be called
a plea in abatement. It is this: the problem of judgment
may be trusted to take care of itself. No reader comes
wholly unprepared to the contemplation of a chapter of
history; he brings with him his own education, his own
moral and philosophical outlook. Nor is the student ever
confined to a single account of any important chapter of
history. We can be confident that historians will differ in
their interpretation of the past and that these differences
will be available and familiar to readers. Errors will be
corrected; wrong opinions will be set right. For every
historian who defends British policy in Ireland, there will

be one to denounce it and reprobate it; for every historian who paints slavery in sunlit terms, there will be one to expose its darkness and cruelty; for every historian who places responsibility for the First World War squarely at the door of the Germans, there will be one to insist that it was the Russians or the French who were really to blame. Let the historian learn humility: the reader is not dependent upon him for the whole of his history; he is not dependent upon him for moral instruction.

That is what the great Italian historical philosopher Benedetto Croce meant when he wrote that "those who, on the plea of narrating history, bustle about as judges, condemning here and giving absolution there, because they think that this is the office of history, are generally recognized as devoid of historical sense."

One final observation is appropriate. We should not confuse moral with professional judgment. In the field of his professional competence the scholar has the same obligation as the judge, the teacher, the physician, the architect. The judge who pronounces sentence, the teacher who gives a grade, the physician who diagnoses an illness, the architect who condemns a building, is not indulging in moral but is exercising professional judgment. So the historian who, after painstaking study of all available evidence and after cleansing himself of all the perilous stuff which might distort his vision, concludes that Lee did right to surrender at Appomattox rather than fight it out in the West, that Roosevelt was not responsible for the attack on Pearl Harbor, that the conduct of the Crimean War was characterized by criminal folly, that the violation of Belgian neutrality in 1914 was an error of the first magnitude, that Cavour rather than Garibaldi deserves credit for Italian unification, that Shakespeare and not Bacon wrote Hamlet, that only the stone and not the inscription on the Kensington runestone is genuine, and that the *Protocols of Zion* are forgeries, is performing

his professional duty. He may be mistaken—but so may
the judge, the teacher, the physician; that is a chance
society takes. His judgments may have moral overtones—it is difficult to keep those out, and we have
learned to discount them. But if it is exasperating to find
a Carlyle or a Motley laying down the moral laws for us,
it is downright frustrating to read comprehensive studies
of controversial subjects which reach no conclusions.
Misuse of evidence is indefensible, but much is to be said
for such opinionated arguments as we find in a Macaulay
or a Churchill, a Beard or a Parrington. For strongly
contested and stoutly defended interpretation contributes,
by its very vigor and independence, to ultimate clarifica-
tion, since it challenges traditional views, excites debate,
and inspires further investigation.

SHOULD THE HISTORIAN WRITE
CONTEMPORARY HISTORY?

"NOTHING in postwar publishing history," says *The New York Times,* "has aroused such outrage as the flood of memoirs about President Kennedy that is cascading toward the bookstalls." "Outrage" is perhaps too strong a term for the reaction; what we have, rather, is dismay and alarm. Is it proper for those who hold positions of confidence, those who have enjoyed the intimacy of men in high places, to reveal the confidences and report the circumstances of the intimacies? The question sounds simple but is really difficult. Is it a question of "confidence" in any genuine sense? Is there any evidence that what Professor Arthur Schlesinger and Theodore Sorensen are now revealing was told them in confidence explicit or implicit? Is it all perhaps merely a matter of timing? Do confidences lose their radioactivity, as it were, with the passing of time? Is it one of right, or of wisdom, or merely of good taste?

Much of the reaction to recent disclosures, particularly

SOURCE: *Saturday Review* (February 12, 1966). Copyright © 1966 by Henry Steele Commager.

those by Arthur Schlesinger, has been superficial and intemperate. This is not "history," we are assured, but something different; it is "keyhole history"; it is "mischievous gossip"; it is a "breach of historical propriety" or a "breach of confidence." But the issues that emerge transcend propriety or taste (the standards here are anything but clear) or even the right of privacy. They involve considerations of the nature of history and the responsibility of the historian, the claims of public interest, and the nature of techniques of censorship.

"Hard cases," Justice Holmes observed, "make bad law." That is nowhere truer than in the broad area of censorship, tangible or intangible. It is almost always the hard case that attracts attention and precipitates an issue; and each case—whether the invasion of privacy, the violation of good taste, or the expression of pernicious ideas—always seems to some vigilant critics so serious that it calls for emergency action regardless of principles or of due process. Thus the Schlesinger and the Sorensen books are discussed as if they constitute new and unique examples of the invasion of privacy, the exploitation of intimacy, or the criticism of public officials by indirection.

But this is not a new problem. Every since Thucydides, historians have been writing about their contemporaries, and no one thinks the worse of Clarendon or Bolingbroke or, for that matter, of Herndon or Badeau, of Hopkins and Ickes, for writing of the administrations they served and the monarchs or the presidents they knew. But there is a new aspect and a new urgency to the problem today. Lincoln must have known that Nicolay and Hay were historical-minded, and Franklin Roosevelt had historians in his official entourage, but no President before Kennedy had chosen an historian as a confidant. Now President Johnson has an historian on his staff, and it is a safe prediction that the historian will become in the future as familiar a feature of the White House landscape as the press secretary or the social secretary. If we are to lay down ground rules for the recording of history, it is a good idea not to formulate them on the basis of emotional reaction to a particular and highly unusual case.

It is Schlesinger's statement that by 1963 President Kennedy "made up his mind to accept Rusk's resignation after the 1964 election, and seek a new Secretary" which has excited the sharpest attention and the most ardent controversy. The objections to this allegation really boil down to a question of "good taste." If the allegation is untrue or misleading, others (like Vice President Humphrey) will challenge it. If it is true, it by no means follows that it weakens Secretary Rusk's position, nor does it commit President Johnson. One President is not required or expected to adopt the views of another; the important thing is that President Johnson has confidence in Mr. Rusk.

Indeed the excitement over revelations of Kennedy's attitude toward Secretary Rusk—an attitude of somewhat exasperated admiration—is for the most part factitious. More important, certainly more relevant to the current situation, are Schlesinger's revelations about Secretary McNamara's lack of foresight and preference for solutions that lent themselves to statistical computation, or Governor Harriman's lack of confidence in the military and particularly in General Krulack. Surely more important is the story—we may almost say the evidence—that the CIA deliberately deceived both Secretary Rusk and Ambassador Stevenson at the time of the Bay of Pigs crisis, and again, that in 1959 the CIA usurped the prerogatives of the State Department and presumably of President Eisenhower in conducting its own foreign policy in Laos, and that at one time the Phoumi regime in Laos was receiving American military aid while the neutralized Souvanna government was receiving economic aid. Assuredly far more sobering than any criticism of Rusk is Schlesinger's verdict on the CIA that "the CIA had its own political desks and military staffs; it had in effect its own foreign service, its own air force, even, on occasion, its own combat forces. Moreover the CIA declined to clear its clandestine intelligence operations either with the State Department in Washington or with the Ambassador in the field" (*A Thousand Days*, p. 427).

It is a good idea to keep in mind that neither Schlesinger nor Sorensen was an "official" historian; neither was under any obligation either to write or to refrain from writing what he saw, heard, and thought; neither was bound to produce just the kind of report that a particular segment of the public happened to want. Assuredly such independence and freedom are desirable: would any of us trust "official" historians, bound in advance to give us only the kind of history guaranteed to hurt no feelings, to reveal no secrets, to shock no sensibilities?

Let us turn, then, to the pros and cons of this debate over the wisdom, propriety, and utility of such revelations as are coming from Schlesinger and Sorensen.

There is, to be sure, no question of overt censorship. Even those who are most outraged do not suggest that. But there is a question of censorship, nevertheless— censorship through the operation of impalpable pressures of critical opinion or professional disapproval, pressures that may discourage future presidents, future historians, from embarking upon such enterprises as now agitate us. Here are some of the arguments that are advanced against encouraging "premature" publication of affairs of state.

There is, first of all, the natural and almost instinctive feeling that this sort of thing simply isn't done—that disclosures of "private" conversations or of confidences, particularly if they reflect ungenerously on others, are in bad taste and that scholars are bound by the canons of good taste. This attitude in turn rests on a series of assumptions—that what is disclosed was indeed confidential; that the rule of silence thus imposed by moral considerations is a continuing one; and that the scholar is bound in his scholarly as in his private conduct to respect conventional standards of good taste.

Closely allied with this is a second consideration, that publication of confidential information may do grave injury or give serious pain to men and women still alive and still in public position—a Dean Rusk, for example, or a General Eisenhower—and that the threat of indiscretions of this kind may therefore dissuade first-rate men from exposing themselves to such risks of public life. Thus society might be deprived by these indiscretions of the services of just the men it most needs.

Third, it is alleged that premature disclosures may do harm to historical truth and understanding. With the best will in the world, historians who make such revelations cannot but be partial, the revelations themselves incomplete and misleading. We know from a hundred earlier examples that anyone may misunderstand or misinterpret what he hears, or that his memory may play him false. Thus to place authority behind a statement of policy or a judgment of character, when he who made it is no longer here to explain or elaborate it, is to harden prematurely the crust, to fix prematurely the pattern, of history.

The very danger that what was said, even if not in confidence but merely in a moment of exasperation or of irritability, might be reported, could well inhibit those in positions of authority from speaking their minds at all and might thus deny them an essential safety valve. Everyone needs such a safety valve, and those who bear heavy burdens need it with special urgency.

It would be absurd to suppose that writers like Professor Schlesinger and Mr. Sorensen have failed to consider all of these objections, to weigh them in the balance against the arguments for publication of what clearly appears to them to be valid history, just as it would be absurd to suppose that they have not in fact exercised discretion and restraint in what they have said or have left unsaid. What are some of the arguments for such publications as Professor Schlesinger's?

First, almost any historical or biographical study of the contemporary scene is bound to leave a trail of hurt feelings and injured *amour-propre*. Where only private persons are concerned and there is no public interest in disclosures that might prove painful, there is a strong case for discretion and even for silence. But with public figures or those whose careers affect the public, the situation is quite different. Disclosures, comments, interpretations of all kinds, just and unjust, generous and ungenerous, are part of the risks of the game, and those who go into public life must be prepared to take the risks. Indeed, if we grant that there is no legitimate public interest in purely private persons, it might be asserted that the more exalted the public person, the more legitimate the public interest.

What of the allegation that early disclosure is bound to be partial and fragmentary and therefore does not so much reveal, as falsify, history? True enough, but this is a criticism of all history, not just of contemporary. Historians can never hope to know the whole truth about the battle of Waterloo, the attack on Fort Sumter, or the negotiations at Munich. If it be said that we should wait until all the evidence is available, it will be answered that all the evidence will never be available. The danger of holding off publication to some distant future is far greater than the danger of "premature" publication, and this for two obvious reasons: first, that the record might never be put down at all (who can doubt that the prospect of publication is an immense stimulus to literary creation?); second, that if we wait until all those who might be embarrassed or chagrined by any disclosures have passed from the scene, there will not be that opportunity for challenge, correction, explanation, and elaboration so essential to arriving at the final verdict. Douglas Freeman used to say that there was nothing like a court-martial for getting at the truth about a battle or a campaign; perhaps charges and countercharges are not less necessary in arriving at the truth about politics or diplomacy.

But there is a larger consideration than any which might be regarded as merely professional. It is the public interest in getting at the truth. In our kind of society the whole public has an obligation and a right to know all that can be known about the conduct of public affairs; only if there is provision for and assurance of this can the principle of "eternal vigilance" operate. Experience has no doubt shown that some things are better arranged without the public—or the television cameras—looking over the shoulders of those who are engaged in hammering out policies. It is not a good idea—to take an extreme example—to let the public in on decision-making in time of war; it is not helpful to have "open diplomacy" if that means letting in the reporters to record the give and take around the conference table. But we all know that secrecy is the first resort of those who do not want to give an account of themselves, and that secrecy is used to cover a multitude of sins of omission and of commission— ineptitude, incompetence, blundering, and even wickedness. As *The Guardian* (Manchester) has recently observed, the British policy of withholding information about government policies for fifty years "seems to be little more than politicians' and civil servants' dislike of being made to feel uncomfortable, together with the national propensity to keep power within a small elite."

We cannot, for example, have much sympathy with those who allege that secrecy is so essential to detecting lawbreakers that officials must be allowed to indulge in wiretapping; the public interest in discouraging wiretapping is greater than its interest in detecting criminals. We cannot have sympathy with those who allege that secrecy is so essential to ferreting out "subversives" that the ancient protections of due process must go by the board: preserving due process is more important than detecting alleged subversives. Those who invoke secrecy in these areas do not come into court with clean hands, and we are justified in thinking the same of those who invoke secrecy in other areas.

Thus there are doubtless risks in premature publication, but these are far less than the risks of tardy publication or of no publication. The risk to men in high places that their ill-considered remarks or opinions may echo in history long after they are gone is real, too; but it is far less serious than the risk that those in positions of power may come to rely on immunity from awkward disclosures.

Much of the current controversy over premature or indiscreet disclosure focuses on Professor Schlesinger's revelations about President Kennedy's attitude toward the State Department, the Pentagon, and the CIA. Now leaving aside the argument of bad taste—for it may be bad taste not to disclose facts to the public—is it really clear that the revelation of the President's disillusionment with the CIA and the Pentagon and his misgivings about the State Department are contrary to public interest? If the President was mistaken (or if Professor Schlesinger proves to be mistaken in his report), it is highly improbable that the position of Pentagon, CIA, or State will be damaged. If the presidential judgment—or disillusionment—was justified, however, it is clearly to the interest of the nation that this be known. Thus if CIA is really deceiving almost everybody in the government from the President down, the sooner the public knows this, the better. In either event the controversy can safely be relied upon to bring out into the open criticisms that have heretofore been covert, and that is all to the good. Finally, if, as has been asserted, President Kennedy's failure to act on his convictions reveals a weakness—rather than mere amiability—in his character, that, too, is a consideration of importance to the student of the executive power.

But it will be asserted that disclosures such as those by Professor Schlesinger suffer from an inherent and ineradicable vice: that no matter how accurate, how well authenticated, they may be, they are still misleading, for they leave out all the atmosphere, the nuances, the tone of voice, the gestures—all those things that suffuse any statement with a special meaning that even the highest literary art can rarely recapture. True enough, but this is true of all historical reporting with a few exceptions such as Boswell's *Johnson* or Herndon's *Lincoln*. Furthermore, there is a built-in protection here: the common sense of readers. Surely none familiar with the literature of politics will be so literal-minded as to accept whatever is reported at face value. Readers can be expected to know something about human nature, even presidential nature, which is not very different, and they will keep in mind that presidents like to blow off steam or indulge their sense of humor or of mischief, just as they will keep in mind that presidents, like other people, are not always masters in their own house: remember Lincoln's wistful remark to the importunate petitioner, "Madame, I have no influence with this administration." As we all allow for the play of personality in ourselves and in our own associates, so we all make allowances for it in public men. Who now holds it against Lincoln that he could never resist telling a good story? Who counts it against Churchill that his wit was irrepressible?

What shall we say of a fourth objection, that the danger of unseemly publication may induce timidity or coun-

sel silence in those who should be encouraged to speak
their minds, and that it will thus invite more stringent
rules about security or about publication? A serious consideration, this, for what we need is less restriction, not
more. But may we not say of this problem what Justice
Holmes said of an analogous situation: "Not while this
court sits"?

These matters are, after all, up to the president, the
secretary, the general, whoever is involved. If he knows
that he is indiscreet, or if he fears disclosures, he may
impose his own security measures, and doubtless he will:
Mr. Schlesinger himself gives some examples of this. The
simplest of all security measures is for the president not
to invite historians or journalists to be part of his official
family, not to give them his confidence. Presidents are,
after all, in command of the situation. If they appoint a
Boswell to act as recorder, they must be presumed to
know what they are about. *We* cannot lay down the rules;
a Roosevelt, a Kennedy, a Johnson will lay down his own
rules, and everything is to be gained from variety and
experimentation.

What of the final objection, that unrestricted or premature disclosure may impair the national security? We
need not take this charge seriously. In the first place, the
kind of men who win the confidence of presidents can be
expected to be quite as patriotic as the rest of us, and
quite as intelligent, too. It is most improbable that they
would knowingly impair the national interest. Second,
the cry of "security" is one that we have learned to discount; it rings out whenever there is anything to conceal.
There is, after all, a national interest in knowing all the
facts of public affairs as soon as possible that overrides
any interest in concealing facts as long as possible. It is
more important, for example, that the pros and cons of
major issues—let us say the Bay of Pigs episode—be
aired and that the public be invited to weigh the charges

of incompetence in the CIA and the Pentagon than that these matters be hushed up or that any branch of government be shielded from publicity and criticism. No serious damage can come from disclosure and criticism, but infinite damage can come from misplaced confidence that permits any individual or department to cover up blunders.

All very well, it will be said, but this assumes that a Roosevelt, a Kennedy, an Eisenhower, a Johnson will be there to impose his wishes on those to whom he gives his confidence. What happens when fate intervenes—as it did in April 1865, in September 1919, in November 1963? There is perhaps no answer to this challenge other than the elementary observation that principles of conduct should not be based on exceptions or on fortuity. Furthermore, in our kind of society much must of necessity be left to the common sense, the intelligence, and the virtue of the individual. We cannot contrive rules to anticipate all conceivable vagaries of human character, but we must allow freedom of expression, even if that freedom is from time to time abused. If we were to discourage or to inhibit the exercise of freedom of speech or press whenever some critics thought the exercise abused or the expression indiscreet, there would be an end to freedom.

We may confidently believe that no president or high official will put his confidence in men palpably wanting in judgment or integrity. We may confidently assume that the public is intelligent enough to disregard writers clearly wanting in judiciousness or integrity. We may be sure, too, that the principle of the countervailing force will operate: that each disclosure will call forth other disclosures, each interpretation inspire other interpretations, and that out of all this something like the truth will eventually emerge. This is the familiar method of history in free societies; the alternative is "official" history.

Those who would directly or indirectly impose restraints upon the historian are for the most part those who believe in censorship in other realms as well—in literature, art, drama, politics, and history. They are the men who are sure that while they can always be trusted to think for themselves, others cannot. They assume that the public is a great booby, easily misled. They know that *they* do not need protection, but they assume that the public does. They are those who believe that government and politics are mysterious things, that politicians and the military operate in some esoteric fashion that can be understood only by the initiate, and that their operations should therefore be shrouded in secrecy. They are basically men of little faith, who do not trust the common sense of their fellow men or the ability of truth to survive the competition of the market place of ideas.

ANDERS SØRENSEN VEDEL:
THE HAMLET OF LILLIEBJERGET

HE was born in 1542 in Vejle, in the kingdom of Denmark, and he took the name of the town for his own. But
it was to Ribe that he belonged, Ribe just fifty miles
across the heath, but looking boldly to the west, not
smugly on the Little Belt. Here he had come as a boy to
study in the famous cathedral school; here he lived in the
formative years of his youth, and the Old Town threw its
spell over him; at the height of his fame it was to Ribe
that he returned, and in the shadow of its cathedral he
lived the ecstasy of aspiration and the tragedy of frustration. No town like Ribe, town of the Valdemars and of
lovely Queen Dagmar; its quays were not so crowded
now, nor its market place so busy, but it still had its
scholars and churchmen, and in all the kingdom there
was no church to compare to the great cathedral, its
mighty tower rising far into the heavens so that storm-
tossed sailors out on the North Sea could see it from afar
and take courage. Here, back in the Dark Ages, Bishop

Source: *Scandinavian Studies*, ed. C. F. Bayerschmidt and E. J.
Friis (Seattle: University of Washington Press; 1965). Reprinted
by permission.

Ansgar had built one of the first churches in the North, and here, seven centuries later, its churchmen had formed the spearhead of the Reformation. The spirit of the mighty Bishop Tavsen still dominated the place, and his disciples filled the canonries and prelacies, preached in the pulpits and taught in the schools.

Jens Grundet's school was famous throughout the kingdom, and young Anders came to study with him and to live with him. It was a severe schooling: he mastered Torrentini and Melanchthon's grammar, read Terence and Vergil and Ovid, Cicero's letters and essays, and elementary Greek; logic and rhetoric were not neglected, and the study of the Old and New Testament was taken for granted. But more important than this formal education was the influence of Grundet himself, and of the scholars and ecclesiastics who frequented his table and study. There was Hans Thomesen, director of the cathedral school, who had just published the first Danish hymnal, and Canon Jens Kansler, who had heard Luther himself at Wittenberg, and whose splendid library was always open to likely students, and Hans Svaning who had been tutor to the King and was the first royal historiographer, and who had many daughters. Svaning was busy with a history of Denmark; there was nothing in existence but Krantz's *Chronica,* and even young Vedel knew how wretched that was, and when he read Thucydides and Plutarch and reflected that Denmark had no such chroniclers, he could not restrain his tears.

In 1561 Hans Thomesen went to teach at the University in Copenhagen, and he took young Vedel with him, and sadly Grundet closed his school; years later Vedel was to pay tribute to this noble scholar and man of learning who had schooled him in the ancient tongues and had not disdained the folklore and ballads of the Danish peasantry. In Copenhagen, Vedel listened to the great Niels Hemmingsen, foremost theologian of his age but flirting, already, with heresies. From this dangerous connection he was rescued by his timely appointment as tutor to young Tycho Brahe, four years his junior; within a year the two young gentlemen were on their way to Leipzig to study jurisprudence and theology. But Tycho Brahe had no stomach for jurisprudence, and Vedel little for theology; conscientiously the tutor tried to persuade his noble pupil to abandon the temptations of mathematics and astronomy, but without avail. Soon the two parted company; Tycho Brahe retained a deep friendship for his brilliant and genial tutor, and Vedel never ceased to admire the one Dane of his generation whom he acknowledged his intellectual equal. Rejecting a position with the Elector of Saxony, Vedel journeyed to Wittenberg, the mecca of Danish students of this century as Göttingen was in the eighteenth, and the center of historical studies. Flaccius had taught here, and Chemnitz and Chytraeus, and here now was the famous Caspar Peucer, who had married the daughter of Melanchthon, and whose versatility was no less astonishing than his learning. He taught mathematics and medicine and history, he had written a continuation of the *Chronici Caronis* which Melanchthon himself had first edited, and he was even then engaged in an investigation of the origin of the name Denmark. Three years Vedel lingered on in Wittenberg; in 1556 he brought out an edition of Jens Grundet's sermons, with a biography and an appreciation of the scholar, and on the basis of this was made Magister.

Back to Copenhagen, then, to become chaplain at the court of the second Frederik, who fancied himself a patron of the arts. Vedel was young and handsome and well-connected, his conversation was no less elegant than were his manners, his reputation was already resounding, and soon he was the darling of the court. The great Chancellor Friis, who loved learning as much as power, befriended him, and threw open to him his magnificent

library and home; Niels Kaas and Bjørn Andersen, coun-
cillors to the King, vied with each other in showing him
favor. Tycho Brahe was here, dreaming of Uranieborg,
and Niels Hemmingsen, not yet forced into retirement,
and Charles Dançey the French legate, a courtier, a man
of the world. Vedel was in his element: he reveled in
patronage, he had for the nobility a respect that bordered
on reverence, and he stood always ready to do their bid-
ding. His sermons were polished and eloquent, no one
could turn out a more graceful poem or a more moving
funeral oration, and in time the prospect of an elegy from
Vedel became something worth dying for.

Soon there were other demands upon his talents. Friis
himself, the chancellor, brought to him a Danish translation of Platina's *Vita Summorum Pontificum* of 1479. A
wretched piece of work, this translation: perhaps Vedel
could do something with it. So Vedel turned from an
investigation into the origin of the name of Yule which
was already beginning to bore him, and undertook an
entirely new translation of Platina. The book grew under
his hands: he added to it and embellished it until it was
an original work, and in 1571 it was published as *Anti-
christus Romanus,* an imposing book of over two hundred
pages of rhyme, and Vedel's name was on every tongue.
He had done this so well that he was called upon for other
things. It was barely fifty years since old Herr Mikkel of
Odense had written his *Vita Hominis,* but so rapidly was
the Danish language changing that it was with difficulty
that the present generation read the book. Dutifully Vedel
brought out a new edition, and the very next year he
compiled a curious collection of fragments from Greek
philosophy. Barely was this pious exercise performed
when he was called upon to enter the theological arena.
The murmurs against Niels Hemmingsen's heresies were
growing more audible; the German churchmen were talk-
ing and there were inquiries from the Lutheran princes.

To set all these at rest Vedel brought out a Latin translation of Hemmingsen's lectures on dogmatics, *Via Vitae;* it was published, not at Copenhagen, but at Leipzig. Perhaps it was not entirely successful, for Hemmingsen shortly retired.

But these were trivia; it was not for this that he had studied under Grundet and Camerarius and Peucer. Shortly after the publication of the *Vita Hominis* Friis had come to him with a project close to his heart—a Danish translation of the greatest of Danish chronicles —*Saxo Grammaticus*. It was the glory of Danish literature and of Danish history, but it had never been rendered into the vernacular. Christiern Pedersen had tried it, to be sure, but without success, and much had been hoped for from the royal historiographer, Hans Svaning. Now Danish nationalism and Danish pride called for a Danish edition, and Vedel was the man for the work. He hesitated, he was modest, he was coy, but finally he was persuaded, and with a high heart and high hopes he set to work on the book that was to insure him immortality.

Vedel's edition of Saxo marks the beginning of Danish literature as Luther's Bible of German. The translation was faithful but idiomatic; in strong, muscular prose Vedel recounted the story of the Danish kings from Dan to Valdemar the Great; each book was prefaced with a succinct summary of events; a genealogical table of the kings was provided in an appendix, marginal notes added criticism and suggestion, and a lengthy dedication pointed the moral and adorned the tale. From this history we may learn, so Vedel wrote, how the nation has been exalted by Christianity, how God has punished evil-doers and rewarded the godly; we may see how the good king is strengthened by the love of his people, and how infidelity, tyranny, and the love of war bring misery. History teaches, too, he continued, that though men and governments may change, human nature does not change; mankind in its habits and its customs and its character remains the same. There was a continuity in history, said Vedel, who himself represented the world that was dying and the world that was coming to life, the medieval world and the renaissance.

The book was a national enterprise: it had been sponsored by the Court and the King himself had lent encouragement; Johan Friis had died, but Niels Kaas extended his patronage, and the young scholar was regarded as a national benefactor. When the work was ready for the printers it was discovered that there was not enough paper in the kingdom, and Tycho Brahe himself wrote an appeal to the women of Denmark to give up their linen to the glory of the state and of learning, and the book was printed.

Vedel was a national hero, and neither unaware nor unappreciative of his position. He had written in his dedication: "It might be that even in our time one might be found who would dare to undertake that which would be to the honor of his God, his King and his country," and he referred to the continuation of Saxo's chronicle, and to himself. He had visited Ribe, and had been excited by Hans Svaning's position and by one of his daughters, and he planned to take both. In 1577 he married the daughter and the same year he began to intrigue for the position of royal historiographer. Svaning had proved a disappointment. In his youth none had been more promising than this farmer lad whom Melanchthon himself had praised. He had returned from Wittenberg to teach at the University in Copenhagen; he had been tutor to the Crown Prince, and had been rewarded by a grateful sovereign by appointment as the first royal historiographer. His compensation was a prelacy at Ribe Cathedral, but the sinecure was fatal and an unkind critic charged that his only

achievement was his family: "liberis quam libris pro-
creandis aptior fuit." Vedel thought better of him. "Vir
prudens, gravis et in omni eruditionis generi excellens,
maxime omnis antiquitatis et historiarum peritissimus,"
he wrote ("a prudent and grave man, excelling in all
kinds of learning and of all antiquarians and historians
the most skillful"). Prudent, grave, and skillful he may
have been, but Vedel wanted his job. It was promised to
him, on condition that he do what Svaning had failed to
do—write the continuation of Saxo.

Vedel was fairly embarked now upon his career as a
historian, and he gave way to that passion for theory
which was to inspire such hopes and such disappoint-
ments. To Niels Kaas he indited a long letter, "Commen-
tarius de scribenda historica Danica." The historian, he
said, must begin with the land and the people—the geography and climate, the towns and villages and countryside, the rivers and the harbors. He must trace the origin
of the people, their migrations, their customs and morals
and character, their language, their literature. His chronology must be exact, every fact in its proper place. Religion was of first importance, wars were only secondary,
and the history of one nation should not be confused with
that of other nations. The writing of national history, he
contended, should be a national enterprise; the work
should proceed by a fixed plan, and should be under the
direction of a single man. He was fascinated with his own
theories of history, and on loose sheets of paper he jotted
down elaborations of his ideas. The historian, he wrote,
has two problems—material and form (res et verba). As
far as material is concerned, he is bound to observe the
facts, for "the soul and life of history is truth," and he
must choose carefully between the significant and the
insignificant. To the facts he might add his own observations, and the observations of others, and he should not

refrain from judgment. As for form, the historian must write in an elegant style, but he might indulge in idioms and homely proverbs.

Meantime there were other things which distracted Vedel's attention from the great work, and besides, the appointment to the prelacy at Ribe had not yet come through. He discovered in the cloister of Sorø the manuscript of Adam of Bremen's *History of the Church in the North*, solved the problem of its authorship, and brought out a new edition with learned notes on a dozen obscure subjects. He collected material for a history of Norway, he organized the chronology of Danish history, he compared the English and the Danish languages. Nor could all of his time be given to history; the demands of the court, the demands of his noble patrons, the demands of society had to be considered. Finally Svaning was removed from his position and its emoluments, and Vedel was given a canonry at the Ribe Cathedral and permitted to leave the capital to take up his duties as historiographer.

And now the great enterprise was about to begin, and all the auspices were favorable. Ribe lacked the resources of Copenhagen, but was free from its distractions. The cathedral library in Bethlehem chapel housed many treasures; Vedel had secured the whole of Svaning's valuable collection of manuscripts, and his own library, he later boasted, was without equal in the whole of the North. Ribe had its men of learning, its churchmen, and its scholars; and in the rich rolling country to the east and the south were the manorial estates of the first families of the kingdom. In Ribe, Vedel had all the social life that was good for him and all the quiet and isolation that he needed, and his circumstances were more than comfortable. From his father-in-law he inherited considerable property; after Maria Svaning had died he had married Mette, daughter of Canon Laugesen of the cathedral, and she had brought with her the handsome estate of Lilliebjerget, which was to have so melancholy a history. As canon and later prelate of the cathedral, and as royal historiographer, Vedel enjoyed a generous income: the clerical and the royal tithes from two parishes, and accountancy monies from over sixty churches.

So Vedel settled into Lilliebjerget and proceeded to make of it a replica of Uranieborg, for he had a sense of the fitness of things. On the old manor house he built a tower, even as Tycho Brahe had done, and from its windows he could look westward across the marches to the North Sea, and northward over the brown and purple heath. One room of Lilliebjerget was a historical museum; here were old coins and weapons and armor, and from the walls hung paintings and maps; in another room he placed his library, rich in manuscripts, records, and documents, bagged in many a hunt where everything was fair game. Over the entrance to the library was a Tabula Bibliothecae Liliomontana with the inscription *Deo ac musis sacer est hic locus,* and a body of Laws, enjoining on the scholar purity in mind and morals, moderation, tolerance, and a reverence for learning; the whole bearing the signatures of nine of the most distinguished men in the kingdom—Tycho Brahe and Niels Kaas and Hans Svaning and Charles Dançey among them. Eventually Vedel added to his establishment a printing press and a printer. Everything was in readiness for the production of the great history.

Everything was ready, but Vedel was not ready. Confidently he drew up a prospectus and gave it to an eager world, but beyond this he was not prepared to go. Nothing more melancholy than this prospectus; it excited the most enthusiastic hopes and remains a symbol of non-fulfillment; for three centuries the shadow of the tower of Lilliebjerget stretched across Danish literature.

The history was to be written in twenty-two books. The first was to describe the geography of the kingdom—the natural and political boundaries, the rivers and valleys, the villages and towns and manorial estates, the churches and cloisters. The second was to embrace ethnology, the third ethnography; in these books Vedel planned to trace the origin of the Danish peoples, their migration into Denmark, their morals and customs, as well those of the common man as of the clergy and the nobility. These books were to form the introduction to the history proper; fifteen books were to be given to the chronicle of political and military and religious events; two concluding books were to contain an exhaustive genealogy of all the Danish kings, and an exact chronology of the history of Denmark and the neighboring kingdoms.

The essential modernity of the conception of history embodied in this plan does not need emphasis. Jean Bodin, to be sure, had anticipated Vedel in his emphasis upon geography, but though his *Methodus ad facilem historiarum cognitionem* had been published in 1566 there is no evidence that Vedel was acquainted with it; Scaliger's *Thesaurus temporum,* the first successful effort to establish a sound secular basis for chronology, did not appear until 1606. Three hundred years later the great historian, Troels-Lund, was to apply to Danish society of the sixteenth century the tests that Vedel had proposed.

Now that Vedel had announced his grandiose scheme he was filled with those forebodings that so often assail the scholar. Omniscience was his ambition and perfection his goal, and he was appalled at his own audacity. How little he knew of the geography of the kingdom, how unfamiliar he was with the life of the common men and women, the farmers and fisherfolk. He must know these things, directly and immediately; he abandoned Lilliebjerget and began the first of those many journeys through the country which were designed to provide a firm foundation for the history. In theory this was to give him mastery of his material; in fact he was already a fugitive.

He persuaded Tycho Brahe to provide him with instruments for surveying; he secured from the Royal Council formal authority to make surveys of the kingdom, and to collect material for his history. Soon he was a familiar figure flitting from parish to parish, from church to church. In 1586 he visited Brahe on the island Hveen, the next year he was in Copenhagen; in 1588 he made the first of his journeys through Slesvig and North Jutland, visiting the libraries of churches and cloisters, the record rooms of city halls, the private libraries of the larger manor houses. In 1589 he extended his surveys to the islands and found time to cross over to Skaane; the cathedral at Lund housed a rich collection of manuscripts, but it was the great tower that attracted him and from its eminence he drew maps of the surrounding country. The next year he was at the cathedral at Roskilde, then back to Jutland again. His collections grew monumentally: maps by the hundred, old manuscripts, copies of church records and of town records, and sometimes the originals, so that protests were not wanting at the thoroughness with which he gutted libraries; to these he was adding epitaphs and inscriptions, popular legends, traditions, folk songs, and ballads. At Uranieborg he had met the Dowager Queen, Sofia; wretchedly treated by the Council, she was finding what consolation she could in marrying off her daughters and in dalliance with the arts. She heard that Vedel had gathered some folk songs and asked to hear them, but he was not ready to make these public and promised instead an extensive collection. There were

delays and promptings, but finally the volume appeared
—*One Hundred Danish Songs*—and it was printed at his
own press in Lilliebjerget.

It was a unique contribution to Danish and to European literature; for a century it was the most popular of
Danish books, and when the indomitable Bishop Grundt-
vig undertook to revive Danish nationalism after the Napoleonic debacle, he turned to this medium of folk song
and ballad. Vedel had a just sense of their significance:
"as for historical facts," he wrote, "even little children
know that they are not to be relied upon," but he valued
them for the revelations of the language, the customs and
habits of an earlier age. "We can read here," he said, "the
deeds and the sentiments, the moods, speech, warfare
and weapons, husbandry, dress, food, marriage and funeral customs of our forefathers, and they preserve for us
the strong old language, the poetry of an older age."
There were other justifications too: when sung by lovely
women they bring delight; when carried by the sojourner
to foreign parts they recall to him his native land; those
who lie abed can read them to while away the time, and
to those who languish in prison he promised that they
would drive away boredom and lighten the passing hours.

But still there was no history, and the murmur of
official disapproval reached his sensitive ears. Boldly he
announced that the great book was all but complete;
within a year it should be published. To prove his industry he printed fragments of the genealogy and the chronology; to placate those in high office he brought out an
edition of his sermons and dedicated it to the Councillor
Hak Ulfstand, who promptly died. An endless stream of
funeral orations flowed from his facile pen, and no marriage or birth but what he contributed a poem for the
occasion.

The history was all but complete. Already he had
moved on to other, and larger, works. He announced a

history of Norway, he announced a history of Slesvig and
of Holstein, he announced a history of the Church in the
North and issued a detailed prospectus; he projected a
history of laws, a history of warfare, a history of the
Danish nobility. He was divorced from all reality, he had
entered a dream world where ideas were the only con-
crete things. Zealously he collected his materials, drew up
tables of contents, and with many a flourish wrote title
page and dedication for each of his many books, and the
work was done.

Fifteen years the state had waited for the history, and
even old Svaning began to appear industrious by contrast.
Christian IV was king now; no nonsense about him, he
was accustomed to having his way. Vedel's patrons were
gone, Friis and Peder Oxe were dead, and Niels Grubbe
and Paasjske had no influence. There were new constella-
tions in the political heavens, new stars on the intellectual horizon.

In 1594 Vedel's last powerful friend, Niels Kaas, died.
Promptly Vedel was dismissed from his position and
young Niels Krag, who had managed so brilliantly the
matrimonial alliance between Princess Anne and James
of Scotland, was appointed royal historiographer and en-
joined to write the history that neither Svaning nor Vedel
had been able to write. But if his predecessor had had too
little energy, Krag had too much. He was invaluable, and
the King could not dispense with his services. In 1597 he
was sent to Poland, the following year to England, and
again to Poland. Finally in 1602 he was appointed Rector
of Sorø Academy that he might find leisure for the history; Providence intervened and removed him from this
earth, the history still unwritten.

There was still Vedel. Anger had given way to melancholy, and Mette wrote to her son that her husband seldom answered when she spoke to him, and that life was
indeed sad. Vedel had not given up his plans; almost

annually he announced the appearance of the long-
awaited history and a score of other volumes as well.
What though his kingdom was lost, all was not lost, and
he retired to the ivory tower of Lilliebjerget, and looked
out over the endless heath and the sea and saw visions
not vouchsafed to other men. For twenty years he lived at
Lilliebjerget while the dust gathered on his manuscripts
and the bells of the great cathedral tolled the passing
hours, and when the creators of Hamlet and Don Quixote
died, he too died.

STRUENSEE AND THE ENLIGHTENMENT: A STUDY IN HISTORIOGRAPHY

THE almost contumacious neglect of smaller states by the historians of modern Europe is, in a sense, a product of modern politics, with its brute emphasis upon power, and of our almost inescapable concern with the more material manifestations of power, the political, the economic, the military. Yet the history of the city-states of ancient Greece, of the cities of Renaissance Italy, of England and the Low Countries in the seventeenth century, of Weimar and Saxony, even of Virginia and Massachusetts, in the eighteenth, should remind us that there is no necessary correlation between size and significance.

The history of Denmark is a case in point. The last volume of the *New Cambridge Modern History*, the volume covering the crucially important years from 1763 to 1793, ignores Denmark altogether. While, on the whole, eighteenth-century Denmark is not undeserving of neg-

SOURCE: Parts of this paper were delivered at the International Conference of Historians in Stockholm in 1960; no part of the paper has ever before been published.

lect, the Denmark of this particular generation most
clearly is, and at least one chapter of that history clamors
for our attention. That is the chapter written by the ad-
venturer who rose so spectacularly to be master of the
kingdom, Johan Friedrich Struensee, the most nearly perfect representative of the principle and practice of enlightened despotism in eighteenth-century Europe.

While the Enlightenment in Denmark—it is not certain that we may even use the term—has nothing like the
intellectual interest that it has in France or in the smaller
states of Germany and Italy, it does present itself to us as
a kind of historical laboratory, all the more useful because of its parochial character, its simplicity, and its
brevity. Indeed Denmark herself is a convenient laboratory of history during these years—and not these years
alone—because she was too small and too weak to engage actively in the wars that filled so many years of
that century, and because her relatively simple political
structure and her simple economy made it possible to
undertake far-reaching experiments (and sometimes reforms) with less difficulty or confusion than attended
larger and more complex economies and societies.

Where indeed can we study the workings of enlightened absolutism more clearly or easily than in Denmark
when Struensee was compressing a generation of reforms
into a few months. Not in France, where the Enlightenment was not really permitted to operate except in the
realms of philosophy and literature. Not in Prussia,
where it was irretrievably mixed up with and largely frustrated by Frederick's military ambitions and activities.
Not in Russia, where, it is increasingly clear, Catherine
was indulging herself in a kind of philosophical games-
manship and where in the end there was really nothing to
show for the contributions of the Enlightenment except
the literary rejoicings of deluded philosophes. Not in Britain nor in America, where the Enlightenment flourished

but not absolutism. Only, perhaps, in two other smaller states: the Portugal of Pombal and the Tuscany of Leopold II; but in both of these states the problem of the Church and the religious orders cut athwart the reform program, and in both these states the achievements, such as they were, were the product of a decade or more of maneuvers.

The Struensee experiment in enlightened absolutism was worked out, so to say, in a pure solution—certainly with less interference from extraneous circumstances than in any other European country, unless perhaps in the little principality of Weimar. Thus for purposes of historical examination it is convenient rather than disconcerting that Struensee was, in a sense, an outsider —this is something the Danish historians invariably insist upon—and that he was unembarrassed by traditional commitments, historical or emotional, that might have interfered with the logic of his administration. His only traditional commitment was, after all, to science and to rationalism, and that was a superficial one; the only emotional commitment that he acknowledged (for he was a cold fish) was to the young queen, Caroline Mathilda, and he never permitted his attachment to her to distract him from his reform program. It is useful, too, to the historian interested in experiments that Struensee functioned in a very considerable isolation: isolation from Denmark through his German past and culture; isolation from the ruling classes of Denmark by his bourgeois antecedents and the character of Danish society ("the world is parcelled out here into nine classes, six of whom I am never to encounter without horror," wrote the English Minister, Robert Keith); isolation from the administrative bureaucracy, because he was a newcomer and because he alienated the bureaucracy by his demands for economy and efficiency; isolation from the middle classes by barriers of language and of faith—or the want of it; isolation from the lower orders, if indeed they had any impact, by his reputed immorality and by those economic policies which, whatever their ultimately benevolent purposes, worked temporary hardship on farmers and workingmen; isolation from the Church by his Rationalism and his impatience with ancient ecclesiastical practices and malpractices; isolation from the army, the traditional defender of dictators, because with a fatuousness which goes far to disprove the notion that he aimed to subvert the state, he liquidated some of the crack regiments; isolation, finally, even from those dissidents and adventurers who had helped him to power because he refused to be their tool and in the end antagonized them.

Finally, for purposes of historical interpretation, it is convenient that Struensee, like Count Rumford of Bavaria (a young man from the colony of New Hampshire), like the Baron d' Holbach, like Condorcet, was a scientist —a scientist who was bemused by the notion that LaMettrie's *Man the Machine* was the last word in philosophy and who almost inevitably approached problems of government and economy with impersonal detachment, ignoring what was human or historical or traditional. Perhaps because Struensee was a professional scientist but only an amateur philosopher, he proceeded with a zeal and a self-assurance that might have been difficult had the weight of these qualities been reversed.

Taking advantage of the special circumstances of Danish politics in 1770—the feebleness of the young king, the infatuation of the younger queen, the ineptitude of the ruling classes and their factional quarrels and enmities—and of his own special position at the Danish Court (that of an outsider with few ties and fewer commitments to any group or faction), Struensee was able to carry through in less than sixteen months reforms more far-reaching than those experienced by any other European nation in that generation. What he did was not wholly new or unanticipated; what he did was by no means comprehensive or conclusive; what he did was often more logical than practical. Even these qualifications make his career instructive. Elsewhere in Europe we have the spectacle of the fluent formulation of philosophical ideas never actually applied; with Struensee we have the spectacle of the application of philosophical ideas never fully formulated. Elsewhere we have a blueprint of a new social order; in Denmark we have—briefly, at least—the new order itself. The blueprint is here as well, in the more than eighteen hundred Cabinet Orders which tumbled out in such torrential disarray, and if all of them were not metamorphosed into practices, enough of them were to revolutionize the administration, the law, the economy, the society, of the little kingdom.

In his cosmopolitanism—a cosmopolitanism that ignored national prejudices as genially as it ignored national vernacular; in his indifference to history and tradition; in his overweening reliance on reason, his faith in logic, his tendency to see men as machines, responding almost automatically to appropriate pressures or instructions; in his curious insensitiveness to individuals and his readiness to subordinate the interests of the individual to those of the state; in his faith in what we would call "planning"; in his combination of moral obtuseness, and even ruthlessness, with genuine benevolence—in all this Struensee was at one with many of the philosophes who spoke their eloquent or dramatic pieces on the stage of the Enlightenment. He was almost the only one of them—Sonnenfels may have shared his role down in Vienna and, briefly, Rumford in Munich—whose lines were translated into laws.

A brief recapitulation of the Struensee reforms shows what could be done by a philosopher of the Enlightenment when he was, for all practical purposes, king.

Beginning with the Cabinet Orders of September 4,

1770, decreeing freedom of the press and putting an end
to the indiscriminate award of titles and honors, Struensee reorganized almost every institution and reformed
almost every practice in the kingdom of Denmark-
Norway. He re-established absolutism in fact—it had
been there in theory for a century—and imprinted upon
it the unmistakable stamp of the Enlightenment. He
struck at the principles and practices of mercantilism,
privilege, and monopoly, and he attempted to restore a
fair balance between industry, commerce, and agricul-
ture, to redress the relations between Copenhagen and
the provinces, to reform the relations between government and governed.

As with so many of the enlightened despots and their
ministers, Struensee's primary concern was with administration—primary in the chronological sense and in the
quantitative, too, though not in the qualitative. He knew
that only through a thorough overhauling of the structure
and machinery of government would he have a chance to
bring some kind of order out of the near chaos that
prevailed in government and economy. His first step was
decisive: to center everything on the king's Cabinet, thus
reducing the historic Privy Council to a nullity; this
meant, needless to say, centering everything on himself,
for the king was mad, and Struensee was his voice and
his hand. All reports were hereafter to be in writing and
directed to the Cabinet; all answers, likewise in writing,
came over Struensee's signature. He insisted on a clear
demarcation of departments and bureaus and on elimi-
nating those that were superfluous or inefficient. For the
first time he gave Denmark a genuine Foreign Office—
heretofore foreign relations had been conducted by the
German chancellery—a centralized and unified financial
administration and budget, and, in the capital at least, a
centralized judiciary. Himself diligent and efficient, he
insisted upon diligence and efficiency not only in the

administration but even in the Army. Delay in making reports subjected any official to a fine and eventual dismissal; thus all criminal cases had to be cleared away within a year. He simplified and speeded up the administration of the customs and established a single department of buildings and grounds with jurisdiction over all governmental construction—buildings, roads, bridges—and with some control even over private building. He reduced expenses in the army, abolished the sale of offices, and decreed promotion on merit. He reorganized the postal system and ended the abuse of the franking privilege. Reform of the civil service brought the elimination of superfluous jobs, the ending of the habit of purchasing offices, or the succession to offices, and of nepotism; an end, too, to extravagant pensions and lavish gifts, which had been such a burden on the all but bankrupt treasury.

Struensee's contributions to land reform were promising rather than effective. He took land reform out of the hands of those who were indifferent to anything but private action and put it in the hands of its friends, fixed by law the amount of service due from the peasant to the proprietor, and did away with the obligation of the *corvée* and other unduly onerous services. He attacked the communal system of land ownership, set up a farmer's loan fund to assist peasant proprietorships, modified the allodial system in Norway, and completely reorganized the administration of the crown lands.

In a year of acute economic distress, 1771, Struensee made energetic though inadequate efforts to relieve victims of bad harvests and unemployment. He provided for the free distribution of grain, set up government bakeshops and sold bread below cost, opened the War Department commissary to the poor, and—like Rumford in Bavaria—set up workshops for them. He attacked Bernstorffian mercantilism by reducing tariffs on imports from

the duchies, opening southern Norway to importations
from outside the kingdom, and relaxing some of the restrictions on trade with the Danish West Indies. Opposed
in principle to guilds and monopolies, he attempted to
reduce their powers and privileges and to insist that all
qualified workers have access to jobs.

Everywhere the administration of justice commanded
the interest of enlightened absolutists and their ministers; in the short time he was in power, Struensee accomplished as much in this area as did any contemporary. He
completely reorganized the judicial system of Copenhagen and the provinces, establishing a single judiciary in
place of the fifty-six separate jurisdictions that had hith-
erto flourished, and he effected a separation between justice and administration. He abolished torture in judicial
proceedings, though not entirely in punishment; amelio-
rated the penal code, ended the death penalty for theft
and for infanticide; did away with civil punishment for
breaches of the moral code—the Church interpreted that
as but another manifestation of his own immorality—
and asserted the right of all citizens to the equal protection of the laws.

With something close to recklessness, Struensee carried through a drastic reorganization of the municipal
government of Copenhagen, doing away with the old,
aristocratic administration and bringing the government
of the capital city under the central administration. Himself a medical doctor, he gave particular attention to all
matters of public health. He improved municipal sanitation, street cleaning, and police; created a department of
public health and welfare to bring together all welfare
activities; set up an inoculation institute and encouraged
universal inoculation by setting the example of inoc-
ulating the crown prince; provided for improvement of
municipal drinking water; required certification of epidemic diseases; removed cemeteries out of the city and

prohibited funerals at night. To cut down on infant mortality, which in Copenhagen, as elsewhere, was appallingly high, he permitted baptism at home and at times convenient to parents; modernized the hospitals of the city; and distributed health information to the provinces. He issued a new Pharmacopoeia, tried to stamp out venereal diseases, and attempted—in vain—to modernize the medical department of the almost moribund University.

Indifferent to religion, Struensee did not seriously concern himself with the Church, nor did he openly attack it. He did, in numerous minor matters, undermine its authority and for this, needless to say, earned its unremitting enmity. He encouraged toleration in religion, invited the Moravian Brethren to settle in Jutland with a promise of toleration, cut down on superfluous holidays—if any holidays are ever superfluous to Danes—and stopped the building of superfluous churches; removed restrictions on worship for special groups of Catholics and Quakers; and insisted that academic degrees be granted without religious tests of any kind.

Perhaps his most famous gesture was his first—the establishment of freedom of the press, best remembered because it inspired a poem from no other than Voltaire. Though Struensee had no very lively interest in cultural matters, he did undertake to reorganize the ancient University in harmony with newer educational ideas, to revitalize the Academy of Sciences, and to transform the Art Academy into a vocational school, both utilitarian and democratic. He tried to break down the exclusiveness of the famous Sorø Academy, throwing it open to students from all classes of society. He did nothing for popular education but, himself a disciple of Rousseau, attempted to educate the crown prince in accordance with the principles of *Émile*.

These were the most important of the reforms which

Struensee inaugurated—it cannot be said that he carried them through—in those brief months while he was in power. Far-reaching as they are, they by no means exhaust the whole of his administrative projects: the eighteen hundred Cabinet Orders addressed themselves to a most bewildering variety of subjects and projects. Here was one of the weaknesses of the Struensee regime, the attempt to do everything at once, the inability to distinguish between the significant and the insignificant. Nor was there any attempt to enlist the support—or even the understanding—either of the ruling classes or of public opinion, if we can use that evanescent term for eighteenth-century Denmark. Yet there is little point in criticizing Struensee for these weaknesses and oversights. Those who had been in power had done little to reform anything; those who did understand public opinion, or public prejudices, did nothing either to educate or to change that opinion. Perhaps only someone with Struensee's lack of commitment to the past, with his impetuousness and tactlessness, could have carried through long-needed reforms.

This is, by any standards, a spectacular record, and Struensee himself is, by any standards, one of the most remarkable figures of the eighteenth-century and certainly of eighteenth-century Denmark, which did not have a superfluity of remarkable figures. Yet for reasons complex rather than elusive, Struensee is by way of being the forgotten man of Danish history. Dead now these two hundred years, the issues he agitated long since irrelevant, the wounds he inflicted long since healed, he might, one should suppose, be forgiven for his sins, if indeed they were sins. The one statesman of his generation who dimly anticipated what Denmark was to become—a welfare state concerned with its domestic affairs—he might, one should suppose, have commanded the sympathetic interest of Danish scholars. Not at all. While biographies of lesser figures pour from the presses, Struensee still lacks a scholarly biography and, except in Edvard Holm's magisterial work on Danish history in the eighteenth century, now over sixty years old, even a scholarly analysis.

The truth is that where Struensee is concerned, Danish historians belong to the catastrophic rather than the evolutionary school. They persist in looking on Struensee as a kind of historical sport, an aberration, a departure from Danish history so convulsive that they can pretend that it never really happened. Danish historians, even to this day, approach this chapter of their history with ostentatious distaste; they glide over it gingerly; they shift historical gear from institutional history to the story of court intrigue, hasten Struensee to the executioner's block with a sigh of relief, and, metaphorically, go with Christian VII to the opera that very night.

The consequence of this combination of distaste and evasion has been not only neglect but misinterpretation of the whole Struensee chapter. The source material is there—the volumes of the Cabinet Orders and of the Judicial Processes, admirably edited by the learned Holger Hansen; the Bernstorff Papers, provided for us by the indefatigable Aage Friis—but Danish historians have been oddly reluctant to use these, and others have passed them by completely. Struensee has suffered, then, both neglect and misinterpretation.

There is, for example, the persistent though often inarticulate assumption that Struensee is somehow an aberration rather than a natural product of Danish and European history. That Struensee was in some ways eccentric will not be denied, nor can we assert with confidence that if Struensee had not come along, someone else would have taken his place; after all, it was to be more than a generation before the main body of his reforms were incorporated into the texture of Danish history. Yet the

Struensee revolution was no more abrupt or unanticipated than the revolution that Gustavus III of Sweden
precipitated at the same time. It is clear that Struensee
represented a very real faction, and a real if not always
a clear interest; that he was encouraged by the anti-
Bernstorff faction, by what was in a sense the "little
Denmark" faction, and by what might without too much
exaggeration be called the liberal faction—all without
any realization on the part of those who used him that he
would be the one to take control. Certainly he could not
have overthrown Bernstorff by himself, nor could he have
ruled Denmark for sixteen months without support and
supporters.

The traditional view of Struensee as an aberration in
Danish history has been in part responsible for that gross
overemphasis on the purely personal aspect of the
Struensee regime which clutters up most of the historical
description of these years. It has meant that the center of
historical attention has not been focused on what Struensee did but on what he was, and not on his far-reaching
program of reform but on the Court intrigues, the relations of Struensee with the king and with the queen, the
struggle for power among followers and opponents, and
adventurers who were both.

And this, in turn, has led to a third misconception, one
that we may call the romantic interpretation of the
Struensee era. It was doubtless important to his position
that Struensee became the lover of Queen Caroline Math-
ilde, and perhaps it was even interesting. But one might
suppose that its romantic aspects could safely be left to
the novelists, the dramatists, and in our day the writers
for television, and that historians could take this love
affair in their stride: after all, it was not the first love
affair in history, even in Danish history. Not only do
Danish historians revel in the lurid details of this rather
prosaic relationship, but they react to it as if they were

moralists rather than historians—and eighteenth-century moralists at that. One gets the impression, somehow, from the thousands of pages of Danish history of this period, that what might have been an amiable weakness in a lord is a cardinal sin in a commoner. The hapless Struensee, who was neither more nor less moral than most of his contemporaries, is presented to us as a very paragon of debauchery, a combination of Casanova and Wilkes. Nor is this the only manifestation of the double standard; there is a national double standard, too, for historians who take it amiss that the queen of Denmark should take a commoner for a lover, are able to record the amours of Catherine of Russia with equanimity.

Certainly there is no evidence that Struensee was unusually dissipated, that he was indolent, that he spent all his time at the theater and the ball. It would have been physically impossible for him to have performed the herculean tasks that he did perform had he not been conscientious and industrious.

One aspect of the campaign—that word suggests, to be sure, something much too calculated—to present Struensee as a historical sport is the insistence on his foreign origin and character. He was, so we are reminded tirelessly, a German. So he doubtless was, though his home town of Altona was in the duchy of Holstein, and he was technically a Danish subject—but so, too, were the Bernstorffs, so were Schimmelmann and Schulin and many others, while the commander-in-chief of the armies, St. Germain, was French. It was, after all, an age when even kings could not speak the language of their country, and if Struensee never learned Danish, neither did King Christian VII! But what is regarded as a gratifying manifestation of cosmopolitanism in a Bernstorff is held up as intolerable contempt for nationalism in a Struensee. Nor is this merely inconsequential astigmatism. The emphasis on Struensee's alien character has served as a kind of

smoke screen to obscure the fact that he was far more
concerned with the internal economy and society of Denmark, and far less with playing a part in international
politics, than either his predecessors or his successors.
Indeed a strong case could be made out for Struensee as
the most Danish-minded prime minister of his generation.

Danish historians are rarely guilty of neglecting economic factors in history—quite the contrary—but their
failure to assess the role of the economy in the collapse of
Struensee is notorious. Struensee was the victim in part
of bad luck—two poor harvests, and the murrain, which
carried off some 400,000 cattle. Worse still for his own
popularity, his policies created suffering in many quarters. The commitment to free trade flooded Denmark
proper with imports from the duchies; the attack on the
guilds antagonized powerful middle-class interests; the
dismissal of superfluous civil servants alarmed the bureaucracy; economies in pensions and in the expenditures
of the court disappointed the nobility; the liquidation of
the guards regiments assured Struensee the hostility of
the army. The enmity of the aristocracy and the upper
classes to Struensee was doubtless unavoidable; hard
times, insecurity, prejudice, and fear deprived him of
support from that growing middle class that might have
formed, in the capital city at least, an effective party.

Danish historians have customarily told the story of
Struensee's rise to and tenure of power in terms of conspiracy, chicanery, ruthlessness, and violence. Their emphasis on violence, like the emphasis of the apologists for
the American South on the alleged violence of the Reconstruction era, may well be an unconscious confession of
guilt for the barbarous punishment meted out to Struensee and his supporters. Struensee was not a conspirator;
he was ruthless only in the administrative arena; he did
not at any time resort to violence: dismissal was his most

severe weapon. He was, in fact, one of the mildest and most humane of eighteenth-century dictators, his *coup d'état* one of the gentlest, his tenure of power one of the most peacable; and his reform program concerned itself pervasively with the amelioration of the savagery and inhumanity of eighteenth-century law and custom.

The central failure of Danish historical writing is, however, the obvious one—failure to deal seriously, critically, and comprehensively with the actual accomplishments of the Struensee regime. Instead of addressing themselves to this record, historians have preferred to concentrate on what is peripheral and even irrelevant. The three stout volumes which house the Cabinet Orders have been available now for forty years, and the four volumes of Hearings by the Judicial Commission that sentenced Struensee to death for thirty, but the story they have to tell has not yet been incorporated into the fabric of Danish or of European history. Danish historians have yet to accept the fact that Johan Friedrich von Struensee is not a case study in the history of morality or even in the consequences of not being Danish, but in the character, operation, potentialities, and limitations of the Enlightenment.

A Note about the Author

HENRY STEELE COMMAGER did his under-
graduate and graduate work at the University
of Chicago. From 1926 to 1938 he taught at
New York University, and for the next twenty
years was Professor of History at Columbia University. He is now Smith Professor of History at
Amherst College. Mr. Commager has held the
Pitt chair of American History at Cambridge
University and the Harmsworth chair at Oxford
University, and has taught at many European
universities. He is an Honorary Fellow of Peter-
house, Cambridge, and Honorary Professor at
the University of Santiago in Chile. Among his
many books are *Theodore Parker; The American
Mind; Documents of American History;* with
Allan Nevins, *A Short History of the United
States;* and with Professor Morison of Harvard
University, *The Growth of the American Repub-
lic,* generally recognized as a classic in its field.

A Note on the Type

THE TEXT of this book was set in a typeface called PRIMER, designed by Rudolph Ruzicka for the Mergenthaler Linotype Company and first made available in 1949. Primer, a modified modern face based on Century broadface, has the virtue of great legibility and was designed especially for today's methods of composition and printing.

Ruzicka was born in Bohemia in 1883 and came to the United States at the age of eleven. During his long career he has been a wood engraver, etcher, cartographer, and book designer. For many years he was associated with Daniel Berkeley Updike and produced the annual keepsakes for The Merrymount Press from 1911 until 1941. From his home in New Hampshire, Ruzicka continues to be active in the graphic arts.

Composed, printed, and bound by
Kingsport Press, Inc., Kingsport, Tenn.

Typography and binding design by

WARREN CHAPPELL